Disarmament Law

This volume seeks to start a revival of the field of disarmament law scholarship.

Law is a fundamental component of disarmament, yet today, most perspectives on the wide range of disarmament issues that exist come primarily from political, diplomatic and public advocacy angles. The aim of this book is to revive the field of disarmament law building on earlier, important and still relevant contributions by international lawyers to the subject. The collection brings together international scholars on various aspects of disarmament. The contributions range across a variety of weapons types, adopt different approaches — doctrinal, historical and critical — to the issues being discussed and taken together, constitute a snapshot of the ideas, concerns and issues that currently occupy disarmament law scholars.

The book will be essential reading for academics, researchers and policymakers working in the area of disarmament.

Treasa Dunworth is an Associate Professor at the University of Auckland. Her work focusses on a range of public international law issues, in particular disarmament law.

Anna Hood is a Senior Lecturer at the University of Auckland. Her work focusses on a range of public international law issues including disarmament law, the history of international law and international law in Aotearoa New Zealand.

Disarmament Law

Reviving the Field

Edited by
Treasa Dunworth and
Anna Hood

Routledge
Taylor & Francis Group
LONDON AND NEW YORK

First published 2021
by Routledge
2 Park Square, Milton Park, Abingdon, Oxon OX14 4RN

and by Routledge
605 Third Avenue, New York, NY 10017

First issued in paperback 2022

Routledge is an imprint of the Taylor & Francis Group, an informa business

Publisher's Note
The publisher has gone to great lengths to ensure the quality of this reprint but points out that some imperfections in the original copies may be apparent.

British Library Cataloguing-in-Publication Data
A catalogue record for this book is available from the British Library

Library of Congress Cataloging-in-Publication Data
A catalog record has been requested for this book

ISBN: 978-0-367-61005-0 (pbk)
ISBN: 978-1-138-34833-2 (hbk)
ISBN: 978-0-429-43672-7 (ebk)

DOI: 10.4324/9780429436727

Typeset in Galliard
by codeMantra

Dedicated to the memory of Fernando Pereira

Contents

Contributors

Emily Camins, University of Western Australia

Anna Crowe, Harvard University

Barry de Vries, Justus Liebig University Giessen

Bonnie Docherty, Harvard University

Associate Professor Treasa Dunworth, University of Auckland

Dr Anna Hood, University of Auckland

Professor Thilo Marauhn, Justus Liebig University Giessen

Professor Masahiko Asada, Kyoto University

Lisa Tabassi, OSCE Secretariat (retired)

Acknowledgements

This book, and the conference that preceded it, would not have been possible without the hard work and support of many people. The project was funded by a very generous grant from the Public Advisory Committee on Disarmament and Arms Control ('PACDAC'). PACDAC is a committee of experts that advises the New Zealand government on disarmament and arms control matters and makes recommendations for granting money to projects that promote understanding of disarmament.[1] Not only did PACDAC provide funding for the project but several members of PACDAC attended our 2018 conference and provided invaluable insights into the papers presented and ideas discussed.

The project was also supported by the Faculty of Law at the University of Auckland. The Faculty's dedicated professional staff ensured that the conference ran smoothly and the Faculty provided funding for the public lecture attached to the conference and research assistants. We would like to specifically acknowledge the time, care and energy that Sabrina Schulte put into assisting us with the conference and this project. Sabrina, we are deeply grateful for your help and penetrating insights on all manner of subjects.

A number of New Zealand disarmament experts have provided advice and guidance on the project. We are very grateful to Tim Caughley, Senior Fellow at the United Nations Institute for Disarmament Research; Kate Dewes, Director of the Disarmament and Security Centre; Kennedy Graham, Director of the New Zealand Centre for Global Studies; Dell Higgie, New Zealand's Ambassador for Disarmament; Kevin J Riordan, Judge Advocate General of the Armed Forces of New Zealand; Lucy Stewart, Coordinator for the Disarmament and Security Centre; and Angela Woodward, Deputy Executive Director of VERTIC. We feel very fortunate to work in a country where there is such a depth of knowledge and expertise on disarmament issues and where those in the field are so generous with their time and thoughts.

It has been a pleasure working with the scholars who have contributed to this project. We really appreciate the hard work, care and dedication that they have put into both the conference and the book. It has been wonderful to engage with

1 *New Zealand Nuclear Free Zone, Disarmament, and Arms Control Act 1987* (NZ), s 17.

each other's work and deepen our ties as scholars. In addition to those whose work appears in this edited collection, Stuart Casey-Maslen, James Fry, Elizabeth Minor and Saroj Nair participated in the initial conference.

Last, but certainly not least, we are indebted to our three research assistants who worked extremely hard on different phases of this project. Anna Zam assisted us with the conference and took detailed notes of all of the discussions that took place at it. Anna, your positivity, can-do attitude and professionalism made a huge difference to the success of the conference. Rachel Buckman and Mohammed Al-Mazrui worked tirelessly on checking references and formatting the chapters. Rachel, we are very grateful for the many hours that you put into the editing process and for your warmth and good humour. Mohammed, thank you for your meticulous work on the chapters in this book, your infectious enthusiasm for the project and your unfailing patience and flexibility.

1 Introduction

Treasa Dunworth and Anna Hood

I Reviving disarmament law

Law is a fundamental component of disarmament. There is a complex web of international treaties, Security Council resolutions and soft law instruments that address the threat posed by weapons, an array of international institutions that work to regulate and eliminate weapons, and a steady stream of disarmament law crises that get aired in the media on a regular basis. Despite all this, in recent decades, the field of disarmament law has received relatively little attention from academics. There is limited discussion or debate about key disarmament law issues, and many issues are not addressed at all in the academic literature.

The dearth of disarmament law scholarship stands in stark contrast to the wealth of scholarship that has emerged in other areas of international law over the last 30 years. Since the end of the Cold War, there has been a rich body of work produced about all manner of international legal topics including international trade law, international environmental law, international human rights law, international criminal law, international refugee law, international law of the sea, international humanitarian law, international economic law and the law of international organisations.

For a number of years, we have been concerned about the relative lack of academic work on disarmament law issues. In our view, there needs to be more doctrinal work that explores how disarmament laws operate and interact with one another as well as with other areas of international law. There are also considerable gaps in the conceptual scholarship on the values that underpin disarmament law, the trends and patterns that have emerged within it over time, and the blind spots that exist within it. Critical and theoretical scholarship as well would allow for identifying, questioning and challenging assumptions within the field and so perhaps lead to better understandings of the myriad dynamics at play in the disarmament law space.

We decided then, in 2017, to begin a project to make space for this scholarship. In making that space, we were mindful of the valuable, and still relevant, work of a host of academics in the first half of the 20th century as they turned their minds to disarmament law issues.[1] Inspired by their work and mindful of the need to engage in more work explaining, developing, critiquing and theorising

1 We are thinking, for example, of the work of Louis Henkin, Richard Falk, Abe Chayes, Anthony D'Amato, Hans Kelsen and Quincy Wright.

the body of disarmament law, we embarked on this project to revive disarmament law. The project had two elements. The first was to convene a conference on disarmament law, bringing together those scholars who were thinking about disarmament law issues to share their work, develop ideas and, in this way, begin building a community of disarmament law scholars. That conference was held in mid-2018 at Auckland Law School. The second element of our project was to produce an edited collection of the papers that were prepared for, and discussed at, the conference. Our hope was (and still is) that the edited collection would provide a snapshot of the ideas, concerns and issues that disarmament scholars were thinking about at the end of the second decade of the 21st century and provide a foundation upon which further scholarship could be built.

As we embarked on the project, one of our first challenges was to define its scope. It was all very well for us to say that we wanted to bring together disarmament scholars to discuss their work, to engage with other international lawyers working in the field or to provide a space to explore trends, blind spots or contradictions in disarmament law. But what, exactly, did we mean by 'disarmament'? In drafting our call for papers, we felt we needed to be able to convey a reasonably clear idea of what we thought fell within the scope of our project. In the end, however, we side-stepped this definitional point, deciding not to define the term 'disarmament law' as we wanted to see how others with an interest in the field might approach it. It is worth noting, we think, that many of our contributors sought to adopt their own understandings of disarmament.

While we chose not to be directive about what lay within 'disarmament', in our call we did explicitly exclude some adjacent areas of international law. We specified that we would not include papers focused on international criminal law or on international humanitarian law. While these bodies of law are connected in certain (and important) ways with disarmament law issues, we see them as distinct areas that are well addressed elsewhere in the literature. This project was about reviving disarmament law and doing so by carving out an independent space for disarmament — that was our core objective.

II Overview of the contributions

We were very fortunate to receive positive responses from across the globe and in June 2018 legal scholars from Austria, Australia, Germany, Hong Kong, Japan, New Zealand, South Africa, the United Kingdom and the United States gathered to share their research and ideas. The eight pieces in this book, which emerged from the conference,[2] touch on a wide variety of disarmament law matters and provide a diverse range of views.

There are some synergies within the chapters that have allowed us to group them into three parts. Part I is entitled 'Disarmament law research agendas'

2 Note that there were two other papers presented at the conference that have not been published in this edition. One was by James Fry and Saroj Nair entitled 'Moral Disarmament: Legacy of the First World War' and the other was by Stuart Casey-Maslen entitled 'Are You Taking the Peace? Disarming Armed Groups During Armed Conflict'.

and contains two chapters that look at broad trends and patterns in disarmament law. The first chapter is Treasa Dunworth's. It surveys contemporary disarmament law work and shows how disarmament practitioners and academics have a tendency to respond to particular crises of disarmament, and how there is a a tendency to focus on disarmament law issues in silos. She terms this state of affairs the 'crisis-silo' dynamic and unpacks what the consequences of these dual preoccupations are for the field before laying out ideas for how the field could break out of this dynamic and adopt new approaches.

The second chapter in Part I is Anna Hood's chapter. It examines the phenomenon of coercive disarmament from 1919 to 2019 and identifies key patterns and themes that have emerged across this sub-field of disarmament law. She focuses in particular on the changes and trends that have emerged within the legal forms that coercive disarmament law measures have assumed, the contexts in which coercive disarmament law measures have appeared and the substantive provisions that coercive disarmament law measures have encompassed. From her findings she identifies new research questions and pathways in disarmament law.

Part II of the book is called 'Humanitarianism and human rights in disarmament'. It explores the implications of the ways in which humanitarianism and human rights are returning to the field. Bonnie Docherty's chapter is the first in this Part and it explores the development and significance of the positive obligations imposed on states parties by three key humanitarian disarmament law treaties — the 1997 *Anti-Personnel Landmines Convention*,[3] the 2008 *Convention on Cluster Munitions* ('*CCM*')[4] and the 2017 *Treaty on the Prohibition of Nuclear Weapons* ('*TPNW*').[5] Specifically, she examines how the provisions in the three treaties that require states to undertake clearance activities and provide victim assistance were conceived and provides important insights into how a humanitarian approach to disarmament ensured that they were embedded in the three treaties despite resistance from some negotiating states. The chapter also assesses the legal and practical impacts of these positive obligations.

Anna Crowe's chapter — the second in Part II — analyses the under-examined relationship between humanitarian disarmament and human rights law. She terms the relationship between the two concepts 'human rights-humanitarianism' and identifies the fact that human rights law contributes legal content to humanitarian disarmament while humanitarianism provides the underlying frame of reducing human suffering. She then examines how human rights-humanitarianism operates in the context of victim assistance provisions in disarmament law treaties. The chapter provides the first in-depth consideration of the connection between humanitarian disarmament and human rights

3 *Convention on the Prohibition of the Use, Stockpiling, Production and Transfer of Anti-Personnel Mines and on Their Destruction*, opened for signature 3 December 1997, 2056 UNTS 211 (entered into force 1 March 1999) ('*Anti-Personnel Landmines Convention*').

4 *Convention on Cluster Munitions*, opened for signature 3 December 2008, 2688 UNTS 39 (entered into force 1 August 2010) ('*CCM*').

5 *Treaty on the Prohibition of Nuclear Weapons*, opened for signature 20 September 2017 (not yet in force) ('*TPNW*').

and offers valuable insights into the complex and, at times, uneasy relationship between the concepts.

The final chapter in Part II — Emily Camin's — also focuses on humanitarian and rights-based issues in disarmament law and compares and contrasts the extent to which two treaties — the *Chemical Weapons Convention* ('*CWC*')[6] and the *CCM* — recognise and protect the rights of victims including the rights of victims to reparations. Her detailed examination of the treaties' texts allows her to conclude that neither treaty confers specific rights on victims which are directly enforceable at international law. Camins concludes by reflecting on some possible future directions in the overall humanisation trend of disarmament law and suggests that even if a human rights-based approach is not adopted or does not emerge, there may yet be scope for better addressing the suffering of victims of mass violence.

The final part of the book — Part III — is entitled 'Making disarmament law'. It contains three pieces that examine issues about some of the key sources of disarmament law. Two focus on treaty interpretation issues and one looks at the significance that soft law can have in a disarmament context. The first chapter to focus on treaty issues is Masahiko Asada's. It looks at what the significance is of the fact that the *Comprehensive Nuclear-Test-Ban Treaty* ('*CTBT*')[7] has still not entered into force nearly a quarter of a century after it was agreed. Specifically, he considers whether *CTBT* signatory and ratifier states are still bound by the obligation in art 18 of the *Vienna Convention on the Law of Treaties* ('*VCLT*')[8] not to carry out 'acts which would defeat the object and purpose of [the] treaty'. To do this he must determine whether the *CTBT*'s entry into force has been unduly delayed and whether any individual signatory state has made it clear that it does not intend to become a party to the *CTBT*. He argues that although it is not possible to conclude that the *CTBT*'s entry into force has been unduly delayed there are a number of complexities around the intention not to become a party provision especially with respect to the United States' practice.

The second chapter in Part III to explore treaty interpretation matters is Barry de Vries and Thilo Marauhn's. It addresses treaty interpretation issues that arise with respect to two other nuclear weapons treaties: the *Treaty on the Non-Proliferation of Nuclear Weapons* ('*NPT*')[9] and the *TPNW*. The authors engage with concerns that have arisen that the *TPNW* may weaken the *NPT*. In

6 *Convention on the Prohibition of the Development, Production, Stockpiling and Use of Chemical Weapons and on Their Destruction*, opened for signature 13 January 1993, 1974 UNTS 45 (entered into force 29 April 1997) ('*CWC*').

7 *Comprehensive Nuclear-Test-Ban Treaty*, opened for signature 24 September 1996, 35 ILM 1439 (not yet in force) ('*CTBT*').

8 *Vienna Convention on the Law of Treaties*, opened for signature 23 May 1969, 1155 UNTS 331 (entered into force 27 January 1980) ('VCLT').

9 *Treaty on the Non-Proliferation of Nuclear Weapons*, opened for signature 1 July 1968, 729 UNTS 161 (entered into force 5 March 1970) ('*NPT*').

dispelling these concerns they argue that: first, there is no formal incompatibility between the two agreements; and second, while there is potential for conflicts to arise between the treaties, these conflicts can be managed by way of interpretation. However, they concede that, given the way in which the two treaties create separate institutional settings each dealing with nuclear weapons, it is possible that political conflicts will emerge which could exacerbate existing tensions between non-nuclear-weapon states and the nuclear-weapon states.

In the final chapter of this Part, Lisa Tabassi and Treasa Dunworth examine the Organisation for Security and Cooperation in Europe ('OSCE'), an organisation that has produced an array of soft disarmament laws. The chapter considers two debates arising in the soft law literature — the extent to which actors that generate soft law can be held to account for the exercise of their power and the extent to which soft law-making processes perpetuate and aggravate existing power inequalities between states. They explore whether these concerns have traction in the context of the OSCE's disarmament law-making, concluding that while there are real difficulties in achieving transparency in such regimes, it is possible to overcome those difficulties. Tabassi and Dunworth also argue that while there are real risks that inequalities among participating states can be perpetuated in soft regimes, those risks are not so alive in the OSCE context due to its particular historical context.

III Reflections

While all of the chapters have been through a rigorous review and editorial process, we have not sought to alter the views of individual authors or ensure consistent approaches are taken to issues throughout the book. In embarking on this project, we did not set out to craft a coherent narrative about disarmament law, or to attempt to get participants to coalesce around singular understandings of any particular issue, or even to work within a particular methodology or approach. Rather, our purpose in creating this collection was to open up a space where different ideas and perspectives could be put forward and tested, and different approaches adopted. We wanted to encourage contributions on many different disarmament law issues from a range of different perspectives and approaches.

To some extent we have achieved that. The following chapters reveal a range of views as between the contributors on certain issues, and engage in a number of contemporary disarmament debates. Different types of scholarship have also emerged in the eight chapters including historical, doctrinal and critical approaches. For example, Hood's chapter is an historical study of coercive disarmament, extending back to the peace treaties at the conclusion of the First World War.[10] Camins, as well, looks to the legacy of chemical weapons use from the

10 For example, the *Treaty of Peace between the Allied and Associated Powers and Germany*, signed 28 June 1919, 13 AJIL Supp 15 (entered into force 10 January 1920) ('*Treaty of Versailles*').

1940s. Other chapters, such as those by Asada and Marauhn and de Vries, are avowedly doctrinal in their approaches. Dunworth's chapter takes a more critical approach.

We were struck by how many of the contributions tackled questions relating to nuclear weapons. The chapters by Asada, and de Vries and Marauhn focus exclusively on nuclear weapons issues while the chapters by Dunworth, Hood, Docherty and Crowe have significant sections on nuclear weapons. Nuclear weapons also feature, although more briefly, in the chapters by Camins, and Tabassi and Dunworth. It is interesting to consider what this strong emphasis on nuclear weapons reveals about the state of disarmament law and/or disarmament law scholarship in 2020. It may simply be that the attention paid to nuclear weapons serves as a snapshot of contemporary concerns and where the focus of disarmament is at this point in time, and in that way, it can be seen as epitomising the crisis-silo dynamic that Dunworth identifies in her chapter. At the time we conceived of the project, the Humanitarian Initiative had borne fruit and the *TPNW* had just been opened for signature. Further, our conference was convened in June 2018, a month after the United States announced its withdrawal from the 'Iran Nuclear Deal'.[11] There is no doubt that we launched this project at a time when nuclear disarmament was high on the international disarmament agenda.

As we bring this project to a close, it is apparent to us that a great deal of work remains to be done. For example, Dunworth's analysis shows that we need more sustained analysis of current disarmament disputes such as the Iranian nuclear programmes and the North Korean missile testing programme. Hood's exploration of coercive disarmament shows that we have only started to scratch the surface of the sub-field of coercive disarmament. The chapters by Camins and Crowe demonstrate that we need much more work to understand the full implications of humanitarianism and human rights re-emerging in the world of disarmament. More broadly, we think that this project has shown that there is a need for sustained theoretical and inter-disciplinary work in disarmament.

We very much hope that the pieces here will inspire further work in the field of disarmament law and that in years to come there will be a much greater variety and depth of disarmament law scholarship from a wide array of approaches.

11 Formally, the *Joint Comprehensive Plan of Action*: SC Res 2231, UN SCOR, 7488th mtg, UN Doc S/RES/2231 (20 July 2015) annex A.

Part I

Disarmament law research agendas

2 Disarmament law

A call to arms

Treasa Dunworth

I Introduction

Since at least the end of the 19th century, disarmament has been an enduring feature of the international legal system and its efforts to secure international peace and security. The Hague Peace Conference in 1899, for example, was convened partly in order to slow the arms race of that time.[1] The League of Nations, formed in the wake of the First World War, was imbued with the idea that peace would come through disarmament — the ill-fated and widely forgotten World Disarmament Conference 1932–34 is testament to the aspirations at that time.[2]

This sensibility was evident too in the early decades of the United Nations era. Although less emphasis was placed on disarmament in the creation of the United Nations, disarmament was one of the objectives of the United Nations, as stipulated in art 26 of the *Charter of the United Nations.* And indeed, the decades right through the Cold War saw a steady development in this sphere. In terms of treaties, states agreed to multilateral treaties such as the *Partial Test Ban Treaty*[3] in 1963, the *Treaty on the Non-Proliferation of Nuclear Weapons* ('*NPT*')[4] in 1968, the *Biological Weapons Convention* ('*BWC*')[5] in 1972, the *Convention on Certain*

1 *Russian Circulate Note Proposing the First Peace Conference, August 1898*, reproduced in James Brown Scott (ed), *Hague Conventions and Declarations of 1899 and 1907: Accompanied by Tables of Signatures, Ratifications and Adhesions of the Various Powers, and Texts of Reservations* (Oxford University Press, 2nd ed, 1915) xv.

2 See, eg, art 8 of the *Covenant of the League of Nations* 1920: 'The Members of the League recognise that the maintenance of peace requires the reduction of national armaments to the lowest point consistent with national safety and the enforcement by common action of international obligations'.

3 *Treaty Banning Nuclear Weapon Tests in the Atmosphere, in Outer Space and Under Water*, opened for signature 5 August 1963, 480 UNTS 43 (entered into force 10 October 1963) ('*Partial Test Ban Treaty*').

4 *Treaty on the Non-Proliferation of Nuclear Weapons*, opened for signature 1 July 1968, 729 UNTS 151 (entered in force 5 March 1970) ('*NPT*').

5 *Convention on the Prohibition of the Development, Production and Stockpiling of Bacteriological (Biological) and Toxin Weapons and on Their Destruction*, opened for signature 10 April 1972, 1015 UNTS 163 (entered into force 26 March 1975) ('*BWC*').

Conventional Weapons ('*CCW*')[6] in 1980, the *Comprehensive Nuclear-Test-Ban Treaty* ('*CTBT*')[7] in 1996 and the *Chemical Weapons Convention* ('*CWC*')[8] in 1993. The United States ('US') and the Soviet Union also agreed to several important bilateral treaties including the *Anti-Ballistic Missile Treaty*[9] in 1972, and the *Intermediate-Range and Shorter-Range Missile Treaty*[10] in 1987.

In the institutional space, as well, there has been considerable activity. Since the inception of the United Nations, the General Assembly has worked on disarmament matters, particularly through its First Committee which meets each year. In addition, the General Assembly convened three Special Sessions on Disarmament in 1978, 1982 and 1988.[11] The Conference on Disarmament (the 'Conference'), the first iteration of which appeared in 1959 created by the General Assembly as the 'Ten Nation Committee on Disarmament', has also had an important role in disarmament, although it has been unable to progress any work in the last 20 years, and would now appear moribund.[12] In its time, however, it was the locus for negotiations of many of today's key treaties, including the *NPT*, the *CWC*, the *BWC* and the *CTBT* (the latter treaty was ultimately adopted by the General Assembly but negotiated in the Conference).[13] All of these treaties are supported by various institutional structures, each of which operates in its own sphere.[14] Other treaties have established 'meetings of the parties' mechanisms, including review conferences, whereby states come together at regular intervals to discuss the respective treaties and their implementation.

6 *Convention on Prohibitions or Restrictions on the Use of Certain Conventional Weapons which may be deemed to be Excessively Injurious or to have Indiscriminate Effects*, opened for signature 10 October 1980, 1342 UNTS 137 (entered into force 2 December 1983) ('*CCW*').

7 *Comprehensive Nuclear-Test-Ban Treaty*, opened for signature 24 September 1996, 35 ILM 1439 (not yet in force) ('*CTBT*').

8 *Convention on the Prohibition of the Development, Production, Stockpiling and Use of Chemical Weapons and on Their Destruction*, opened for signature 13 January 1993, 1975 UNTS 45 (entered into force 29 April 1997) ('*CWC*').

9 *Treaty on the Limitation of Anti-Ballistic Missile Systems*, Soviet Union–United States of America, signed 26 May 1972, 944 UNTS 13 (entered into force 3 October 1972). Note that the United States withdrew from this treaty in 2002, so it is no longer in force.

10 *Treaty between the United States of America and the Union of Soviet Socialist Republics on the Elimination of Their Intermediate-Range and Shorter-Range Missiles*, Soviet Union–United States of America, signed 8 December 1987, 27 ILM 1186 (entered into force 1988).

11 Randy Rydell, 'A Historical Perspective on the General Assembly's Three Special Sessions on Disarmament' (Statement, Open-Ended Working Group on the Fourth Special Session of the General Assembly Devoted to Disarmament, 26 March 2016).

12 See generally, Tim Caughley, 'Conference on Disarmament: Breaking the Ice' (UNIDIR, 2010). See also John H King, 'Transforming the Conference on Disarmament: Multilateral Arms Control and Disarmament for a Pluralistic World' (UNIDIR, 2011).

13 See Masahiko Asada, 'CTBT: Legal Questions Arising from Its Non-Entry-Into-Force' (2002) 7(1) *Journal of Conflict and Security Law* 85, 86.

14 The International Atomic Energy Agency ('IAEA') for the *NPT*; the Organisation for the Prohibition of Chemical Weapons ('OPCW') for the *CWC*; the Implementation Support Unit for the *BWC* and the Preparatory Commission for the Comprehensive Test Ban Treaty Organization ('CTBTO') for the *CTBT*.

Such treaties include the *CCW*, the *Anti-Personnel Landmines Treaty*[15] and the *Convention on Cluster Munitions*.[16] When and if the *Treaty on the Prohibition of Nuclear Weapons* ('*TPNW*')[17] enters into force, there will also be a mechanism in place for biennial meetings of the states parties to that treaty.

Academic interest and discourse has been less consistent but nevertheless has also endured. In the first decades of the new United Nations legal order, many of the leading academic international lawyers acknowledged disarmament as a key issue.[18] However, there does appear to have been a falling away of interest from international lawyers from the mid-1970s. For example, a review of the index of the Proceedings of the Annual Meeting of the American Society of International Law suggests that from the mid-1970s, disarmament was not a core research interest in the academy generally.[19]

My focus in this chapter is on contemporary attention to disarmament (roughly, the last two decades) and I show how contemporary academic literature, as well as the practice of disarmament, is marked by two tendencies. First, there is a tendency for both academics and practitioners to pay attention to weapons or disarmament when a particular issue reaches a 'crisis' point. Thus, that discussion is generally very narrow in focus and often the event or development in question is poised to collapse into armed conflict (for example, the allegations around Iraq's possession of weapons of mass destruction and the consequent 2003 Iraq war). A second feature of contemporary disarmament practice and scholarship is what I term 'sectoral', by which I mean that the scholarship and

15 *Convention on the Prohibition of the Use, Stockpiling, Production and Transfer of Anti-Personnel Mines and on Their Destruction*, opened for signature 3 December 1997, 2056 UNTS 211 (entered into force 1 March 1999) ('*Anti-Personnel Landmines Convention*').

16 *Convention on Cluster Munitions*, opened for signature 3 December 2008, 2688 UNTS 39 (entered into force 1 August 2010) ('*Convention on Cluster Munitions*').

17 *Treaty on the Prohibition of Nuclear Weapons*, opened for signature 20 September 2017 (not yet in force) ('*TPNW*'), art 8(2).

18 For example, Richard Baxter, a leading international lawyer at the time and future judge of the International Court of Justice, wrote in a 1963 book review that 'the intellectual world has its fashions too, and books on disarmament are now in flood': R R Baxter, 'Book Review' (1963) 57(1) *American Journal of International Law* 153, 155. Writing the following year, Adrian S Fisher expressed the view that the 'law relating to arms control and disarmament is a novel subject, however, in the sense that only in recent years has intense, systematic attention been devoted to it': Adrian S Fisher, 'Arms Control and Disarmament in International Law' (1964) 50 *Virginia Law Review* 1200, 1200. The first panel in the 1962 Meeting of the American Society of International Law was devoted to disarmament.

19 There were some notable exceptions to this. For example, on the occasion of the 25th anniversary of the United Nations in 1970, the Annual Meeting of the American Society of International included a panel on disarmament: *Proceedings of the Sixty-Fourth Annual Meeting of the American Society of International Law*, New York, 24–26 April 1970, published in (1970) 64(4) *American Journal of International Law* 191–211; and the 1982 proceedings including a spirited call for engagement by lawyers in the nuclear weapons debate: Francis A Boyle, Burns H Weston and Roger Fisher, 'The Role of Lawyers in Preventing Nuclear War' (1982) 76 *Proceedings of the ASIL Annual Meetings* 332–49. Further, there have been some academics, Richard Falk for example, who have always maintained a strong research profile in this area.

practice focuses on particular weapons types and/or particular weapons regimes. This might include analysis on a particular treaty (for example, the *Anti-Personnel Landmines Convention*), or a discussion of the use of a particular weapon (for example, the use of chemical weapons in Syria). As I will show, the institutional structures for disarmament also lend themselves to a sectoral approach.

I argue that, taken together, these two tendencies — what I call the silo-crisis approach (that is, the focus on crises and the sectoral approach) — give rise to at least three troubling consequences. First, I suggest that the attention given to weapons' crises lends an air that disarmament generally, or disarmament law specifically, is not effective in that the law or a legal framework will not be able to achieve desired outcomes (a reduction or elimination of weapons). That is, the literature and policy responses implicitly suggest that this area of law is ineffectual. This in turn perpetuates and reinforces a dismissal of the area of law.[20] A second consequence of the silo-crisis approach that concerns me is that these apparent failures of disarmament practice and policy are presented in such a way as to lend themselves to an imperative of military action. That is, when disarmament 'fails', a military response somehow seems inevitable, as it appears to be the only realistic way to address the problem.[21] That in turn creates a sense that disarmament would in fact be dangerous because without weapons, or sufficient weapons, there then could be no resort to force to counter some other states having certain weapons. The third consequence of the silo-crisis approach to disarmament is the way in which it obscures structural imbalances and inequities in the development of disarmament law.[22] By that I mean that in always narrowing the focus to a particular weapon or a particular issue, the wider institutional and normative framework is unseen. Like any system of law, disarmament law contains its own biases, blind spots and hegemonic tendencies. A failure to examine the system more holistically means that these go unnoticed and often unchecked.

My discussion is structured as follows: Parts II and III demonstrate my core assertions on which my chapter rests — that is, first, that disarmament law and practice is infused with crisis and second, that the area is dominated by regime-specific analysis. Part II attends to the crisis argument, drawing out two illustrations of the crisis dynamic in action: the use of chemical weapons in Syria from 2013 and the dispute regarding Iran's nuclear programme. In Part III, I show how the literature and practice in recent decades is very regime-specific and thus siloed in its approach. I draw on a range of examples to show how in a variety of disarmament-related contexts, there is little, if any, holistic thinking. In Part IV, I explore the three troubling consequences of the silo-crisis approach

20 See generally, Neil Cooper, 'Putting Disarmament Back in the Frame' (2006) 32(2) *Review of International Studies* 353.

21 See generally, Anne Orford, *Reading Humanitarian Intervention: Human Rights and the Use of Force in International Law* (Cambridge University Press, 2003).

22 See generally, Hilary Charlesworth, 'International Law: A Discipline of Crisis' (2002) 65(3) *Modern Law Review* 377.

identified above. I conclude in Part V with a call to arms: a call for a renewed, more ambitious research agenda that moves beyond consideration of narrow categorisations and uncritical acceptances of various crises.

II Disarmament as crisis

Writing in 2002 in the wake of the Kosovo War, Hilary Charlesworth argued that international lawyers tend to focus on crises in their work.[23] She identified a disciplinary pattern whereby scholars and practitioners often flit from crisis to crisis without pausing to consider or deeply reflect on the broader contexts in which these crises are playing out.[24] International lawyers are drawn to crisis, she surmised, because it gives a sense of immediacy and real-world relevance to their work and scholarship.[25] However, she identified a number of negative consequences of the tendency towards crisis. These include the way in which such an approach can perpetuate a truncated understanding and presentation of the 'facts' of any given crisis; and — of particular relevance to this chapter — a failure to engage in more fundamental considerations of the operation of international law and in particular structural injustices and biases of the system.[26]

In the specific context of disarmament law, there are many illustrations of this crisis dynamic at play and, in this part, I explore two: first, the use of chemical weapons in the Syrian War and the subsequent disarmament of Syria in respect of its chemical weapons; and second, the advent and, at the time of writing, the unravelling of the 'Iran Nuclear Deal'.[27] In Part IV, I return to the idea of a crisis dynamic to show how it supports Charlesworth's concern about the way in which crisis obscures more fundamental structural concerns. For now, I am simply illustrating its operation in disarmament discourse.

A Syria and chemical weapons

Even before chemical weapons were used in Syria, the prospect of their use was presented as a crisis when, in 2012, then United States President Barak Obama declared that any use of chemical weapons in the Syrian War would be a 'game changer' and would constitute a 'red line' in terms of how the United States would approach the conflict.[28] Concerns that government forces would use chemical weapons were not without foundation: Syria remained one of only a small number of states to remain outside the *CWC* and it was generally

23 Ibid.
24 Ibid., 382.
25 Ibid.
26 Ibid.
27 Formally the *Joint Comprehensive Plan of Action* ('*JCPOA*'): SC Res 2231, UN SCOR, 7488th mtg, UN Doc S/RES/2231 (20 July 2015) annex A.
28 Mark Landler, 'Obama Threatens Force against Syria', *New York Times* (New York, 20 August 2012) A 7.

understood in the arms control community that Syria did in fact possess chemical weapons.[29]

In August 2013, the Syrian chemical weapons crisis escalated when sarin was used in an attack in Ghouta, a suburb of Damascus, which resulted in at least several hundred deaths and possibly as many as 1,500 deaths.[30] The attack was particularly significant for two reasons.[31] First, the chemical weapon used in this attack was sarin, a chemical which acts on the central nervous system and is therefore among the most toxic and dangerous of chemical weapons. In contrast, the earlier attacks had seemed to involve less toxic chemicals, including chlorine. The second significance of the Ghouta attack was one of timing. It happened as a United Nations team was in Damascus preparing to investigate the earlier allegations regarding the use of chemical weapons in the conflict.[32] Consequently, the investigators were able to be in Ghouta within days and confirmed without doubt that significant quantities of sarin had been used.[33] In this way, the discourse shifted from one of conjecture to confirmed scientifically verified fact.

The immediate response to the Ghouta attack was one of crisis, with no room to doubt that President Obama's 'red line' had been crossed. Responding to the actual use of sarin, President Obama said: 'if we really do not want to turn away from taking appropriate action in the face of such an unspeakable outrage, then we must acknowledge the costs of doing nothing'.[34] The United Kingdom ('UK') issued a legal opinion within days describing the attack as 'the most egregious single incident of the conflict'.[35] The opinion asserted the legal authority of the UK 'to take exceptional measures in order to alleviate the scale of the overwhelming humanitarian catastrophe in Syria by deterring and disrupting

29 Philipp C Bleek and Nicholas J Kramer, 'Eliminating Syria's Chemical Weapons: Implications for Addressing Nuclear, Biological, and Chemical Threats' (2016) 23(1–2) *The Nonproliferation Review* 179, 198–201. The other states outside the treaty at the time were Angola, Democratic People's Republic of Korea, Egypt and Somalia. Israel and Myanmar were signatories but not states parties.

30 These figures are taken from Ralf Trapp who makes the point that it was, and remains, difficult to verify exact figures, despite varying reports in the media and from a variety of sources: Ralf Trapp, 'The Use of Chemical Weapons in Syria: Implications and Consequences' in Bretislav Friedrich et al. (eds), *One Hundred Years of Chemical Warfare: Research, Deployment, Consequences* (Springer, 2017) 363, 366.

31 Noting that it was far from the only use of chemical weapons in the Syrian War. See Alicia Sanders-Zakre, 'Timeline of Syrian Chemical Weapons Activity, 2012–2019' *Arms Control Association* (Web Page, March 2019) <https://www.armscontrol.org/factsheets/Timeline-of-Syrian-Chemical-Weapons-Activity>.

32 Trapp, The Use of Chemical Weapons in Syria: Implications and Consequences (n 30) 366.

33 Ibid., 367.

34 Barrack Obama, 'Statement by the President on Syria' (Statement, The White House, 31 August 2013) (Web Page) <http://www.whitehouse.gov/the-press-office/2013/08/31/statement-president-syria>.

35 Prime Minister's Office, 'Chemical Weapons Use by Syrian Regime: UK Government Legal Position (Policy Paper, 29 August 2013) (Web Page) < https://www.gov.uk/government/publications/chemical-weapon-use-by-syrian-regime-uk-government-legal-position> para 5(i).

the further ruse of chemical weapons by the Syrian regime'.[36] In France, there was Presidential talk of 'avenging the massacre' of civilians.[37]

International law academic commentary as well saw the Ghouta attack as a crisis. First, the language of exceptional outrage featured prominently in responses.[38] Second, much of the commentary focused on whether a military response to the atrocity would be lawful, thus heightening the sense of crisis by focusing on (and often justifying) possible military responses.[39] Even those authors rejecting recourse to military action were still immersed in the crisis paradigm because even as they resisted arguments that a military response would be lawful or appropriate, their engagement with the arguments on a doctrinal level left unchallenged the premise that Ghouta was, in fact, a crisis.[40] Thus, however approached, a common feature of the discourse was the way in which it took seriously and devoted consideration to violent responses to the violence.

B Iran and nuclear weapons

The dispute about Iran's nuclear programme is the second instance of showing crisis in the context of discourse around disarmament law and practice. As with the Syrian situation, both in diplomatic and political circles, as well as among international law academics, the language of crisis has prevailed in this context.

A state of crisis has persisted around Iran's alleged nuclear weapons programme since at least 2002 when it came to light that Iran was operating a uranium enrichment site at a nuclear power facility in Natanz, some 300 kilometres south of Tehran, and a heavy water plant at Arak, a town to the south west of the capital.[41] Although these were not unlawful activities per se (the operations could have been for the development of nuclear energy explicitly permitted under the *NPT*), they had not been declared to the International Atomic Energy Agency ('IAEA') as required by Iran's Safeguards Agreement with the IAEA.[42] Following further inspections conducted under that Safeguards Agreement, in 2003 the IAEA determined that Iran was in non-compliance with its obligations on

36 Ibid., para 4.

37 John Gaffney, 'Political Leadership and the Politics of Performance: France, Syria and the Chemical Weapons Crisis of 2013' (2014) 12(3) *French Politics* 218.

38 See, eg, Christopher M Ford, 'Syria: Can International Law Cope? Workshop Report' (2016) 92 *International Law Studies* 340. For an exploration of the various responses to Syria, see Tim McCormack, 'Chemical Weapons and Other Atrocities: Contrasting Responses to the Syrian Crisis' (2016) 92 *International Law Studies* 512.

39 Michael P Scharf, 'Striking a Grotian Moment: How the Syria Airstrikes Changed International Law Relating to Humanitarian Interventions' (2019) 19(2) *Chicago Journal of International Law* 586.

40 McCormack (n 38) 537.

41 Daniel H Joyner, 'Iran's Nuclear Program and International Law' (2013) 2(2) *Penn State Journal of Law and International Affairs* 282, 282.

42 IAEA, Text of the Agreement between Iran and the Agency for the Application of Safeguards in Connection with the Treaty on the Non-Proliferation of Nuclear Weapons, IAEA Doc INFCIRC/214 (13 December 1974).

account of the non-disclosure of these activities but also because of the discovery of undeclared uranium (which was required to be declared under the Safeguards Agreement).[43] In 2006, the IAEA referred the matter to the Security Council,[44] which ordered Iran to cooperate with the IAEA and to suspend its enrichment programme.[45] When Iran refused to comply, still insisting that its programme was peaceful and that it was within its rights to conduct such a programme, the Council imposed sanctions which escalated over the following years.[46]

The stand-off continued until 2015, when the permanent members of the Security Council ('P5'), along with Germany and the High Representative of the European Union for Foreign Affairs and Security Policy, entered into an agreement on a way forward with Iran — the Joint Comprehensive Plan of Action ('JCPOA' or 'Iran Nuclear Deal').[47] Iran agreed to significant limits on its civilian programme as well as to submitting to and cooperating with an enhanced inspection regime which was to be conducted by the IAEA. In return, the permanent members of the Council, along with Germany, agreed to the phased, coordinated lifting of sanctions. Additionally, a 'Roadmap Agreement' was agreed between Iran and the IAEA, the aim of which was to work towards resolving past and present outstanding disputes and concerns. By the end of 2015, the Board of Governors of the IAEA accepted that there was 'no credible indications of activities in Iran relevant to the development of a nuclear explosive device after 2009'.[48] It also concluded that there were 'no credible indications of the diversion of nuclear material in connection with the possible military dimensions to Iran's nuclear programme'.[49] Sanctions started to be lifted as envisaged by the Roadmap Agreement.

The course of the dispute changed again in 2017 when the incoming US Administration unilaterally re-imposed sanctions and placed pressure on its European allies to cease trading with Iran.[50] At the time of writing, the crisis

43 Joyner (n 41) 283. See Board of Governors of the IAEA, 'Implementation of the NPT Safeguards Agreement in the Islamic Republic of Iran' (Resolution GOV/2003/81, IAEA, 26 November 2003) (Web Page) <https://www.iaea.org/sites/default/files/gov2003-81.pdf>.

44 Mohamed El-Baradei, *Report by the Director General of the IAEA to the Board of Governors: Implementation of the NPT Safeguards Agreement in the Islamic Republic of Iran* (Report GOV/2006/27, IAEA, 28 April 2006). See discussion by Christine Gray, 'The Use of Force to Prevent Proliferation' (2009) 52 *Japanese Yearbook of International Law* 101, 117.

45 SC Res 1696, UN SCOR, 5500th mtg, UN Doc S/Res/1696 (31 July 2006).

46 Joyner (n 41) lists all the resolutions in his footnote 12. See also the detailed discussion by Asli Ü Bâli, 'Negotiating Nonproliferation: International Law and Delegation in the Iranian Nuclear Crisis' (2014) 61(2) *University of California Law Review* 232.

47 *JCPOA* (n 27). See Hood, Chapter 3 as she characterises this as coercive disarmament).

48 IAEA Board of Governors, *Final Assessment on Past and Present Outstanding Issues regarding Iran's Nuclear Programme* (Director-General Report GOV/2015/68, IAEA, 2 December 2015) para 87.

49 Ibid., para 88.

50 Donald J Trump, 'Remarks by President Trump on Iran Strategy' (Statement, The White House, 13 October 2017) (Web Page) <https://www.whitehouse.gov/briefings-statements/remarks-president-trump-iran-strategy>. Because the United States was only one party to the

continues to escalate. By mid-2019, there were standoffs between the UK and Iran regarding seizures of oil tankers and, in September 2019, allegations that Iran was behind, or directly responsible for, drone strikes on the state-owned Saudi Aramco oil-processing facilities in Saudi Arabia.[51]

Both in practice and in scholarship, the dispute has been presented in terms of a crisis (notwithstanding that the 'crisis' has now endured for almost 18 years). In practice, particularly the rhetoric emanating from the United States has been crisis focused[52] and the sense of crisis has also been evident from within the United Nations.[53] With a few notable exceptions,[54] legal scholarship, as well, has been firmly in crisis mode.[55] Most attention has been paid in the periods when the dispute boiled over into outright military confrontation, with little thorough consideration of the broader issues of the history of the dispute.[56]

---

six-party arrangement, this change in position did not result in a complete collapse of the Iran Nuclear Deal at this point.

51 The Houthis, the Iran-aligned rebel army in Yemen, claimed responsibility, but many Western governments believed that Iran was behind the attack. See Michael Safi and Graeme Wearden, 'Everything You Need to Know about the Saudi Arabia Oil Attacks' *The Guardian* (online, 16 September 2019) (Web Page) <https://www.theguardian.com/world/2019/sep/16/saudi-arabia-oil-attacks-everything-you-need-to-know>.

52 United States Secretary of State, Mike Pompeo, described the attack as an 'unprecedented attack on the world's energy supply', thus implicitly making the claim that this was an attack on the whole international community and in some way exceptional. See 'Pompeo: Iran Behind Attack on Saudi Oil Facilities That Will Reduce Kingdom's Output' *The Guardian* (online,15 September 2019) (Web Page) <https://www.theguardian.com/world/2019/sep/14/pompeo-iran-saudi-arabia-oil-yemen-houthi>. United States President Trump responded by Twitter, stating that the US was 'locked and loaded' and ready to respond. See: 'US "Locked and Loaded" after Saudi Oil Attack: Trump' Al Jazeera (online, 17 September 2019) (Web Page) <https://www.aljazeera.com/news/2019/09/saudi-oil-attack-reignites-fears-iran-conflict-gulf-190915200146301.html>.

53 Speaking at a briefing to the Security Council in December 2019, the Under-Secretary-General for Political Affairs referred to the oil tanker attack saying that those developments had 'dangerously brought the region closer to a serious confrontation. Such an eventuality would be devastating and must be prevented at all cost': 'Iran and US both undermining nuclear deal says UN political affairs chief' *UN News* (online, 19 December 2019) (Web Page) <https://news.un.org/en/story/2019/12/1054071>.

54 See, eg, Bâli (n 46). Daniel Joyner's work is another example, especially through his blog Arms Control Law, which follows all the related developments closely with clear and thorough assessments of the issues. See *Arms Control Law* (Web Page) <https://armscontrollaw.com>.

55 See, eg, Michael Glennon, 'Pre-empting Proliferation: International Law, Morality, and Nuclear Weapons' (2013) 24(1) *European Journal of International Law* 109 who says that '[n]uclear proliferation therefore poses a threat to both the United States and the international community. This threat is now presented most immediately by the nuclear programmes of Iran and North Korea': at 110.

56 Shampa Biswas also bemoans the way in which the historical background to the dispute is either ignored or presented in 'clash of civilisations' terms: Shampa Biswas, 'Iran v "the International Community": A Postcolonial Analysis of the Negotiations on the Iranian Nuclear Program' (2018) 26(3) *Asian Journal of Political Science* 331, 335–6.

The sense of crisis has been sustained and heightened by the way in which Iran has been pitted against the 'international community'. By this I mean that Iran's transgressions as regards its obligations under its Safeguards Agreement with the IAEA, and its alleged nuclear weapons programme, are portrayed as a threat to the 'international order' or to some imagined international community.[57] For example, President Barak Obama, speaking on the occasion of the initial agreement, wove the language of a global order and solidarity of the international community into the specific concerns of the United States:

> ... for many years, Iran has been unwilling to meet its obligations to the international community.
>
> ... If Iran seizes this opportunity, the Iranian people will benefit from rejoining the international community. ... This would provide Iran with a dignified path to forge a new beginning with the wider world based on mutual respect.
>
> ... The world is united in support of our determination to prevent Iran from developing a nuclear weapon.
>
> It won't be easy, and huge challenges remain ahead. But through strong and principled diplomacy, the United States of America will do our part on behalf of a world of greater peace, security, and cooperation among nations.[58]

III The sectoral approach in disarmament discourse and practice

The second tendency in contemporary disarmament law practice and discourse that I want to draw out in this chapter is what I term a sectoral approach. By sectoral approach I mean that work on particular issues or regimes (in both the academy and in practice) tends to take place in silos or in over-specialised segregated compartments. In other words, there is a paucity of cross-cutting analysis in disarmament scholarship and few opportunities to transcend the sectoral approach.[59]

57 Ibid. See as well Glennon's invocation of the international community (n 55).

58 Barack Obama, 'Statement by the President on First Step Agreement on Iran's Nuclear Program' (Statement, The White House, 23 November 2013) (Web Page) <https://obamawhitehouse.archives.gov/the-press-office/2013/11/23/statement-president-first-step-agreement-irans-nuclear-program>.

59 A notable exception is the work of the United Nations Institute for Disarmament Research ('UNIDIR'). Established in 1980, UNIDIR is an autonomous institution within the United Nations, mandated to carry out independent research on disarmament. While much of its work is sectoral, UNIDIR has produced a number of important studies on disarmament that transcend sectoral approaches, including work on gender and disarmament, disarmament as humanitarian action and analysis of the institutions for disarmament negotiations, especially the Conference on Disarmament. See 'Publications' UNIDIR (Web Page) <https://www.unidir.org/publications>.

A Sectoral disarmament discourse in academia

Turning first to the academic work in the area, the assertion that research is predominately sectoral is difficult to categorically prove. However, a review of the contents of one of the leading journals devoted to security issues — the *Journal of Conflict and Security Law* — which explicitly includes in its mandate 'arms control and disarmament',[60] shows that of the 58 articles dealing with disarmament published in the period 1996 (when the journal began) to 2019, the vast majority addressed a specific regime (such as the *NPT*, the *BWC* or the IAEA for example), or a specific incident or event (such as the Iran dispute, the use of chemical weapons in Syria or particular Review Conferences of the *NPT*) without reference to the broader system of disarmament and arms control. There were articles which addressed more general questions of disarmament, but even these stayed close to their specific subject matter and did not adopt a cross-cutting methodology. Those works included the customary international humanitarian law study's provisions on weapons,[61] and the general law of treaties in the context of arms control treaties.[62] Of the 58 articles published in the life of the journal, only two adopted a cross-cutting holistic view of disarmament.[63]

Looking now at a generalist international law journal — the *International and Comparative Law Quarterly* — a search on Westlaw of its indexes returned 87 hits for the terms 'disarmament' spanning the years 1986–2019.[64] Of those, ten hits can be discounted because they were using the word in a completely different sense (for example, 'disarming informality') or in a citation.[65] A further 46 articles did mention disarmament in the intended sense, but only in passing. For example, disarmament might be listed as one item in a list of activities of an organisation. Of the 31 remaining articles, all except one (which was a book review on the non-proliferation of weapons of mass destruction ('WMD'))[66]

60 See the evaluation by Cooper discussed below in Part IV(A) (n 89).

61 David Turns, 'Weapons in the ICRC Study on Customary International Humanitarian Law' (2006) 11(2) *Journal of Conflict and Security Law* 201.

62 Andrew Michie, 'The Provisional Application of Arms Control Treaties' (2005) 10(3) *Journal of Conflict and Security Law* 345–77; Guido den Dekker and Tom Coppen, 'Termination and Suspension of, and Withdrawal from Weapons of Mass Destruction Arms Control Agreements in Light of General Law of Treaties' (2012) 17(1) *Journal of Conflict and Security Law* 25.

63 John Freeman, 'Is Arms Control Law in Crisis?' (2004) 9(3) *Journal of Conflict and Security Law* 303; Erwin Dahinden, 'The Future of Arms Control Law: Towards a New Regulatory Approach and New Regulatory Techniques' (2005) 10(2) *Journal of Conflict and Security Law* 263.

64 The search was run on 22 November 2019.

65 For example, a citation to *R (on the application of the Campaign for Nuclear Disarmament) v Prime Minister* [2002] EWCH 2777 (Admin), a case which did not involve issues of disarmament but rather was an (unsuccessful) challenge in the United Kingdom to the proposed invasion of Iraq.

66 Daniel H Joyner and Marco Roscini (eds), *Non-Proliferation Law as a Special Regime: A Contribution to Fragmentation Theory in International Law* (Cambridge University Press, 2012); reviewed in: Dirk Pulkowski, 'Book Review' (2016) 65(2) *International and Comparative Law Quarterly* 521.

were sectoral in that they dealt with either a particular weapon type in isolation (for example, nuclear weapons, chemical weapons or cluster munitions), or a particular situation (the various Iraqi crises, the situation with North Korea or discussions on the Advisory Opinions of the International Court of Justice relating to nuclear weapons).

To take a regional journal (and from a region that is especially affected by weapons and disarmament law issues),[67] a search of the indices for the *Asian Journal of International Law*, published since 2011, reveals only one article on arms control.[68] That article was examining the question of arms control in space, so in that sense it too was a 'sectoral' analysis and did not consider the issues in the broader context of disarmament law.

Turning then to scholarship outside of journals, the same pattern emerges. While there are some instances of attempts to consider disarmament generally, these tend to be unusual.[69] Some specific examples illustrate the point: of approximately 67 titles in the Oxford Monographs in International Law, only two — Daniel Joyner's *International Law and the Proliferation of Weapons of Mass Destruction*[70] and James Busuttil's *Naval Weapons Systems and the Contemporary Law of War*[71] — address disarmament-related issues. Both of these are sectoral, although Joyner's book does capture weapons of mass destruction, rather than one single category of weapon. The international law catalogue of Routledge shows a similar result. Of around 400 titles (covering all areas of international law), less than a handful address disarmament.[72] Of those, only the *Guide to International Disarmament Law* eschews a sectoral approach.[73]

67 I am thinking here of the Hiroshima and Nagasaki bombings, the on-going concerns with the nuclear weapons development by North Korea, the legacy of the use of landmines and herbicides in Vietnam, Lao PDR and Cambodia, and the history of use of incendiary weapons during the Korean War.

68 Jinyuan Su, 'Space Arms Control: Lex Lata and Currently Active Proposals' (2017) 7(1) *Asian Journal of International Law* 61.

69 See John Kierulf, *Disarmament Under International Law* (McGill-Queen's University Press, 2017); Treasa Dunworth, *Humanitarian Disarmament: An Historical Enquiry* (Cambridge University Press, 2020). Joyner and Roscini (n 66). I have included this latter contribution as a generalist text because while it is confined to weapons of mass destruction and their delivery systems, it brings discussions about non-proliferation into a more general discussion of international law.

70 Daniel Joyner, *International Law and the Proliferation of Weapons of Mass Destruction* (Oxford University Press, 2009).

71 James Busuttil, *Naval Weapons Systems and the Contemporary Law of War* (Oxford University Press, 1998).

72 Stuart Casey-Maslen and Tobias Vestner, *Guide to International Disarmament Law* (Routledge, 2019); Morse Tan, *North Korea, International Law and the Dual Crises* (Routledge, 2018); Alan Bryden, *International Law, Politics and Inhumane Weapons* (Routledge, 2017) and Alexander Breitegger, *Cluster Munitions and International Law: Disarmament with a Human Face?* (Routledge, 2013).

73 Casey-Maslen and Vestner (n 72).

B Sectoral approach in disarmament practice

Outside of that admittedly incomplete snapshot of academic work, the practice of disarmament is also often sectoral. The tendency towards a sectoral approach emerged very strongly in the early work of the United Nations for a number of reasons.[74] First, almost immediately, discussions were split into those relating to 'atomic weapons and all other major weapons adaptable to mass destruction' which would be discussed in the Atomic Energy Commission[75] on the one hand; and on the other hand, those that would take place in the Commission for Conventional Armaments, which had the mandate to achieve 'general regulation and reduction of armaments and armed forces'.[76] Thus an early split emerged between weapons of mass destruction (particularly nuclear weapons) and all other categories of weapons, although of course the second category falling under the Commission for Conventional Armaments was very broad. Nonetheless, this early division, which can be explained by the advent of nuclear weapons and the special risks they were deemed to pose, heralded an increasingly sectoral approach in disarmament practice.

Second, a sectoral approach was an inevitable consequence of the fact that as states concluded negotiations on various treaties, those treaties in turn often created self-contained regimes, and this has naturally led to sectoral activity. For example, the *CWC* established the Organisation for the Prohibition of Chemical Weapons ('OPCW');[77] the states parties to the *BWC* over time have developed a system of 'confidence building measures' including reports to an Implementation Support Unit;[78] and the *CTBT* created the Comprehensive Nuclear-Test-Ban Treaty Organization ('CTBTO').[79]

74 In the League of Nations, disarmament issues were considered sectorally – think of naval disarmament for example – but there was also a strong sense (from some states) that disarmament should be considered more holistically, hence the convening of the World Disarmament Conference from 1932 until its collapse in 1934. See generally, Lara Steiner, *The Lights That Failed: European International History 1919–1933* (Clarendon Press, 2005) ch 14.

75 *Establishment of a Commission to Deal with the Problems Raised by the Discovery of Atomic Energy*, GA Res 1/1, UN GAOR, 1st sess, 17th plen mgt, UN Doc A/Res/1/1 (24 January 1946).

76 *Regulation, Limitation and Balanced Reduction of All Armed Forces and All Armaments; International Control of Atomic Energy*, GA Res 502 (VI), UN GOAR, 6th sess, 358th plen mtg, UN Doc A/RES/502(VI) (11 January 1952).

77 *CWC* (n 8) art VIII.

78 The confidence-building measures emerged from a decision of the Second Review Conference: *Final Declaration*, Second Review Conference of the Parties to the Convention on the Prohibition of the Development, Production and Stockpiling of Bacteriological (Biological) and Toxin Weapons and on Their Destruction, UN Doc BWC/CONF.II/13/1 (18–26 September 1986) 4–5, which were further developed in subsequent Review Conferences. The Implementation Support Unit was established at the Sixth Review Conference: *Final Document*, Sixth Review Conference of the Parties to the Convention on the Prohibition of the Development, Production and Stockpiling of Bacteriological (Biological) and Toxin Weapons and on Their Destruction, UN Doc BWC/CONF.VI/6 (20 November – 8 December 2006) Part III, paras 5 and 6.

79 *CTBT* (n 7) art II. The Organization is not yet in legal existence as the *CTBT* itself is not yet in force. However, in fact preparatory and verification work does progress through the

A third possible explanation for the pervasive sectoral approach lies in the dysfunction of the institutional framework created by the *CCW*. In essence that treaty is an umbrella treaty whereby (initially) three categories of weapons were dealt with by means of a series of three protocols to the treaty (non-detectable fragments; mines, booby-traps and other devices; and incendiary weapons).[80] Institutionally, a mechanism of meetings of the states parties was established to oversee the treaty and to agree to further protocols.[81] However, that mechanism became dysfunctional as further real agreement (either to strengthen the existing protocols or to develop additional ones) was impossible in large part due to the consensus rule of decision-making.[82] As such, there have been instances of 'breakouts' to pursue ad hoc processes which in turn have created further regimes for particular weapons, for example, for anti-personnel landmines[83] and cluster munitions.[84]

Despite the prevalence of sectoral practice, there are important institutions in which disarmament is considered more holistically. The foremost instance of this is the work of the General Assembly. Tasked in the *Charter of the United Nations* with addressing disarmament issues,[85] most of the work of the General Assembly in disarmament takes place in its First Committee, established in 1946 and mandated to deal with matters of disarmament and international peace and security.[86] Another non-sectoral instance of disarmament is the Conference on Disarmament, which was intended to be an avenue for disarmament negotiations which would transcend particular sectors.[87]

However, neither the First Committee nor the Conference on Disarmament has managed to entirely transcend the impetus towards sectoral approaches. This is due in large part to the pragmatic need to organise work into defined

Preparatory Commission for the Organization including through its Provisional Technical Secretariat. See generally: CTBTO (Web Page) <https://www.ctbto.org/the-organization>.

80 For a contemporary assessment, see Malcolm Shaw, 'The United Nations Convention the Prohibitions or Restrictions on the Use of Certain Conventional Weapons, 1981' (1983) 9(2) *Review of International Studies* 110.

81 *CCW* (n 6) art 8(2).

82 See John Borrie, 'Tackling Disarmament Challenges' in Jody Williams, Stephen Goose and Mary Wareham (eds), *Banning Landmines: Disarmament, Citizen Diplomacy, and Human Security* (Rowman and Littlefield, 2008) 263, 275.

83 *Anti-Personnel Landmines Convention* (n 15) art 7 (Transparency measures), art 8 (Facilitation and clarification of compliance) and art 11 (Meetings of the States Parties).

84 *Convention on Cluster Munitions* (n 16) art 7 (Transparency measures), art 8 (Facilitation and clarification of compliance) and art 11 (Meetings of the States Parties).

85 *Charter of the United Nations* art 11.

86 *Rules of Procedure of the General Assembly*, UN Doc A/520/Rev.18 (21 February 2017) Rule 98. And see the confirmation by the General Assembly at its First Special Session on Disarmament that the First Committee should deal only with disarmament and related security matters: *Final Document of the First Special Session on Disarmament of the General Assembly*, UN Doc A/S-10/4 (23 May – 3 June 1978), para 117.

87 *Final Document of the Tenth Special Session of the General Assembly*, S-10/2, (23 May – 3 June 1978) para 120 referring to the Conference on Disarmament as a 'multilateral disarmament negotiating forum'. See generally Caughley (n 12).

categories in their respective programmes of work. A flow-on consequence of this is that even in the general debate segment of the work of the First Committee, statements lean towards addressing (sectoral) issues in sequence, rather than actually engaging in a debate that is free-ranging and holistic.[88]

IV Consequences of the crisis-silo dynamic in disarmament

The foregoing part has shown what I see as two tendencies in disarmament discourse and practice: a tendency to react and respond to particular incidents or crises of disarmament; and a tendency to consider disarmament law issues in a sectoral way — de-linking consideration of the specific issue, weapon or treaty being discussed from the broader disarmament canvas. In this part, I explore three consequences of these tendencies. In Part IV(A), focusing on the crisis dynamic, I argue that it contributes to the pervasive sense that disarmament is ineffectual and therefore utopian — that it is a hopeless pursuit and doomed to failure. I explore this idea by analysing the way in which the sense of crisis about the use of chemical weapons in Syria obscured what was, in fact, a disarmament success. In this way, the failure narrative overall for disarmament remains unchallenged. In Part IV(B), I explore the idea that the combined crisis-silo dynamic gives rise to an 'imperative of action', and I show how that action is generally military in nature. In this way, disarmament becomes militaristic. I draw on both the Syrian and Iranian examples to illustrate my point. Finally, in Part IV(C), using the Iranian situation as an illustration, I argue that the combined silo-crisis dynamic renders invisible and therefore leaves unexplored and unexamined broader issues of disarmament law, in particular issues of control and hegemony.

A Disarmament as failure

Neil Cooper has shown how a sense of failure about disarmament has been propagated in the field of international relations.[89] While the dynamics explored by Cooper have resonance in the international legal literature, my argument here

88 Statements from the General Debate of the First Committee can be found at: *UN Web TV* (Web Page) <http://webtv.un.org/meetings-events/general-assembly/main-committees/1st-committee/>.

89 Cooper (n 20) 354. Cooper explains that one of the ways in which the sense of failure is projected is by differentiating between 'arms control', which the literature defines as being international restraints adopted or imposed on states' armaments policies, and 'disarmament', which the literature defines as being the reduction or abolition of arms: at 356. Thus, instead of seeing the two areas as forming part of a whole, 'disarmament' is understood very narrowly, as meaning only the elimination of a category of weapon or, at its most extreme, the complete elimination of all weapons. By separating out 'arms control' and 'disarmament' in this way, Cooper argues that it allows disarmament to be dismissed as being unrealistic and as having no real-world relevance, in contrast to the practical and pragmatic arms control approach. In these

is that the crisis dynamic, described in Part II above, also plays a large part in creating a pervasive sense of disarmament as failure. In this section, I use the Syrian example to explore this dynamic. I first show why despite its portrayal in the literature, Syria can and should be understood as a disarmament success story. I then explore some thoughts on how the crisis dynamic obscures this understanding of Syria as a success and instead creates a sense of failure.

The dismantling and destruction of Syria's chemical weapons can be fairly claimed as a disarmament success. It seemed, in the immediate aftermath of the Ghouta attack, that a military response was inevitable. President Obama's red line had been well and truly crossed and key allies were primed for taking action.[90] Instead, a joint US-Russia deal was brokered whereby Syria joined the *CWC*, declared its chemical weapons and related production and storage facilities, and then cooperated with the treaty's implementation body, the OPCW, to have those stockpiles and facilities destroyed.[91] Within a year, all declared chemical weapons had either been destroyed or removed from the jurisdiction for destruction.[92] The OPCW also disabled and partly destroyed the chemical weapons production facilities that had been declared by Syria.[93] This is not to suggest that the chemical weapons disarmament of Syria has been straightforward, uncomplicated or fully realised even today, more than six years on. However, the progress that has been made is remarkable and has resulted in the destruction of Syria's declared chemical weapons and related facilities (although obviously some weapons remained undeclared given the subsequent instances of use).[94]

Despite this, in my view, the focus by practitioners and academics on the use of chemical weapons in Syria in 2013 (and subsequently — this was by no means the last use of chemical weapons in the conflict) has obscured the disarmament

ways, Cooper shows how the disarmament-as-failure dynamic is established and maintained: anything that is successful is co-opted as 'arms control' and anything that fails is 'disarmament'.

90 As discussed above, Part II(A).

91 McCormack (n 38) 518.

92 The details of the process are in Ralf Trapp, *Lessons Learnt from the OPCW Mission in Syria Submitted to the Director-General of the Technical Secretariat of the OPCW* (Report, OPCW, 16 December 2015) ('Lessons Learnt').

93 Ralf Trapp, 'Compliance Management under the Chemical Weapons Convention' (Research Paper, UNIDIR, 5 December 2019) 19.

94 See the periodic reports of the OPCW-UN Joint Mission established to oversee the elimination of the Syrian chemical weapons programme available on: 'Mission Updates' *OPCW* (Web Page) <https://opcw.unmissions.org/mission-updates>. The OPCW Fact Finding Mission was also set up (and is still operating) to establish facts surrounding allegations of alleged use of chemical weapons, many of those allegations arising even after the chemical weapons destruction process was pronounced completed: see 'Fact Finding Mission' *OPCW* (Web Page) <https://www.opcw.org/fact-finding-mission>. A third entity was established by the Security Council – the OPCW-UN Joint Investigative Mechanism – with the purpose of identifying the perpetrators of the attacks that had been confirmed by the Fact Finding Mission. However, the Mechanism's mandate was not renewed by the Security Council and so expired in November 2017.

success that came about as a result of the Ghouta attack.[95] In other words, the use of chemical weapons is what is mostly understood and remembered about the role of chemical weapons in the Syrian War, while the unexpected and remarkable disarmament success has been sidelined and obscured.[96] While the Security Council and the OPCW co-operated closely to identify, locate, and render inoperable or destroy the weapon stockpiles, those operations did not garner the same level of attention either in academic commentary or in public discourse.[97] Overwhelmingly, the academic scholarship has focused on the (admittedly unlawful) use of chemical weapons.[98] Once the immediate crisis in 2013 had passed, international law scholars turned their attention elsewhere, returning to Syria only when, in yet another crisis point of the conflict, chemical weapons were used again on a large scale in 2017 and 2018.[99] The disarmament process, in all its tedious, technical detail, could not compete for attention with the immediacy and urgency of the use of the weapons.

By only focusing on the crisis of the use of the weapons (and especially the subsequent attacks), a sense of failure emerged: how could the disarmament exercise be considered a success when clearly *some* weapons remained in the hands of the government forces? Thus, because there was not absolute and complete disarmament success, the entire exercise could easily be dismissed as failure. In this way, we see how a sense of crisis about the use of chemical weapons obscured actual disarmament success in Syria.

B Disarmament as militaristic

In this section, I argue that the combined silo-crisis dynamic in disarmament law can give rise to, and exacerbate, militaristic tendencies. First, I show how disarmament can become militaristic and then I go on to show how both the crisis dynamic and the sectoral tendencies in disarmament discourse perpetuate this tendency. I illustrate this happening in the specific contexts of Syria and Iran.

The idea that disarmament might be militaristic seems counter-intuitive given that the essence of disarmament is to reduce, or even eliminate, weapons.

95 I join with Makdisi and Hindawi in acknowledging the difficulties about describing this as a 'success' given the subsequent deaths and injuries from chemical weapons after 2013: Karim Makdisi and Coralie Pison Hindawi, 'Exploring the UN and OPCW Partnership in Syrian Chemical Weapons Disarmament' (2019) 25(4) *Global Governance* 535, 537 n 5.

96 See, eg, Geoffrey Chapman, Hassan Elbahtimy and Susan B Martin, 'The Future of Chemical Weapons: Implications from the Syrian Civil War' (2018) 27(4) *Security Studies* 704, 719, who refer only in passing to the disarmament of Syria — noting only that it limited and complicated Syria's ability to use chemical weapons — but who go no further in their analysis.

97 There are of course excellent reflections in the more technical/scientific literature — see particularly the work of Ralf Trapp: Trapp, 'Lessons Learnt', (n 92) and Trapp, 'Compliance Management under the Chemical Weapons Convention' (n 93).

98 See, eg, McCormack (n 38), and Chapman, Elbahtimy and Martin (n 96).

99 See, eg, Ash Stanley-Ryan, 'Achieving Chemical Weapons Convention Compliance in the Aftermath of Khan Shaykhun' (2018) 16 *New Zealand Journal of Public and International Law* 39.

Nonetheless, we see repeated examples of states resorting to the use of force in order to forcibly reduce or eliminate the weapons' stockpiles of another state.[100] For example, in 1981, Israel attacked an Iraqi nuclear reactor in Osirak, aimed at disrupting any potential Iraqi nuclear weapons development.[101] In 1984, Iraqi missiles targeted the Iranian Bushehr Nuclear Power Plant.[102] During the 1990s, there were several attacks by the United States against various Iraqi nuclear plants.[103] In 2003, the Iraq War, led by the United States and the United Kingdom, was very much premised on the need to disarm Iraq from its supposed WMD stockpiles.[104] In 2007, Israel carried out an airstrike on Syria's nuclear facility.[105]

This dynamic, termed 'preventive war' by some commentators,[106] is also evident in more recent practice in Syria. While a military response was avoided in 2013, as explained in Part IV(A), that was not the case in subsequent instances of chemical weapons use. In April 2017, the United States launched 59 missiles against an alleged chemical weapons storage facility in Syria,[107] and the following year, joining with the United Kingdom and France, the United States launched 103 missiles against various targets in Syria including alleged chemical weapons storage facilities and a chemical weapons scientific research facility based in Damascus.[108]

In the Iranian situation, as well, the tone and approach has been militaristic. Prior to the Iran Nuclear Deal, there were a number of attacks (although not direct military engagement) against Iran's nuclear programmes. For example, in 2010, Stuxnet, a computer virus, attacked Iran's centrifuges, damaging 1,000 of 6,000 nationwide.[109] This cyber-attack is widely understood to have been carried out by the US and Israel.[110] Between 2007 and 2013, at least five nuclear

100 See Hood, Chapter 3 on coercive disarmament. Here I am only considering instances of actual or threatened use of military action to force a state to disarm, whereas the idea of 'coercive disarmament' is much wider. For an overview of instances of use of force relating to nuclear facilities, see Matthew Fuhrmann, 'Preventive War and the Spread of Nuclear Programs' in Henry Sokolski (ed), *Nuclear Nonproliferation: Moving Beyond Pretense* (Nonproliferation Policy Education Centre, 2012) 33, 34–8.

101 Gray (n 44) 110.

102 IAEA, 'Correspondence between the President of the Atomic Energy Organization of Iran and the Director General' (Information Circular INFCIRC/318, September 1984).

103 Fuhrmann (n 100) 35.

104 *Iraq's Weapons of Mass Destruction: The Assessment of the British Government* (Report, September 2002).

105 Andrew Garwood-Gower, 'Israel's Airstrike on Syria's Al-Kibar Facility – Pre-emptive Self Defence' (2011) 16(2) *Journal of Conflict and Security Law* 263.

106 See, eg, Joseph Cirincione, 'Can Preventive War Cure Proliferation?' (2003) 137 *Foreign Policy* 66.

107 Scharf (n 39) 591.

108 Ibid., 592.

109 Biswas (n 56) 340.

110 Ellen Nakashima and Joby Warrick, 'Stuxnet Was the Work of US and Israeli Experts, Officials Say' *The Washington Post* (online, 2 June 2012) (Web Page) <https://cyber-peace.org/wp-content/uploads/2013/06/Stuxnet-was-work-of-U.S.pdf>.

scientists were assassinated, and these assassinations are widely understood to have emanated from Israel.[111] Throughout the crisis, the language of military attack and bellicosity has been pervasive from both the US and Iran.[112]

With these examples, we can see that when states resort to the use of military force (or threaten to use force) to either prevent proliferation, or to eliminate suspected weapons stockpiles of other states, it can lead to disarmament becoming militaristic.[113] In my view, the pervasive sense of crisis about the use of chemical weapons in Syria, and the suspected nuclear weapons development by Iran, makes it easier to justify and defend (in political, if not in legal terms) exercises of military force by one state, or a group of states, against the military capabilities (or suspected capabilities) or weapons' stockpiles of other states. In other words, the sense of crisis exacerbates the militaristic tendencies embedded in disarmament discourse.

The sense of crisis is heightened when the language of exceptional risk and humanitarian suffering is introduced (as opposed to a crisis which 'just' poses a national security threat).[114] That was precisely the dynamic with the use of chemical weapons in Syria. It was not so much that Syria was a threat to, for example, the United States itself, but that the suffering which would be endured by the Syrian people simply had to be prevented.[115] In this way, the already militaristic tendency within disarmament is woven into a language of humanitarianism, thus implicitly, and at times explicitly, bringing the debate around 'preventive war' into the language of humanitarian intervention.[116]

The sectoral tendency in disarmament practice and scholarship further exacerbates the militaristic dynamic. For example, anti-personnel landmines, cluster munitions and other weapons are earnestly and persistently presented

111 Patrick Cockburn, 'Just Who Has Been Killing Iran's Nuclear Scientists?' *The Independent (UK)* (online, 6 October 2013) (Web Page) < https://www.independent.co.uk/voices/comment/just-who-has-been-killing-irans-nuclear-scientists-8861232.html>.

112 See, eg, the examination of the media reports and public discourse in 'US versus Iran: Tension over the Airwaves', *The Listening Post* (Al Jazeera, 2020) (Web Page) <https://www.aljazeera.com/programmes/listeningpost/2020/01/iran-tension-airwaves-200110234248448.html>.

113 There is of course a debate as to the legality of such exercises of force, but that is not my concern here.

114 This insight is drawn from the work of Anne Orford (n 21).

115 In his statement on the Ghouta attack, then President Obama said 'the world watched with horror as men, women and children were massacred in Syria' and later 'we cannot turn away from the massacre of countless civilians with chemical weapons': Barack Obama, 'Remarks by the President in Address to the Nation on Syria' (Statement, The White House, 31 August 2013) (Web Page) < https://obamawhitehouse.archives.gov/the-press-office/2013/08/31/statement-president-syria>.

116 Scharf's article 'Striking a Grotian Moment' (n 39) is a very clear example of this. In discussing the military strikes against Syria, he argues that they form part of the formation of customary international law of humanitarian intervention because of the suffering wrought by chemical weapons. In Iraq, in 2003, this melding of security and humanitarianism was also evident from the statement of the United Kingdom asserting the legality of any use of military force: above n 105. Christine Gray suggests that the earlier instances of state practice in this area were more firmly couched in the language of state security and self-defence: see Gray (n 44) 110.

by academic commentators and those in the diplomatic disarmament arena as constituting humanitarian crises,[117] and yet there is often no engagement of the broader consequences of such framing. A possible consequence of framing the use of a particular weapon as a humanitarian crisis is that the door is then opened to considering whether the use of a particular weapon could warrant the deployment of military force in the name of humanitarian intervention. But because of the sectoral approach, the flow-on effects of presenting the use of a weapon as a humanitarian harm are not seen or considered.

In the practice of disarmament as well, it is difficult in a sectoral context to manage (or even anticipate) potential militaristic consequences. This is because by definition agencies dealing with weapons (for example, the OPCW) have no authority to work outside their mandate, or comment on any broader consequences of their findings or conclusions. Thus, if a finding that chemical weapons have been used is made, it is not for the OPCW to consider any broader implications of that.

C *Disarmament as structural injustice*

A third consequence that I can see arising from the crisis-silo dynamic is the failure to examine disarmament more systematically particularly in terms of its structural injustices and imbalances which are left obscured, unacknowledged and unexplored. This concern builds on Hilary Charlesworth's exploration of crisis in international law, in which she points out that one of the costs of a crisis paradigm in international law is that it diverts attention from structural injustice.[118] Our preoccupation with crises, she argues, means that 'international law steers clear of analysis of longer-term trends and structural problems'.[119] In my view, this dynamic also afflicts disarmament law. The combined tendencies towards crisis and sectoral studies mean that, in Charlesworth's words, we stay 'glued to specific climatic events, and fail to see the larger picture'.[120] In this section, I will take the example of Iran to explore this point.

In discussing the 'Iran crisis' we get locked into a binary discussion about whether or not Iran is or is not developing nuclear weapons; whether or not the Security Council can or should respond, either by means of further sanctions or ultimately by using military force. Meanwhile, there is little or no discussion of

117 As one example: Human Rights Watch, *Flooding South Lebanon: Israel's Use of Cluster Munitions in Lebanon in July and August 2006* (Report, Vol. 20 No 2(E), February 2008).

118 Charlesworth (n 22) 382.

119 Ibid., 389. Dianne Otto builds on that work and suggests that crises are constructs, created and exploited to justify systems of control: see Dianne Otto, 'Decoding Crisis in International Law: A Queer Feminist Perspective' in Barbara Stark (ed) *International Law and Its Discontents: Confronting Crises* (Cambridge University Press, 2015) 115, 115. See also Anna Hood's work exploring how this dynamic plays out in the context of the power of the Security Council: Anna Hood, 'The Security Council's Legislative Phase and the Rise of Emergency International Law-Making' (PhD Thesis, University of Melbourne, 2014).

120 Charlesworth (n 22) 386.

the broader context in which the situation has unfolded. In my view, there are three significant dynamics that are relevant to understanding the dispute once it is considered in its broader context. The first relates to the broader framework of nuclear law, in particular, the so-called 'grand bargain' of the *NPT*. The second relates to the US-Iran relationship in areas outside of nuclear energy/weapons. The third relates to the internal structures and membership of the international institutions involved in the dispute. I will discuss each one in turn.

(i) The broader framework of nuclear law

The first dynamic that is obscured by the focus on the immediate nuclear crisis is the broader legal framework of nuclear law generally and the *NPT* specifically. In the crisis mode, a common starting point of analysis (and indeed, often the only point of analysis) is Iran's legal obligation not to develop nuclear weapons. It is correct that, as a state party to the *NPT*, Iran is prohibited from developing or possessing nuclear weapons.[121] However, that prohibition (which also applies to the other non-possessor states parties to the treaty) is one of a number of inter-locking rights and obligations carefully constructed in the 'grand bargain' of the *NPT*.

Another essential provision in the *NPT*, and the second pillar of the overall bargain underpinning the treaty, is the legal right of all states (including Iran) to develop peaceful nuclear energy programmes. This emanates from art IV(1) of the *NPT* which provides that:

> Nothing in this Treaty shall be interpreted as affecting the inalienable right of all Parties to the Treaty to develop research, production and use of nuclear energy for peaceful purposes without discrimination and in conformity with Articles I and II of this Treaty [not to transfer, receive, manufacture or acquire nuclear weapons].

The third pillar — the so-called disarmament pillar — is also neglected when adopting a crisis mode to the Iran dispute. This arises from art VI of the *NPT* which provides:

> Each of the Parties to the Treaty undertakes to pursue negotiations in good faith on effective measures relating to cessation of the nuclear arms race at an early date and to nuclear disarmament, and on a treaty on general and complete disarmament under strict and effective control.

Article VI was included in the treaty in order to at least partially redress the discrimination inherent in the regime whereby the treaty acknowledges nuclear weapons possession by five states and prohibits all other states from developing

121 *NPT* (n 3) art II.

nuclear weapons.[122] It was an essential concession sought by the non-nuclear-weapon states when the *NPT* was being negotiated. If they were to forego what was their sovereign right to choose to develop nuclear weapons, they needed an undertaking from the nuclear-weapon states that there would be good faith attempts to negotiate towards nuclear disarmament.[123]

With this bargain, and the three inter-locking pillars, the world is divided into two groups: those acknowledged by the *NPT* as being possessors of nuclear weapons; and those proscribed from possessing or developing nuclear weapons.[124] The division was a necessary compromise in the late 1960s. However, it gave rise to a festering dispute within the *NPT* regime as the years, and then decades, passed with no meaningful progress towards nuclear disarmament. Indeed, in 2005, the year before the IAEA referred the dispute with Iran to the Security Council, discord among the states parties to the *NPT* was so bad that states attending the *NPT* Review Conference were unable to reach agreement on a Final Document.[125] A key part of the failure to adopt a Final Document was frustration on the part of the non-nuclear-weapon states, including Iran, with the slow pace of progress towards this neglected disarmament pillar of the treaty.[126]

Thus, while it is undoubtedly the case that Iran is prohibited from developing a nuclear weapon, the focus on this one pillar (non-proliferation) distorts our understanding of the overall dispute and ignores the carefully constructed balance of other rights and obligations in the overall system.

(ii) The broader US-Iran relationship

The second dynamic that is obscured by the focus on the immediate nuclear crisis is the broader US-Iran relationship. It is now often forgotten that prior to 1979, Iran had pursued a peaceful nuclear energy programme with the explicit and direct support of the United States.[127] Indeed, the cooperation between the United States and Iran in the first decade of the *NPT*'s life can be seen as an exercise of the 'peaceful purposes' pillar of the treaty.[128] That peaceful and cooperative relationship came to a dramatic end in 1979 with the Iranian revolution and subsequent siege of the United States Embassy in Tehran, resulting

122 Harald Müller, 'A Treaty in Troubled Waters: Reflections on the Failed NPT Review Conference' (2005) 40(3) *The International Spectator* 33, 41.

123 Ibid. See as well for a discussion of the *NPT* negotiations: Mohamed Ibrahim Shaker, *The Nuclear Non-Proliferation Treaty* (Oceana Publications, 1980) Vol. 2, at 556–9.

124 See Marauhn and de Vries, Chapter 8.

125 Müller (n 122).

126 Chamundeeswari Kuppuswamy, 'Is the Nuclear Non-Proliferation Treaty Shaking at Its Foundations? Stocktaking after the 2005 NPT Review Conference' (2006) 11(1) *Journal of Conflict and Security Law* 141, 146.

127 Mustafa Kibaroglu, 'Iran's Nuclear Ambitions from a Historical Perspective and the Attitude of the West' (2007) 43(2) *Middle Eastern Studies* 223, 225. See also Biswas (n 56).

128 Captured in *NPT* (n 4) art IV.

in 52 Americans being held hostage for well over a year.[129] A particularly tragic episode came in July 1988 when the USS Vincennes shot down an Iranian airliner, killing all 290 civilians on board.[130] That was part of simmering hostilities through the 1980s and into the 1990s between the two states.[131] In January 1984, the US State Department designated Iran as a State Sponsor of Terrorism,[132] and consequently various sanctions were imposed on Iran.[133] In 2002, in the opening years of the American-led war on terror, the US declared Iran — along with North Korea and Iraq — to be part of an 'axis of evil'.[134]

The fraught and deteriorating relationship between the two states is an important dynamic in understanding the nuclear debate because it reframes the nuclear dispute from being one in which a rogue state (Iran) is attempting to procure a prohibited weapon for evil purposes to one that allows us to see that the nuclear dispute is yet another chapter in a hostile and troubling relationship between the US and Iran.

(iii) Internal structures and membership of international institutions

A third dynamic that becomes visible when the broader framework of the Iran dispute is considered relates to the membership and structure of the IAEA and the Security Council. The IAEA was established in 1957 to promote the peaceful use of atomic energy.[135] Its safeguards system is a means of the IAEA verifying that states are not diverting their peaceful nuclear programmes to unlawful nuclear weapons programmes.[136] However, the Board of Governors

129 The incident led to the United States commencing proceedings against Iran at the International Court of Justice: *United States Diplomatic and Consular Staff in Tehran (United States of America v Iran) (Judgement)* [1980] ICJ Rep 3.

130 *Aerial Incident of 3 July 1988 (Islamic Republic of Iran v United States of America) (Order on 22 February 1996)* [1996] ICJ Rep 9. The case was discontinued in 1996 when the parties settled out of court.

131 See, eg, *Oil Platforms (Islamic Republic of Iran v United States of America) (Judgement)* [2003] ICJ Rep 161.

132 See Office of the Spokesperson, 'Designation of the Islamic Revolutionary Guard Corps: Fact Sheet' *US Department of State* (Web Page, 8 April 2019) <https://www.state.gov/designation-of-the-islamic-revolutionary-guard-corps>.

133 See, eg, *Iran and Libya Sanctions Act* 50 USC §1701 (1996).

134 George W Bush, 'State of the Union Address' (Speech, United States Capitol, 29 January 2002) (Web Page) < https://georgewbush-whitehouse.archives.gov/news/releases/2002/01/20020129-11.html>.

135 *Statute of the IAEA* art II:

> The Agency shall seek to accelerate and enlarge the contribution of atomic energy to peace, health and prosperity throughout the world. It shall ensure, so far as it is able, that assistance provided by it or at its request or under its supervision or control is not used in such a way as to further any military purpose.

136 *NPT* (n 4) art III.

of the IAEA — the executive body that receives the reports of IAEA inspections — is not representative, comprising only 35 states at any given time. Also, while the IAEA is generally seen, and positions itself, as a technocratic impartial arbiter, it is notable that, in practice, all the five acknowledged nuclear-weapon states always have a seat on the Board of Governors. This means that the dispute between the IAEA and Iran is not so much a dispute between Iran and the imagined 'international community'[137] but is rather a dispute between Iran and the five acknowledged nuclear-weapon states and their allies taking place within an ostensibly multilateral setting.[138]

This 'imagined community' problem also plays out with the Security Council. The referral to the Security Council by the IAEA Board of Governors is proper process in terms of the governing law.[139] However, all five permanent members of the Security Council are nuclear-weapon states, and so it is misleading to characterise the Security Council as representing the 'international community' in this regard.[140] Seen in this light, the referral by the IAEA, although entirely proper in terms of legal process, further enhanced and privileged the power of the nuclear-weapon states.

I am not suggesting that the situation is 'unfair' to Iran (it may be, but that is not my concern here), much less that because the permanent Security Council members have nuclear weapons, Iran should be permitted to as well. As a matter of treaty law (and perhaps customary international law, but the point does not need to be addressed here), Iran is prohibited from developing or possessing nuclear weapons. My point is simply that by taking a broader view of the situation, it might be possible to see structural biases and injustices. We might, in this way, come to the realisation that if we want meaningful engagement on nuclear disarmament (all nuclear disarmament, not simply just for Iran), those structural issues need to be acknowledged and addressed.

V A call to arms

The argument I have advanced in this chapter is simple: that disarmament law scholarship and practice is driven by a sense of crisis and is studied and practised in segmented categories isolated from broader themes and dynamics; and that these dynamics taken together have resulted in an overly narrow scholarship and a diplomatic practice that often seems paralysed. Some of the consequences of these dynamics have been explored in Part IV, specifically that disarmament is presented as failure; can become militaristic; and that the structural injustices in disarmament are obscured from view. These intuitions lead me to a call to

137 See Part II(B) drawing particularly on the work of Biswas (n 56).

138 See the critique of the IAEA by Gabrielle Hecht, 'Negotiating Global Nuclearities: Apartheid, Decolonization, and the Cold War in the Making of the IAEA' (2006) 21(1) *Osiris* 25.

139 *Statute of the IAEA* art XII.C. Although note that the Board 'shall' refer to both the Security Council and the General Assembly.

140 See Biswas (n 56).

arms: a call to deepen our scholarship, to reassess the way in which we practise disarmament and to widen our views on disarmament.

If we imagine disarmament as a system of law, rather than simply as an unconnected series of diplomatic practices, what other avenues of exploration would be open to us? Consider for example the work within the umbrella of Third World Approaches to International Law ('TWAIL'). That work has canvassed a broad scope of international law activity and thought from trade, to human rights, to international criminal law, to global health, to the environment and counter-terrorism.[141] As a theoretical school[142] that questions existing hierarchies and the production of knowledge, what might a TWAIL analysis say about the imbalances in disarmament law's focus? A feminist analysis might also reveal complexities in weapons discourse.[143] Innovative thinking in the environmental law arena might make for interesting transplants to the world of disarmament. Finally, might other accounts of international law — law as an iterative process,[144] or law as discursive practice[145] — allow us to reimagine and bring new life and energy into the field of disarmament law? It might be that such lines of enquiry could not only enlighten and enliven our thinking about disarmament, they could enlighten and enliven our understandings of international law itself.

141 See James Gathii, 'TWAIL: A Brief History of Its Origins, Its Decentralized Network, and a Tentative Bibliography' (2011) 3(1) *Trade Law and Development* 26. See also Deborah Cass 'Navigating the New Stream: Recent Critical Scholarship in International Law' in Gerry Simpson (ed) *The Nature of International Law* (Ashgate Publishing, 2002).

142 If indeed it can be considered as a theoretical 'school'. See Gathii (n 141) 30.

143 See, eg, Claire Duncanson and Catherine Eschle 'Gender and the Nuclear Weapons State: A Feminist Critique of the UK Government's White Paper on Trident' (2008) 30(4) *New Political Science* 545. See also the work of UNIDIR on gender and disarmament: UNIDR (Web Page) <www.unidir.org>.

144 Jutta Brunnée and Stephen J Toope, 'Interactional International Law: An Introduction' (2011) 3(2) *International Theory* 307.

145 For example, see Sidra Hamidi, 'Law as a Discursive Resource: The Politics of the Nuclear/Non-Nuclear Distinction in the Non-Proliferation Treaty' (2019) *European Journal of International Relations* 1.

3 The under-explored and evolving landscape of coercive disarmament 1919–2019

Anna Hood

I Introduction

Traditionally, when international lawyers have turned their minds to disarmament, they have focused on voluntary disarmament initiatives where states have come together in bilateral or multilateral fora to give up or limit their supply of weapons. Far less attention has been paid to a different form of disarmament: coercive disarmament. Exactly what comes within the parameters of the term coercive disarmament will be discussed below in Part II, but broadly it can be defined as a phenomenon whereby a state or states (including states working together through the auspices of an international organisation) force another state to give up, restrict or limit its weapons.[1] At various times in history, coercive disarmament measures have been embedded in treaties, in the decisions of international organisations and sanctions regimes, and connected to threats to use, or uses of, force.[2]

The little work that has been done to date by international lawyers on the concept of coercive disarmament has tended to focus on discrete forms or instances of coercive disarmament in isolation from each other. For example, James Fry has written about the idea that the Security Council has adopted coercive disarmament measures,[3] Coralie Pison Hindawi has examined coercive disarmament in the Iraqi and Iranian contexts in the last 30 years[4] and Roger Smith has considered the legality of force or threats of force being used 'to either eliminate

1 Of course, the term can also encompass the disarmament of non-state actors, but as will be discussed in Part II below, this falls outside the scope of the present discussion.

2 For more details about each of these categories, see the discussion in Parts II and III below.

3 James D Fry, 'Dionysian Disarmament: Security Council WMD Coercive Disarmament Measures and Their Legal Implications' (2008) 29(2) *Michigan Journal of International Law* 197 ('Dionysian Disarmament'); James D Fry, 'Of Pinpricks and Cannon Shots: UN Arms Embargoes and Peacekeeping as Coercive Disarmament Measures' (2011) 17(2) *UC Davis Journal of International Law and Policy* 213 ('Of Pinpricks and Cannon Shots').

4 Coralie Pison Hindawi, 'The Controversial Impact of WMD Coercive Arms Control on International Peace and Security: Lessons from the Iraqi and Iranian Cases' (2012) 16(3) *Journal of Conflict and Security Law* 417.

or restrict the production or deployment of certain classes of weapon systems'.[5] There has not, however, been an international lawyer who has examined the array of international law coercive disarmament measures that have been developed over history, their relationship to each other or the idea that together they form a field or sub-category of international law.[6]

In this chapter, I want to begin to look at, and think about, the field of coercive disarmament law as a whole. While work that focuses on specific forms or instances of coercive disarmament is valuable, there is also value in thinking about the many different forms of coercive disarmament that exist in the international legal system as an interconnected field. Such work will enable the consideration of a wide range of issues including: connections and differences between the various forms of coercive disarmament law; how the field has evolved over time; the ideas and philosophies that have permeated the field; the role that coercive disarmament law performs in the international system; and the differences that exist between the objectives, methods and players connected to coercive disarmament law and those associated with voluntary disarmament law. Indeed, turning attention to coercive disarmament has the potential to alter our understanding of disarmament law as well as our understanding of broader ideas in public international law.

In this chapter, it is not possible to set out and analyse all of the insights and value that may come from viewing coercive disarmament as a field of international law. It is possible, however, to start to explore the potential that viewing coercive disarmament as an interconnected field has and the many research pathways to which it could give rise. It is to this end that the chapter is focused.

The chapter begins in Part II by exploring how the term 'coercive disarmament' is best understood and what sorts of international legal measures come within it so that there is clarity around the term and a strong foundation for the rest of the chapter. Parts III and IV then turn to show some of the potential that lies in viewing coercive disarmament law as an interconnected field. Part III reveals some of the insights that can be gleaned from studying how particular elements of coercive disarmament law have developed and evolved over the last century: Part III(A) considers the legal forms that coercive disarmament law measures have assumed; Part III(B) analyses the contexts in which coercive disarmament law measures have emerged and Part III(C) examines the

5 Roger K Smith, 'The Legality of Coercive Arms Control' (1994) 19 *Yale Journal of International Law* 455, 457.

6 Historians have conducted some studies of coercive disarmament over time. See, eg, Fred Tanner (ed), *From Versailles to Baghdad: Post-War Armament Control of Defeated States* (UNIDIR, 1992); Philip Towle, *Enforced Disarmament: From the Napoleonic Campaigns to the Gulf War* (Clarendon Press, 1997). Note, however, that these studies have not been comprehensive and have tended to focus on discrete instances of coercive disarmament rather than understanding them holistically and/or comparing and contrasting them.

substantive provisions that coercive disarmament law measures have encompassed. I argue that key patterns and themes have emerged within each of the three elements over the last hundred years and that these patterns and themes give rise to a host of rich research questions about disarmament law and the international legal system more broadly, which provide the basis for an array of future academic projects. Part IV argues that when coercive disarmament law is studied as an interconnected field rather than a series of isolated measures, it becomes possible to see the various roles it has played in the international legal system over the last hundred years. While it is often assumed that the primary role of coercive disarmament has been to promote international peace and security, I argue that it has also served as a tool for implementing collective punishment and allowing the Great Powers of the day to control and order others in the international system.

Before commencing the substantive parts of the chapter, it is necessary to say something about the selected time period for this study (1919–2019). I wanted this project to be an historical study because in order to understand coercive disarmament law practices as an interconnected field and see how productive this could be, it is helpful to examine coercive disarmament law measures across time. Indeed, as the turn to history in international law scholarship over the last two decades has shown,[7] often it is only when we take a look at an area of law over time that important trends and insights emerge. In any historical study, decisions regarding the time period on which to focus are contentious. The timeframe placed on a project affects what is seen and understood, what is excluded and what conclusions are drawn. There is a long history of coercive disarmament stretching back to Ancient Greece and Rome[8] and consequently a wide range of choices from which to determine the temporal limits of the project. The principal reason for focusing the study on the period of 1919–2019 is that it captures a period when coercive disarmament underwent significant legal changes in the international system. As will become apparent in Parts III(A)–(C) below, in 1919, coercive disarmament measures were primarily ensconced in peace treaties that were developed at the conclusion of conflicts, a situation that had remained the same since coercive disarmament was first juridified in the 18th century. From the mid-20th century on, however, the legal forms that coercive disarmament measures

7 See, eg, James Crawford and Martti Koskenniemi (eds), *The Cambridge Companion to International Law* (Cambridge University Press, 2012); Samuel Moyn, *The Last Utopia: Human Rights in History* (Belknap Press, 2010); Gerry J Simpson, *Law, War and Crime: War Crimes, Trials and the Reinvention of International Law* (Polity Press, 2007); Anne Orford, *Reading Humanitarian Intervention: Human Rights and the Use of Force in International Law* (Cambridge University Press, 2003); Antony Anghie, *Imperialism, Sovereignty and the Making of International Law* (Cambridge University Press, 2005); Treasa Dunworth, *Humanitarian Disarmament: An Historical Enquiry* (Cambridge University Press, 2020).

8 See, eg, Towle (n 6) 5–6.

assumed, the contexts in which they arose and the substance of the measures within them changed significantly. Analysing the practice from 1919 to 2019 allows us to see a number of interesting patterns and themes emerge in coercive disarmament law and provides strong examples of the productive research questions that can eventuate from viewing coercive disarmament law measures as an interconnected field.

II Understanding the scope of coercive disarmament

Before exploring how productive understanding coercive disarmament law measures as an interconnected field can be, it is necessary to settle on a definition of coercive disarmament and consider what sorts of legal measures come within it. Consequently, this part sets out to determine the meaning of the term 'coercive disarmament' before mapping some of the key legal measures that come within its parameters. As will become apparent, a large number of measures can fit within the definition of 'coercive disarmament' — too many to canvas well in a study of this size. In light of this, the part concludes by explaining why certain forms of coercive disarmament measures will be excluded from Parts III and IV of the study.

A Defining coercive disarmament

Given how little attention coercive disarmament has received from international lawyers to date, it is perhaps not surprising that there is no clear understanding of the scope of the concept.[9] Both 'coercive' and 'disarmament' are amorphous terms that are employed in an array of different ways. This section will set out the possible parameters of both terms before turning to explain how they will be understood in this chapter.

At the heart of 'disarmament' is the idea of reducing or completely abolishing weapons.[10] However, it can also refer to preventing an entity from developing certain weapons (for example, through testing or weapons programmes)[11] and preventing weapons from being delivered to a particular entity (for example, by

9 As will be discussed below, James Fry has examined the concept of 'coercive' in the context of disarmament in depth but has not focused specifically on the contours of 'disarmament'.

10 'Disarmament', *Encyclopedia Britannica* (Web Page, 25 November 2019) <https://www.britannica.com/topic/disarmament>; Ray Acheson and Beatrice Fihn, 'Disarmament and Development', *Reaching Critical Will* (Web Page) < http://www.reachingcriticalwill.org/resources/fact-sheets/critical-issues/4646-disarmament-and-development>; 'Disarmament', *Peace Palace Library* (Web Page) < https://www.peacepalacelibrary.nl/research-guides/war-and-peace/disarmament>.

11 An example of this form of disarmament is the UN Security Council resolutions that have sought to halt the development of Iran's nuclear programme and activities. See Fry 'Dionysian Disarmament' (n 3) 271–2.

putting arms embargoes in place).[12] Further, some definitions of disarmament extend beyond a focus on weapons and encompass demilitarisation, that is, the reduction, abolition or restriction of armed forces.[13] Finally, disarmament may be applied to the government of a state or to armed groups within a state (for example, Disarmament, Demobilisation and Reintegration ('DDR')).[14]

There is no single understanding of the term 'coercive' in international law. In the context of work on coercive disarmament, however, James Fry has distilled the essence of the word 'coercion' from a range of legal and philosophical texts. He suggests that 'coercion' is 'a means beyond persuasion that "agents (coercers) can use to get other agents (coercees) to do or not do something"'.[15] In other words, it is a form of pressure.[16] It may involve the use, or threat, of force but equally could entail measures such as sanctions, the suspension of aid and the imposition of fines.[17] It is important to note that coercion may be present even when a state appears to voluntarily consent to a particular initiative (for example, when a state signs a treaty under pressure) as well as when consent appears to be absent or at least very remote.[18]

B Mapping coercive disarmament

Combining the terms, it becomes apparent that a significant number of measures that emerged in the international system between 1919 and 2019 may fall within the concept of coercive disarmament, when both terms are broadly construed. There are some disarmament measures that will fall clearly within the ambit of 'coercive' while there are others where matters are not so clear. In light of this, it may be helpful to think of coercive disarmament measures on a spectrum ranging from those that clearly qualify as coercive to those where there is uncertainty or debate as to their coercive nature.

Peace treaties in which the victorious states require the vanquished state(s) to disarm — for example, the treaties signed between the Allied Nations and

12 Fry, 'Of Pinpricks and Cannon Shots' (n 3) 215–6.

13 The *Oxford English Dictionary*, for example, provides that disarmament means 'the action of disarming esp the reduction of an army or navy to the customary peace footing' *Oxford English Dictionary* (2nd ed, 1989) 'disarmament'; *Peace Palace Library* (n 10).

14 'Disarmament, Demobilization and Reintegration', *United Nations Peacekeeping* (Web Page) < https://peacekeeping.un.org/en/disarmament-demobilization-and-reintegration>; 'What Is DDR?', *United Nations Disarmament, Demobilization and Reintegration Resource Centre* (Web Page) <http://www.unddr.org/what-is-ddr/introduction_1.aspx>.

15 Fry 'Dionysian Disarmament' (n 3), 202.

16 Ibid.

17 Ibid., 202–4.

18 An example of very remote state consent is when the Security Council issues a resolution imposing disarmament measures on a UN member state. The extent to which the target state can be said to have consented to the measures is highly questionable. It is highly unlikely that the target state voted for the Security Council resolution but by virtue of the fact they are a UN member state, they have agreed, pursuant to article 25 of the *Charter of the United Nations* to carry out decisions of the Security Council.

Germany,[19] Austria,[20] Bulgaria,[21] Turkey[22] and Hungary[23] at the end of the First World War — are likely to be towards the more coercive end of the spectrum because they are created in circumstances where the vanquished state has little power to negotiate or resist particular treaty terms. Where other treaties and agreements requiring disarmament appear on the spectrum will depend on the particular circumstances of each case. Examples of particularly coercive treaties and agreements include those where the state being disarmed is not a party to the treaty or agreement. A prime example of this category was the *Potsdam Agreement*[24] between the United Kingdom ('UK'), the United States ('US') and the Soviet Union in 1945 that provided for the forcible disarmament of Germany following the Second World War.[25] Another was the *Munich Agreement*[26] when, in 1938, the UK, France, Italy and Germany agreed to allow Germany to take over the Sudetenland complete with armaments that Czechoslovakia had installed there — thus in effect 'disarming' Czechoslovakia.[27]

Beyond treaties and agreements that provide for coercive disarmament, there is an array of United Nations ('UN') Security Council resolutions that impose disarmament obligations on states. Most of them sit comfortably at the coercive end of the spectrum. One group of Council resolutions encompasses resolutions in which states are required to give up their weapons' programmes. The resolutions issued against Iran and North Korea to address nuclear weapons concerns are illustrative of this form of resolution.[28] A second group of Security Council resolutions that can be understood as encompassing coercive disarmament measures are resolutions that impose arms embargoes on

19 *Treaty of Peace between the Allied and Associated Powers and Germany,* signed 28 June 1919, 13 AJIL Supp 15 (entered into force 10 January 1920) ('*Treaty of Versailles*').
20 *Treaty of Peace between the Allied and Associated Powers and Austria*, signed 10 September 1919, 14 AJIL Supp 1 (entered into force 16 July 1920) ('*Treaty of Saint Germain-en-Laye*').
21 *Treaty of Peace between the Allied and Associated Powers and Bulgaria*, signed 27 November 1919, 14 AJIL 185 (entered into force 9 August 1920) ('*Treaty of Neuilly-sur-Seine*').
22 *Treaty of Peace between the Allied Powers and Turkey*, signed 10 August 1920, 15 AJIL Supp 179 (never entered into force) ('*Treaty of Sèvres*').
23 *Treaty of Peace between the Allies and Associated Powers and Hungary*, signed 4 June 1920, 15 AJIL Supp 1 (entered into force 31 July 1921) ('*Treaty of Trianon*').
24 *Potsdam Agreement: Protocol of Proceedings*, Soviet Union–United States–United Kingdom, adopted 1 August 1945 ('*Postdam Agreement*').
25 Ibid., II(3), II(15).
26 Towle (n 6) 14.
27 A series of attempts to conclude agreements providing for coercive disarmament outside of the peace treaty setting took place at the end of the First World War when the Great Powers tried to force the smaller allied nations (Czechoslovakia, Romania, Yugoslavia, Poland and Greece) to disarm. Their efforts, however, were met with strong resistance and ultimately failed. See Document, 'Notes of a Meeting Held at President Wilson's House in the Place des Etats-Unis, Paris, on Thursday, June 5, 1919, at 4 p.m.' (1919) 6 *Papers Relating to the Foreign Relations of the United States: The Paris Peace Conference: 1919* 1, 202–9.
28 See, eg, SC Res 1696, UN SCOR, 5500th mtg, UN Doc S/Res/1696 (31 July 2006); SC Res 1718, UN SCOR, 61st sess, 5551st mtg, UN Doc S/Res/1718 (14 October 2006); SC Res 1737, UN SCOR, 5612th mtg, UN Doc S/Res/1737 (27 December 2006).

states.[29] Interestingly, such resolutions are coercive not because they impose obligations on the target state but because they require all other states to deny the target state access to weapons. A third category of coercive disarmament resolutions issued by the Security Council is when the Council requires UN peacekeepers to implement DDR measures and disarm armed groups or militias within a country.[30]

Coercive disarmament can also occur through the imposition of sanctions (either dictated by the United Nations Security Council or imposed unilaterally by states) and other diplomatic measures. Where such measures appear on the spectrum will depend on the particular case and it may not always be clear. An example of a state disarming in response to sanctions where opinions differed as to whether the disarmament was voluntary or coercive was Libya's announcement in 2003 that it would abandon its nuclear, chemical and biological weapons programmes after years of US sanctions.[31] Reports at the time spoke of Libya's 'voluntary' decision to forgo these weapons programmes.[32] However, the fact that the state had been diplomatically isolated and placed under severe sanctions for so long suggests that in fact the decision was made because of pressure, not mere persuasion.[33]

A similar case was the conclusion of the Joint Comprehensive Plan of Action ('JCPOA') that was agreed to by Iran, the United States, United Kingdom, Russia, France, China, Germany and the High Representative of the European Union for Foreign Affairs and Security Policy in 2015.[34] The JCPOA set down provisions to ensure Iran's nuclear programme remained peaceful and, at face value, appeared to have been entered into voluntarily by all parties. On closer examination, however, it is apparent that it was concluded against the backdrop of Iran being subject to stringent United Nations Security Council sanctions and the prospect of those sanctions being lifted if it agreed to the JCPOA.[35] The existence of these sanctions, and the promise to lift them if it signed the agreement, suggests that Iran was not 'merely persuaded' to commit to a peaceful nuclear programme but in fact was under significant pressure to do so thus making the agreement coercive at least to a certain degree.

A final way that coercive disarmament can arise is states using force, or threats of force, to disarm another state. Such actions are likely to be classified at the

29 See Fry 'Of Pinpricks and Cannon Shots' (n 3).

30 As James Fry has noted, not all DDR measures are coercive in nature. It is only where the Council requires peacekeepers to carry out disarmament measures in an enforcement capacity: ibid., 223–4.

31 Flynt L Leverett, 'Why Libya Gave Up on the Bomb', *Brookings Institution* (Web page, 23 January 2004) < https://www.brookings.edu/opinions/why-libya-gave-up-on-the-bomb>.

32 'Libya to Give Up WMD', *BBC* (online, 20 December 2003) (Web Page) <http://news.bbc.co.uk/2/hi/3335965.stm>.

33 In addition to the sanctions and international isolation, it is suggested that Libya's decision was also influenced by its concern that it may be attacked by the United States and its allies as Iraq was in March 2003: Leverett (n 31).

34 SC Res 2231, UN SCOR, 7488th mtg, UN Doc S/Res/2231 (20 July 2015) annex A ('JCPOA').

35 Indeed once the JCPOA had been concluded, the UN Security Council passed Resolution 2231 which lifted the sanctions that had been in place against Iran: ibid., [7].

coercive end of the spectrum. An example of force being used to disarm a state was Israel's 1981 attack on the Osirak nuclear reactor that was being built in Iraq.[36] Additionally, the invasion of Iraq by the 'Coalition of the Willing' in 2003 to destroy Iraq's supposed weapons of mass destruction might be understood as a form of attempted coercive disarmament through the use of force. The word attempted is included because, of course, the invading powers found no evidence of weapons of mass destruction once they had entered Iraq.[37]

C *Forms of coercive disarmament discussed in the remainder of the study*

In a small study such as this, it is not possible to cover all forms of coercive disarmament measures, and I am therefore limiting the scope of my discussion. First, I am omitting coercive demilitarisation. While the restriction, limitation and abolition of weapons and armed forces are related, it is possible to draw a clear distinction between the two concepts and I am particularly interested in understanding the patterns that have emerged over time in relation to weapons. Second, I am only looking at instances where states have been required to take action, or refrain from taking action, with respect to their own weapons or weapons' programmes. This excludes two sets of measures from my analysis. First, it leaves out analyses of arms embargoes which do not focus on preventing the target state from doing anything related to its weapons nor require the targeted state to do anything with respect to its weapons but rather place obligations on other members of the international community not to deliver weapons to the target state.[38] Second, it excludes discussion of DDR programmes as they are primarily focused on the disarmament of armed groups, not states.

Thus the remainder of the study analyses coercive disarmament measures that have involved states or international organisations limiting, restricting or abolishing states weapons between 1919 and 2019.

III Examining coercive disarmament law as an interconnected field

Having established a definition of 'coercive disarmament', the chapter now turns to examine the idea that there is value in seeing coercive disarmament law

36 David K Shipler, 'Israeli Jets Destroy Iraqi Atomic Reactor; Attack Condemned by US and Arab Nations', *New York Times* (online, 9 June 1981) (Web Page) <https://www.nytimes.com/1981/06/09/world/israeli-jets-destroy-iraqi-atomic-reactor-attack-condemned-us-arab-nations.html>.

37 Julian Borger, 'There Were No Weapons of Mass Destruction in Iraq' *The Guardian* (online, 7 October 2004) (Web Page) <https://www.theguardian.com/world/2004/oct/07/usa.iraq1>.

38 I appreciate that some states that are subject to arms embargoes may well have other coercive disarmament obligations placed on them. For example, a state that is subject to an arms embargo may also have a Security Council resolution issued against it that requires it to forgo its nuclear weapons programme. Under the parameters I have set up for this chapter, however, it is not relevant to examine the arms embargo.

measures as an interconnected field. In order to do this it looks at some of the key elements of disarmament law across the period of 1919–2019. It explores the patterns and themes that have emerged within each element and the sorts of research questions that might arise out of them. In this way, it highlights the potential that lies in moving beyond analysing coercive disarmament measures in isolation from each other.

A *Examining the legal forms coercive disarmament measures assume*

The first element of coercive disarmament law that this part considers is the legal form that coercive disarmament measures assumed between 1919 and 2019. This section sets out one of the main patterns that emerges when the legal form of coercive disarmament over the course of the century is considered, namely, that the legal form of coercive disarmament measures has changed significantly. It then turns to consider the potential significance of the changes in legal form and the sorts of research projects to which these changes could give rise.

1 *The changes in the legal forms of coercive disarmament measures*

Between 1919 and 2019, the legal form that coercive disarmament measures took underwent significant development. In the first half of the 20th century, coercive disarmament measures were embedded within the legal framework of treaties generally, and peace treaties in particular. This was a practice that dated back to the 1700s when coercive disarmament was first juridified.[39] Between the 18th century and the mid-20th century, it was common for peace treaties to contain provisions dictating which arms vanquished states needed to forgo in the aftermath of wars and what limits were to be placed on states rearming in the years ahead.[40] The peace treaties that were developed at the end of the First World War exemplified this practice. The *Treaty of Versailles*, for example, required Germany to ensure that its navy did not exceed six battleships, six light cruisers, 12 destroyers and 12 torpedo boats,[41] and that its armed forces did not include any military or naval air forces.[42] In addition to coercive disarmament

39 Prior to the 18th century, coercive disarmament was an extra-legal practice that took place outside the juridical sphere. From the Roman Empire through to the 1700s, victorious armies would disarm their vanquished enemies by, for example, setting fire to armaments and sinking armoured fleets without regard for the law. Such actions were frequently complemented by the victors committing mass murders and/or ethnic cleansing, enslaving the vanquished population, pillaging the area and colonising territory. Over time, states began to legalise the aftermath of wars and much of the behaviour that once took place — mass murder, ethnic cleansing, enslavement, pillaging and colonisation — was outlawed. In contrast, however, coercive disarmament was juridified and began appearing in peace treaties: Towle (n 6) 2–6.

40 Ibid.

41 *Treaty of Versailles* (n 19) art 181.

42 Ibid., art 198.

measures appearing in peace treaties, in the early to mid-20th century, they were also occasionally inserted into other forms of treaties and international agreements.[43]

In the second half of the 20th century, the propensity of states to embed disarmament measures in treaties declined dramatically[44] and a more diverse array of legal forms emerged. These forms included Security Council resolutions, economic sanctions and the use, or threat of use, of force. The extent to which some of these new mechanisms complied with international law was at times queried. For example, when the Security Council first began issuing resolutions that required states such as Iraq to abandon its nuclear, chemical or biological weapons programmes,[45] and Iran[46] and North Korea[47] to abandon their nuclear programmes, there was disquiet about the Council creating and imposing law on states without their consent and debates ensued as to whether the *Charter of the United Nations* ('*UN Charter*') permitted such actions.[48]

43 As set out above, two agreements in this period contained coercive disarmament provisions which involved the Great Powers agreeing to the forcible disarmament of other states without their consent: the *Munich Agreement* that forced Czechoslovakia from the Sudetenland and the weapons it had installed there; and the *Potsdam Agreement* (n 24) that provided for the forcible disarmament of Germany.

44 This chapter is only examining international peace treaties (not peace treaties signed after civil wars) because of the focus on the coercive disarmament of states. One of the reasons that coercive disarmament measures being embedded in peace treaties declined is because there was a significant decline in the number of peace treaties concluded. For a discussion of the decline in peace treaties in the second half of the 20th century generally, see Tanisha M Fazal, 'The Demise of Peace Treaties in Interstate War' (2013) 67 (Fall) *International Organization* 695. One of the rare peace treaties in the second half of the 20th century to include coercive disarmament was the Camp David Accords which provided for both Israel and Egypt to limit their arms: *The Framework for Peace in the Middle East*, Egypt–Israel, signed 17 September 1978; *Framework for the Conclusion of a Peace Treaty between Egypt and Israel,* Egypt–Israel, signed 17 September 1978.

45 SC Res 687, UN SCOR, 2981st mtg, UN Doc S/RES/687 (3 April 1991).

46 See (n 28).

47 Ibid.

48 It was asserted by many states and academics alike that the Council's role was to protect international peace and security, not to create new international laws. While the legality of the Council's early coercive disarmament resolutions remains questionable, the fact that it has now repeatedly issued resolutions containing such measures over three decades and the fact that these resolutions have been endorsed or at least acquiesced to by the vast majority of states means that it is possible to argue that the Council's subsequent practice has transformed its powers to allow it to pass such measures. See generally Anna Hood, 'The United Nations Security Council's Legislative Phase and the Rise of Emergency International Law-Making' in Hitoshi Nasu and Kim Rubenstein (eds), *Legal Perspectives on Security Institutions* (Cambridge University Press, 2015) 141; Axel Marschik, 'Legislative Powers of the Security Council' in Ronald St John Macdonald and Douglas M Johnston (eds), *Towards World Constitutionalism: Issues in the Legal Ordering of the World Community* (Martinus Nijhoff Publishers, 2005) 457; Eric Rosand, 'The Security Council as "Global Legislator": *Ultra Vires* or Ultra Innovative' (2005) 28(3) *Fordham International Law Journal* 542; Paul C Szasz, 'The Security Council Starts Legislating' (2002) 96(4) *The American Journal of International Law* 901; Daniel H Joyner, *International Law and the Proliferation of Weapons of Mass Destruction* (Oxford University Press, 2009).

Similarly, when the US, UK, Australia and other supporting states used force to invade Iraq in 2003, ostensibly to rid the country of its weapons of mass destruction, very serious concerns were put forward about the legality of these states' actions.[49] Specifically, states and academics raised concerns that the UN Security Council had not authorised the use of force, and the use of force was not justified under the doctrine of self-defence in art 51 of the *UN Charter* because there had not been an armed attack, nor was the prospect of one imminent.[50] For our purposes, whether these coercive disarmament measures were legal is not the primary concern (although it is an issue worthy of further consideration in future projects). What is significant here is that the states and international organisations carrying out the coercive disarming were seeking to use legal forms and felt compelled to legally justify their actions. Thus coercive disarmament continued to be seen as a legal matter; states and international organisations just adapted and developed the particular legal forms they employed to pursue the practice.

2 *A research agenda on changing legal forms of coercive disarmament measures*

The observation that the legal forms that are used for coercive disarmament have changed over the last century is interesting and goes some way by itself to showing the value in examining coercive disarmament measures together as a whole. However, it also gives rise to a range of questions and issues that are worthy of further research. This section sets out some of these questions and issues to provide an indication of the sort of work that scholars could engage with in years to come if we continue to view coercive disarmament law as an international legal field.

To start with, future research projects could explore the various actors, law-making processes and contexts that have been involved with each coercive disarmament legal form. While such matters may appear somewhat pedestrian and technical, they in fact may give rise to significant insights. Which actors are involved in crafting coercive disarmament measures affects the substance, scope and targets of those measures. For example, the permanent members of the Security Council (all of whom possess nuclear weapons) are likely to have very different priorities to other states that may be interested in coercive disarmament measures. Further, if certain legal forms place restrictions on which states can participate in their construction and are used repeatedly in certain periods, it may well be that the legal form assists with the construction of hierarchies and hegemony in the international system. Indeed, legal form can often have a

49 Matthew Craven et al., 'We Are Teachers of International Law' (2004) 17(2) *Leiden Journal of International Law* 363.

50 See, eg, Sean Murphy, 'Assessing the Legality of Invading Iraq' (2004) 92(2) *Georgetown Law Journal* 173.

profound effect on shaping international relations and the power politics at play in the international system.[51]

Second, simply reflecting on the fact that there have been significant changes and innovations in legal form might generate insights into what the states and international organisations driving such changes and innovations were hoping to achieve: did changes in legal form promise different results, did they obscure certain practices or open up particular possibilities? Third, what should be made of the fact that the legality of some of the legal forms adopted in the second half of the 20th century and early 21st century was questioned and contested? What does this tell us about the practice of coercive disarmament at that time and perhaps disarmament law more broadly?

Finally, it is interesting to observe that while one of the legal forms above (treaties) is a traditional, ordinary form of international law, the others can be understood as emergency forms of international law because they are made in times of crisis when there are international threats to peace and security.[52] Thinking about the idea that there has been a move from coercive disarmament as a normal form of international law-making to it being an emergency form of international law-making opens up an array of avenues for further exploration. Why has the phenomenon come to be seen as an exceptional matter? What might emergency law theories reveal about the contemporary practice of coercive disarmament? And what risks might come with a move to emergency law-making in this sphere?

B The contexts in which coercive disarmament occurs

A second aspect of coercive disarmament law that gives rise to interesting patterns, themes and research questions is the changing contexts in which coercive disarmament law measures have been produced over the last century. This section explores the main contextual changes that have occurred around coercive disarmament law measures since 1919 before suggesting some research pathways to which these changes give rise.

1 The changing contexts of coercive disarmament law

Over the last century, there has been a shift from coercive disarmament measures emerging in the aftermath of wars to them being implemented either outside the context of war or as a rationale for going to war. In the first part of the 20th

51 For a discussion of how the legal form of nuclear weapons laws affected both the construction and maintenance of the Cold War and Post-Cold War periods, see Anna Hood, 'Nuclear Weapons Law and the Cold War and Post-Cold War Worlds: A Story of Co-Production' in Matthew Craven, Sundhya Pahuja and Gerry Simpson (eds), *International Law and the Cold War* (Cambridge University Press, 2020) 98.

52 For general discussions about emergency law-making in the international arena see Hood, 'The United Nations Security Council's Legislative Phase and the Rise of Emergency International Law-Making' (n 48) 141.

century, coercive disarmament initiatives were primarily embedded in treaties at the conclusion of conflicts.[53] The treaties at the end of both world wars provide strong evidence of this. Since the end of the Second World War, however, the vast majority of instances where coercive disarmament has occurred have been where there have been concerns about the threat posed by a state's weapons' programme but no actual conflict has broken out. Examples of this occurring include the Security Council's resolutions against North Korea and Iran, and Israel's use of force against Iraq's nuclear reactor in 1981. There are a handful of exceptions to this trend such as at the conclusion of the Gulf War in 1991 when the Security Council passed Resolution 687 requiring Iraq to disband its nuclear, chemical and biological weapons programmes.[54] For the most part, however, coercive disarmament measures have not been implemented at the conclusion of hostilities.

2 A research agenda on the changing contexts of coercive disarmament law

Paying attention to the idea that the context in which coercive disarmament measures emerge has changed, opens up numerous lines of enquiry. To start with, there are questions about the relationship between the changes in legal form and the changes in context. The change from coercive disarmament measures emerging in post-war contexts to pre-war or non-war contexts appears to map closely onto the shift from coercive disarmament measures appearing in peace treaties to them emerging in other legal forms. This raises questions as to whether the change in form drove the change in context, the change in context encouraged a change in form or whether the two factors were mutually constitutive.

Another line of enquiry that a focus on the changing context invites is whether, and if so how, the phenomenon of coercive disarmament fits within broader trends in international affairs. One possible trend it may fit within is the broad shift that occurred at international law across the 20th century from a punitive paradigm to a preventative or regulatory one. Gabriella Blum has explained how until the early 20th century, international law permitted and condoned states collectively punishing other states for violations of international law.[55] Over the course of the century, however, collective punishment fell out of favour and states shifted (at least rhetorically) to trying to prevent violations of international law through a variety of means.[56] The move from states coercively

53 An exception was the *Munich Agreement* which required Czechoslovakia to abandon the Sudetenland, and the armaments it had installed there, in an attempt to appease Hitler and prevent war from breaking out in Europe: see Towle (n 26).

54 SC Res 687, UN SCOR, 2981st mtg, UN Doc S/RES/687 (3 April 1991).

55 Gabriella Blum, 'The Crime and Punishment of States' (2013) 38(1) *Yale Journal of International Law* 57, 58.

56 Ibid.

disarming other states at the end of conflicts (when international law had invariably been violated and harm perpetrated), to states seeking to coercively disarm states prior to conflict occurring, appears to accord with this paradigm. As will be seen below in Part IV, there are reasons to question the extent to which all pre- or non-war coercive disarmament measures should in fact be understood as not involving a form of punishment.[57] However, the prima facie correlation between what has happened in coercive disarmament law and Blum's theory makes it worthy of further consideration. This is especially so as Blum herself has drawn attention to the idea that the turn to prevention at international law has been primarily a theoretical and rhetorical one that at times has obscured the fact that, in reality, states are often still motivated by the desire to enact punitive measures.[58]

A further research pathway that opens up in this area is considering the consequences of changing coercive disarmament law contexts. It would be interesting to consider whether the change in contexts has resulted in a growing prevalence of coercive disarmament law measures and the measures becoming a more significant feature in the international system. Such a consequence seems plausible because when coercive disarmament law measures were confined to post-war contexts there were a limited number of opportunities for such measures to be produced. The fact, however, that in recent times they have emerged in pre-war and non-war contexts means there are far more opportunities for them to be developed. Research on this issue as well as other possible consequences of the shift in contexts would thus be worthy of examination.

C The substance of coercive disarmament measures

A third element of coercive disarmament law that shows how valuable it is to see coercive disarmament law as an interconnected field is the substance of coercive disarmament law measures. This section examines how the substance of coercive disarmament law measures has evolved since 1919 and how this evolution reveals a promising research agenda.

1 The changing substance of coercive disarmament law

Similarly to the other factors considered so far in this part, there has been a transformation in the substance of coercive disarmament measures that have been targeted at states over the last century. One hundred years ago the practice involved the reduction, limitation or abolition of a wide range of arms. In the last 50 years, there has been a shift to coercive disarmament measures that focus almost exclusively on targeting nuclear weapons, and occasionally chemical and biological weapons, but very rarely conventional weapons.

57 See below Part IV(B).
58 Blum (n 55) 59.

In the period after the First World War, the treaties containing coercive disarmament measures included provisions that required limitations on the conventional armaments of target states[59] as well as provisions that prevented those states from possessing, manufacturing and importing asphyxiating, poisonous or other gases, and all similar liquids, materials or devices.[60] Similarly, the *Potsdam Agreement* and the peace treaties between the Allies and smaller Axis powers at the end of the Second World War combined limitations on conventional weapons with prohibitions on nuclear, chemical and biological weapons. For example, art 51 of the *Treaty of Peace with Italy* (1947) provided:[61]

> Italy shall not possess, construct or experiment with (i) any atomic weapons, (ii) any self-propelled or guided missiles or apparatus connected with their discharge ..., (iii) any guns with a range of over 30 kilometres, (iv) sea mines or torpedoes of non-contact types actuated by influence mechanisms, (v) any torpedoes capable of being manned.

Article 54 of the same treaty limited the number of tanks that Italy could have to 200.

In more recent decades, coercive disarmament measures have been directed at states' nuclear, chemical and biological weapons programmes rather than their stocks of conventional weapons or their capacity to manufacture conventional weapons.[62] However, in this period, conventional weapons did feature in arms embargoes and DDR programmes. As set out above, these coercive disarmament mechanisms have been excluded from this study because they are not directed at requiring *states* to take action with respect to disarmament.[63] There is scope, however, for future projects to document and reflect on the changing forms that coercive disarmament measures have assumed in relation to non-state actors.

2 *A research agenda on the changing substance of coercive disarmament law*

The shift from coercive disarmament measures targeting all types of weapons to targeting primarily nuclear, chemical and biological weapons raises a host of questions for further research. Chief among them is what has driven this change? Have those implementing coercive disarmament measures lost interest in controlling conventional weapons because they pose little risk in the nuclear age? Is coercive disarmament an effective mechanism for nuclear-weapon possessor states (that is, those that are entitled to possess nuclear weapons under the

59 See, eg, *Treaty of Saint Germain-en-Laye* (n 20) Part V.

60 See, eg, ibid., art 135.

61 *Treaty of Peace with Italy*, signed 10 February 1947, 49 UNTS 3 (entered into force 15 September 1947).

62 See, eg, SC Res 687, UN SCOR, 2981st mtg, UN Doc S/RES/687 (3 April 1991) para 8.

63 See above Part II(C).

international legal system)[64] to employ to stop other states from acquiring such weapons without themselves having to give up their nuclear stockpiles as they might have to in voluntary disarmament contexts? Or is this shift explicable by reference to other, broader trends in the international legal arena over the last 70 years?

Another important factor to consider is that, as noted above, the apparent shift within coercive disarmament to an almost exclusive focus on weapons of mass destruction is disrupted when arms embargoes and DDR measures are brought into the frame. It would be interesting to explore the idea that coercive disarmament involving conventional weapons has not disappeared completely but has simply moved into different sorts of contexts including, most prominently, contexts involving non-state actors. There is room to consider what the significance of this move might be and what we can learn from analysing it in detail.

One further angle that is worthy of consideration is what a shift towards coercive disarmament measures focusing on nuclear, chemical and biological weapons (at least with respect to state actors) means for voluntary disarmament initiatives around these sorts of weapons.

IV The roles that coercive disarmament law plays in the international legal system

Understanding coercive disarmament law as an interconnected legal field not only enables us to generate insights into how the different elements of the practice have evolved over time but also allows us to consider what roles the practice has played in the international legal system. In this part, I examine some of the key roles coercive disarmament law has played in the international legal system since 1919 and identify areas for further research in this space. I argue that the orthodox account of the role that coercive disarmament law measures play is that they further international peace and security. I assert, however, that there is a real need to interrogate this account and question both the extent to which coercive disarmament measures in fact aid international peace and security, and whether there are other roles that the practice might play in the international system. I suggest that if we look behind the dominant rhetoric put forward about the practice, it becomes apparent that coercive disarmament law measures provide an avenue to implement collective punishment and for the Great Powers of the day to order and control other players in the international legal system.

A The quest for peace and security

In the days of Ancient Rome and Greece, one of the primary reasons coercive disarmament was purportedly pursued was to appease the gods in the aftermath

64 *Treaty on the Non-Proliferation of Nuclear Weapons*, opened for signature 1 July 1968, 729 UNTS 161 (entered into force 5 March 1970).

of war by offering them the weapons of the vanquished.[65] In recent times, it appears that those engaged with coercive disarmament have stopped fearing the wrath of the gods. Instead, in the 20th and 21st centuries, the most commonly and publicly articulated reason that states and international organisations have put forth for implementing coercive disarmament law measures is the attainment of international peace and security. Since 1919, states and international organisations have consistently argued that they have imposed coercive disarmament measures on other states in order to end conflict, prevent it from occurring and keep states and individuals safe generally.

For example, in the aftermath of the First World War, Clemencau, Wilson, Orlando and George defended the extensive disarmament measures they imposed on the Central Powers by arguing that they needed to weaken the threat that the Central Powers posed, and enhance not only their own security but the security of the international community generally.[66] Their primary argument for seeking to forcibly disarm the minor allies was also centred on peace and security matters. They determined that because they were requiring the disarmament of the new state of Austria, the states around Austria should also be disarmed so that they could not threaten Austria.[67] Similarly, the rationale for forcing Czechoslovakia from the Sudetenland in 1938 was to prevent Germany from initiating war[68] and, in 1945, the measures in the *Potsdam Agreement* were seen as necessary to weaken Germany through disarmament in order to maintain peace.[69]

In the second half of the 20th century and the early decades of the 21st, concerns about security have continued to underpin many of the explanations for enacting coercive disarmament measures. For example, in one of the Security Council debates surrounding the need to limit Iran's nuclear programme, the US stated that 'Iran's pursuit of nuclear weapons capability constitutes a grave threat'[70] and Russia noted that there was a need to pass a Security Council resolution restricting Iran's programme to ensure the 'establishment of solid regional and international security and stability'.[71] Similarly in the Security Council debates about North Korea in 2006, China explained that coercive disarmament measures were needed because North Korea's nuclear actions were

65 Towle (n 6) 5.

66 Ibid., 66, 68–9, 72; Frédéric Dessberg, 'The Versailles Peace Settlement and the Collective Security System' in Thomas W Zeiler and Daniel M DuBois (eds), *A Companion to World War II* (Blackwell Publishing Ltd, 2013) vol. 1, 29, 29; David Stevenson, 'Britain, France and the Origins of German Disarmament, 1916–19' (2006) 29(2) *Journal of Strategies Studies* 195, 195–7; Towle (n 6) 94.

67 Sir Maurice Hankey, 'Notes of a Meeting Held at President Wilson's House in the Place des Etats-Unis, Paris, on Thursday, May 15, 1919, at 11 a.m.' (1919) 5 *Papers Relating to the Foreign Relations of the United States: The Paris Peace Conference: 1919* 1, 627–8, 634.

68 Towle (n 6) 94.

69 Ibid., 165–6.

70 UN SCOR, 61st sess, 5612 mtg, UN Doc S/PV.5612 (23 December 2006) 3.

71 Ibid., 2.

'not conducive to peace and stability in North-East Asia'[72] and the US justified the Council's measures by noting that North Korea's 'proclaimed test of a nuclear device … unquestionably poses one of the gravest threats to international peace and security that the Council has ever had to confront'.[73]

While the states and international organisations that have implemented coercive disarmament law measures have consistently asserted that they have done so to further international peace and security, there is a need to probe and question these assertions. To start with, to what extent can we really trust the public rationales offered by those pursuing coercive disarmament law agendas and what other motivations might inform decisions to engage with the practice? Second, even if we accept that international peace and security concerns have been a factor in decisions to implement coercive disarmament law measures, to what extent have they in fact furthered international peace and security? Whose peace and security? And are there times that coercive disarmament law measures have in fact (contrary to the public justifications offered) actually generated instability, tension and conflict? Third, if we move beyond the rhetoric of international peace and security, what other roles might we see coercive disarmament law measures performing in the international sphere? Unfortunately, it is not possible to delve into all of these questions in this chapter. In the closing sections, however, I would like to briefly consider two roles beyond international peace and security that I think coercive disarmament law measures have played in the international system since 1919.

B A mechanism for collective punishment

While the goal of international peace and security has always been the primary explanation that states have put forward to justify coercive disarmament measures, if we look beyond the public rhetoric, it becomes apparent that there have been other motivations animating coercive disarmament measures. Chief among these other measures has been the desire of the Great Powers to punish states that have wronged them, violated international law or threatened the international system.

Leaders have always been fairly reticent about publicly declaring that they are imposing coercive disarmament measures for punitive ends. The time when leaders were most open about their punitive intentions was in the early decades of the 20th century when, as discussed above in Part III(B), ideas of collective punishment were more accepted in international law than they are today.[74] When the *Treaty of Versailles* was being drafted, the leaders of the Great Powers at times intimated that its provisions were designed to punish Germany for the devastation it had brought to Allied Nations. Such statements were more often

72 UN SCOR, 61st sess, 5551 mtg, UN Doc S/PV.5551 (14 October 2006) 4.
73 Ibid., 2.
74 Blum (n 55) 58.

made to domestic audiences, who were seeking revenge for the harm they had suffered, as opposed to being made in international fora.[75]

As the acceptability of collective punishment declined across the 20th century, so too did the willingness of leaders to suggest that coercive disarmament measures were punitive in nature. However, this has not stopped states, academics and the media from asserting that a number of coercive disarmament measures in recent decades have in fact been punitive, at least in part. For example, many viewed the coercive disarmament measures inflicted on Iraq by the Security Council in Resolution 687 at the conclusion of the Gulf War as punitive and comparable in some ways to the measures imposed on Germany in the *Treaty of Versailles.*[76]

Additionally, Iran has repeatedly expressed the view that the Security Council action taken against it in relation to its nuclear programme has been punitive in nature.[77] Iran's vocal concerns about the punitive intent behind the Council resolutions have driven other nations to deny Iran's allegations. Most prominently, in a 2007 Security Council debate, Indonesia, the United States, Russia and China all explicitly rejected the idea the Council's actions were punitive in nature.[78] However, there were a number of comments in the Security Council debates about the resolutions imposed on Iran that suggest a number of states were motivated, at least in part, by a desire to punish Iran for its nuclear programme and transgressions of international law. For example, in a 2006 debate about a Security Council resolution directed at Iran's nuclear programme, the United Kingdom emphasised that 'Iran has simply thumbed its nose at the Council and defied international law'.[79]

There is room for future studies to delve further into the potentially punitive nature of modern coercive disarmament measures. Such studies could move beyond the assertions of states and other players about whether a particular measure was punitive in nature and develop objective criteria for determining whether a measure is punitive as well as methodologies for assessing competing claims about the punitive nature of coercive disarmament measures. Further, regard could be had to the implications of coercive disarmament measures

75 Dessberg (n 64) 32; Alan Sharp, 'The "Big Four" – Peace-Making in Paris in 1919' [2009] (65) *History Review* 14, 15. It is interesting to note that there was a tension in the aftermath of the First World War between laying the blame for the war at the feet of the Kaiser and seeking individual punishment through the international criminal law lens, and laying the blame for the War with the German people as a whole and thus pursuing collective punishment measures such as coercive disarmament. Ultimately in this era, collective punishment succeeded and individual criminal justice measures did not: Towle (n 6) 72–3.

76 See, eg, James D Fry, *Legal Resolution of Nuclear Non-Proliferation Disputes* (Cambridge University Press, 2013) 113.

77 UN SCOR, 61st sess, 5500th mtg, UN Doc S/PV.5500 (31 July 2006) 10; UN SCOR, 61st sess, 5612 mtg, UN Doc S/PV.5612 (23 December 2006) 9; UN SCOR, 62nd sess, 5647th mtg, UN Doc S/PV.5647 (24 March 2007) 16.

78 UN SCOR, 62nd sess, 5647th mtg, UN Doc S/PV.5647 (24 March 2007).

79 UN SCOR, 61st sess, 5612 mtg, UN Doc S/PV.5612 (23 December 2006) 5.

exhibiting punitive elements in an era where notions of collective punishment are frowned upon in international legal circles and states purport to have moved beyond them.

C *A form of international control or ordering*

A third role that coercive disarmament law measures have performed over the last century is that they have given the Great Powers of the day a means to control and order the international system. Coercive disarmament can be understood as a means of control or ordering in a number of ways. First, it can be seen as a tool that Great Power states wield to consolidate and augment their power and position in the international system while weakening the power and position of other states.[80] Second, it can be understood as a method that states employ to signal who is accepted within the international community and who has been cast out. Further, at times, coercive disarmament measures may be seen as providing a road to redemption for those states that have been cast out. They can be reintegrated into the international community, albeit in a subservient position, if they abide by the dictated disarmament measures and forgo particular weapons.

Whether state leaders actively think about coercive disarmament as a form of control or ordering is difficult to prove as states, unsurprisingly, do not make statements that suggest they are imposing coercive disarmament law measures to strengthen their own position in the international system. However, regardless of the specific intent of Great Power leaders, in practice their coercive disarmament actions often operate to enhance their states' geo-political positions and ostracise the target states.[81] Understood in this way, coercive disarmament can be seen as contributing to the phenomenon that Gerry Simpson has termed 'legalised hegemony'.[82] This is the idea that the Great Powers, acting in concert, have a superior status in the international system that is supported by international law.[83] Here, the legal measures containing coercive disarmament measures (for example, treaties and Security Council resolutions) are working to enhance the power and dominance of the Great Powers.

It is apparent then that coercive disarmament measures have performed an array of roles in the international system over the last century. It would be interesting for future projects to consider the extent to which each of the different

80 The use of coercive disarmament in this way goes beyond a concern with international peace and security as it involves states trying to strengthen their own positions geopolitically.

81 States being ostracised through coercive disarmament measures can be seen from the way that the First and Second World War peace treaties significantly weakened the geopolitical standing and power of the vanquished states for a number of years as well as the way Security Council resolutions against Iraq, North Korea and Iran have undermined their international standing and positioned them as pariah states.

82 Gerry Simpson, *Great Powers and Outlaw States* (Cambridge University Press, 2004) 67–8.

83 Ibid.

roles coercive disarmament has performed has complemented or undermined the aims of other disarmament law endeavours. Are coercive disarmament measures that are punitive in nature consistent with voluntary disarmament measures? Are coercive disarmament measures that are contributing to legalised hegemony in the international order compatible with attempts to achieve general and complete disarmament? Are the notions of peace and security that underpin coercive disarmament measures the same as the ideas around peace and security that inform voluntary disarmament activities?

V Conclusion

The aim of this chapter has been to illustrate the value that lies in viewing coercive disarmament law measures as an interconnected field of international law rather than as a series of isolated incidents. I have sought to provide examples of the sorts of insights and understandings that might be generated from seeing coercive disarmament as a holistic field and to set out some research questions that other disarmament law scholars might like to pursue. I have suggested that the way the field has developed over time and the different ideas embedded within it have implications, not only for how we understand and think about disarmament law, but also for how we comprehend trends and ideas in international law as a whole. I look forward to engaging with other scholars in the years ahead about the issues that have been raised in this piece as well as many other coercive disarmament law matters that have not yet come to the fore.

Part II

Humanitarianism and human rights in disarmament

4 Completing the package

The development and significance of positive obligations in humanitarian disarmament law

*Bonnie Docherty**

I Introduction

The adoption of the *Anti-Personnel Landmines Convention*[1] in 1997 marked the beginning of a remarkable era in disarmament, which continues to thrive today. While humanitarian concerns have long informed the regulation of weapons, that treaty, followed by those that banned cluster munitions and nuclear weapons, established a distinctive approach known as 'humanitarian disarmament'.[2] Humanitarian disarmament seeks to address the human and environmental harm inflicted by arms through the establishment and implementation

* The author participated actively in the negotiations of the *Convention on Cluster Munitions* and the *Treaty on the Prohibition of Nuclear Weapons*. She is grateful to Elizabeth Minor, advisor at Article 36, for her collaboration on a paper prepared for the Auckland Law School conference that laid the groundwork for this chapter. She also wishes to thank Minor and Steve Goose of Human Rights Watch for offering comments on this chapter.

1 *Convention on the Prohibition of the Use, Stockpiling, Production and Transfer of Anti-Personnel Mines and on Their Destruction*, opened for signature 3 December 1997, 2056 UNTS 211 (entered into force 1 March 1999) ('*Anti-Personnel Landmines Convention*').

2 *Convention on Cluster Munitions*, opened for signature 3 December 2008, 2688 UNTS 39 (entered into force 1 August 2010) ('*CCM*'); *Treaty on the Prohibition of Nuclear Weapons*, opened for signature 20 September 2017 (not yet in force) ('*TPNW*'). For a discussion of the role of humanitarian concerns in earlier weapons treaties, see, eg, Treasa Dunworth, *Humanitarian Disarmament: An Historical Enquiry* (Cambridge University Press, 2020); Nik Hynek, 'Re-Visioning Morality and Progress in the Security Domain: Insights from Humanitarian Prohibition Politics' (2018) 55(3–4) *International Politics* 421, 427–8; Tim Caughley, 'Tracing Notions about Humanitarian Consequences' in John Borrie and Tim Caughley (eds), *Viewing Nuclear Weapons through a Humanitarian Lens* (UNIDIR, 2013) 14, 15–8. For a discussion of the new humanitarian approach to disarmament, see, eg, Markus Reiterer and Cornelia Kratochvil, 'Introduction to the Agora on Humanitarian Disarmament' (2013) 15 *Austrian Review of International and European Law* 3; Patrick McCarthy, 'Deconstructing Disarmament: The Challenge of Making the Disarmament and Arms Control Machinery Responsive to the Humanitarian Imperative' in John Borrie and Vanessa Martin Randin (eds), *Alternative Approaches in Multilateral Decision Making: Disarmament as Humanitarian Action* (UNIDIR, 2005) 51, 56–7.

of norms.[3] It is people-centred in its purpose, process, and provisions. The humanitarian nature of this approach shifts the focus from advancing perceived national security interests to ending civilian suffering. Civil society organisations and survivors, in partnership with like-minded states and international organisations, advance this goal through 'citizen diplomacy'.[4] The instruments that result establish comprehensive standards for protecting civilians.[5]

Humanitarian disarmament law may be best known for its absolute prohibitions on the use, production, development, and stockpiling of specific weapons, but they represent only part of the package. Obligations to respond to the ongoing effects of past use are equally important to achieving humanitarian aims. The 1997 *Anti-Personnel Landmines Convention*, the 2008 *Convention on Cluster Munitions* ('*CCM*'), and the 2017 *Treaty on the Prohibition of Nuclear Weapons* ('*TPNW*') all include requirements (positive obligations) to adopt remedial measures.[6] These treaties oblige states parties to undertake clearance activities, notably the cleanup of contaminated areas and other measures to protect civilians from exposure to explosive or toxic remnants of war.[7] They also mandate that states parties provide victim assistance to people who have suffered the humanitarian consequences of banned weapons.[8]

This chapter analyses the development and significance of remedial measures in humanitarian disarmament law. Part II explores the negotiating history and legal content of clearance and victim assistance provisions. Part III identifies the challenges presented by states' reluctance to break new ground, concerns about feasibility, and resistance to assuming responsibility. Part IV examines

3 The definition in this paragraph comes from one developed by an international group of humanitarian disarmament experts at a Harvard Law School conference on the topic. See 'About', *Humanitarian Disarmament* (Web Page) <https://humanitariandisarmament.org/about>. See also Bonnie Docherty, 'A "Light for All Humanity": The Treaty on the Prohibition of Nuclear Weapons and the Progress of Humanitarian Disarmament' (2018) 30(2) *Global Change, Peace & Security* 163, 163–4 ('A "Light for All Humanity"'); Reiterer and Kratochvil (n 2); McCarthy (n 2) 56–7.

4 Jody Williams and Stephen D Goose, 'Citizen Diplomacy and the Ottawa Process: A Lasting Model?' in Jody Williams, Stephen D Goose and Mary Wareham (eds), *Banning Landmines: Disarmament, Citizen Diplomacy, and Human Security* (Rowman & Littlefield Publishers, 2008) 181, 181.

5 The humanitarian approach has expanded beyond the three ban treaties to encompass a range of efforts to reduce arms-inflicted suffering. It informed the negotiation and content of the *Arms Trade Treaty*, opened for signature 3 June 2013, 3012 UNTS (entered into force 24 December 2014). It has also influenced current campaigns to ban fully autonomous weapons, to end the use of explosive weapons with wide area effects in populated areas, and to increase protections for humans and the environment from toxic remnants of war.

6 This chapter uses the terms 'remedial measures' and 'positive obligations' interchangeably to refer to clearance and victim assistance requirements. Legally, the term 'positive obligations' refers to any action a state party is required to perform, as opposed to prohibited actions. In disarmament law, stockpile destruction and reporting are other common positive obligations. During the *TPNW* negotiations, however, 'positive obligations' became used as shorthand for provisions related to clearance and victim assistance, and this chapter adopts the same approach.

7 *Anti-Personnel Landmines Convention* (n 1) arts 4–6; *CCM* (n 2) arts 4, 6; *TPNW* (n 2) arts 6–7.

8 *Anti-Personnel Landmines Convention* (n 1) art 6(3); *CCM* (n 2) arts 5–6; *TPNW* (n 2) arts 6–7.

how humanitarian disarmament countered these challenges through three distinguishing characteristics: a humanitarian purpose, an inclusive process, and a new framework of law and practice. Part V assesses the legal and practical impacts of the obligations to clear remnants of war and assist victims. The chapter shows how the humanitarian approach to disarmament drove the development of the positive obligations, and how they in turn are helping humanitarian disarmament to fulfil its promise.

II Development of clearance and victim assistance provisions

Over the past 20 years, clearance and victim assistance have become integral parts of humanitarian disarmament. The negotiating histories of the treaties banning anti-personnel landmines, cluster munitions, and nuclear weapons show that the development of the positive obligations presented challenges. As time passed, however, the remedial measures grew stronger, due to the inclusion of more detailed obligations and their adaptation to different circumstances.

A Anti-Personnel Landmines Convention

The desire for a legal prohibition on anti-personnel landmines inspired the negotiations of the *Anti-Personnel Landmines Convention*, but participants recognised from the beginning that fully addressing the humanitarian concerns associated with weapons demanded more. Designed to be detonated by human contact once emplaced on or under the ground, anti-personnel landmines were causing an increasingly large number of casualties in the 1990s.[9] In 1996, many states became frustrated with the failure to deal comprehensively with these weapons in a United Nations ('UN') forum and committed to addressing the issue in an independent one.[10] They initiated the Ottawa Process, a series of diplomatic conferences that culminated in the adoption of the *Anti-Personnel Landmines Convention*. The *Ottawa Declaration*[11] that launched this process

9 Stuart Maslen, 'The Role of the International Committee of the Red Cross' in Maxwell A Cameron, Robert J Lawson and Brian W Tomlin (eds), *To Walk without Fear: The Global Movement to Ban Landmines* (Oxford University Press, 1998) 80, 84; *Anti-Personnel Landmines Convention* (n 1) art 2(1) defining anti-personnel mine.

10 That year, states parties to the *Convention on Prohibitions or Restrictions on the Use of Certain Conventional Weapons Which May Be Deemed to be Excessively Injurious or to Have Indiscriminate Effects (with Protocols I, II and III)*, opened for signature 10 October 1980, 1342 UNTS 137 (entered into force 2 December 1983) ('*CCW*') reached consensus on amending *CCW Protocol II* on landmines, but many of these states along with the International Committee of the Red Cross ('ICRC') and civil society considered the revised protocol inadequate: Maslen (n 9) 85–6; Kenneth R Rutherford, *Disarming States: The International Movement to Ban Landmines* (Praeger, 2011) 81–2.

11 Ottawa Conference, *Ottawa Declaration on Anti-Personnel Land Mines*, 5 October 1996 ('*Ottawa Declaration*'), reprinted in Stuart Maslen, *Commentaries on Arms Control Treaties Volume 1: The Convention on the Prohibition of the Use, Stockpiling, Production, and Transfer of*

not only called for a ban on anti-personnel landmines, but also noted that 'the international community must provide significantly greater resources to mine-awareness programs, mine-clearance operations and victim assistance'.[12] Negotiators understood that an absolute prohibition would prevent further production, proliferation, and use of anti-personnel landmines. It would, however, neither stop already emplaced anti-personnel landmines from creating new victims, interfering with development, or blocking the return of displaced persons, nor would it help survivors in a holistic and sustained way.[13]

Participants in the Ottawa Process agreed on the need for a requirement to clear landmines, although their views on what form that requirement should take diverged in some ways. A provision mandating clearance appeared in the first draft of the *Anti-Personnel Landmines Convention* and was fleshed out over the months that followed.[14] Key points of discussion were the length of the deadline for clearance and the differences in duties regarding minefields and mined areas, a distinction that was ultimately abandoned.[15]

The final text of the *Anti-Personnel Landmines Convention* highlights the importance of clearance by addressing it in five places. The preamble expresses the belief that states parties must 'do their utmost to contribute in an efficient and coordinated manner to face the challenge of removing anti-personnel mines placed throughout the world, and to assure their destruction'.[16] Article 1 places the requirement to clear contamination on a par with the treaty's prohibitions by listing destruction of anti-personnel mines, whether emplaced or stockpiled, among the treaty's general obligations. Article 5 obliges states parties to 'destroy or ensure the destruction of all anti-personnel mines in mined areas under [their] jurisdiction or control' within ten years of entry into force, unless they receive an extension.[17] In the interim, states parties must ensure that mined areas are marked, monitored, and fenced in order to exclude civilians.[18]Article 6 requires all states parties 'in a position to do so' to help affected states parties meet their obligations by providing assistance for clearance. Article 7 mandates

---

Anti-Personnel Mines and on Their Destruction (Oxford University Press, 2nd ed, 2005) appendix 3, 381 ('*Anti-Personnel Landmines Convention Commentary*').

12 *Ottawa Declaration* (n 11) [4]-[5].

13 South African Ambassador Jacob Selebi, who served as president of the final negotiations, described the clearance and victim assistance provisions as 'central to the comprehensiveness of the treaty': Jacob S Selebi, 'Foreword by Ambassador Jacob S Selebi' in Louis Maresca and Stuart Maslen (eds), *The Banning of Anti-Personnel Landmines: The Legal Contribution of the International Committee of the Red Cross* (Cambridge University Press, 2000) xxi, xxii.

14 'Convention on the Prohibition of Anti-Personnel Mines (First Austrian Draft Text)', art 5, reprinted in Maslen '*Anti-Personnel Landmines Convention Commentary*' (n 11) appendix 4, 428.

15 Maslen '*Anti-Personnel Landmines Convention Commentary*' (n 11) 167–71 [5.4]–[5.13]. According to the draft texts, minefields, unlike mined areas, contained mines whose locations were recorded, facilitating clearance: at 169 [5.8].

16 *Anti-Personnel Landmines Convention* (n 2) preamble para 2.

17 Ibid., art 5(1)

18 Ibid., art 5(2).

detailed reports regarding the location of contaminated areas, progress on clearance, and warnings to the population.

While the adoption of clearance obligations was largely uncontroversial during the Ottawa Process, victim assistance measures encountered significantly more difficulties.[19] The *Ottawa Declaration* referenced victim assistance, but early drafts of the treaty did not contain any relevant provisions. Support for including victim assistance came largely from the International Campaign to Ban Landmines ('ICBL'), a global civil society coalition, the International Committee of the Red Cross ('ICRC'), and states from the Global South. The declaration of an international civil society conference held in Maputo, Mozambique, in February 1997 called for greater assistance to survivors.[20] The June 1997 Brussels Declaration, which outlined the main elements of the treaty in advance of the negotiations, did not, however, mention assistance for mine victims.[21] Several African states objected to the omission, and it led to 'a diplomatic row between Belgium and South Africa'.[22] In the lead-up to the final negotiations, the ICRC recommended including victim assistance among the treaty's general obligations, a proposal that ultimately failed.[23] Negotiators inserted a requirement to provide international cooperation and assistance for victims only towards the end of the process after 'heated discussions' regarding its content.[24]

Ultimately, victim assistance appeared in the *Anti-Personnel Landmines Convention* in two places. Consistent with the treaty's humanitarian aims, the preamble articulates states parties' wish 'to do their utmost in providing assistance for the care and rehabilitation, including the social and economic reintegration of mine victims'.[25] Article 6(3) requires states parties 'in a position to do so' to provide such assistance for victims through a range of organisations.[26] The treaty does not impose a specific obligation on affected states parties to assist victims in their territory. Despite this limitation, art 6(3) proved to be an influential element of the treaty because its text and later implementation measures laid the foundation for the growth of victim assistance over the following years.

19 See generally Jerry White and Ken Rutherford, 'The Role of the Landmine Survivors Network' in Maxwell A Cameron, Robert J Lawson and Brian W Tomlin (eds), *To Walk without Fear: The Global Movement to Ban Landmines* (Oxford University Press, 1998) 99.

20 Maslen '*Anti-Personnel Landmines Convention Commentary*' (n 11) 32 [0.60].

21 Brussels Conference, *Declaration of the Brussels Conference on Anti-Personnel Landmines*, 24–27 June 1997, reprinted in Maslen '*Anti-Personnel Landmines Convention Commentary*' (n 11) appendix 3, 397–401.

22 Ibid., 57–8 [0.111].

23 'Comments of the ICRC on the Third Austrian Draft (13/5/97) of the Convention on the Prohibition of Anti-Personnel Mines', reprinted in Louis Maresca and Stuart Maslen (eds), *The Banning of Anti-Personnel Landmines: The Legal Contribution of the International Committee of the Red Cross* (Cambridge University Press, 2000) 548, 548–9.

24 Maslen '*Anti-Personnel Landmines Convention Commentary*' (n 11) 190 [6.8].

25 *Anti-Personnel Landmines Convention* (n 2) preamble para 3.

26 This paragraph also requires international assistance for mine awareness programmes.

B Convention on Cluster Munitions

Remedial measures played an even greater role in the Oslo Process, which consisted of five diplomatic conferences that produced the *CCM*.[27] Cluster munitions are large weapons that disperse dozens or hundreds of smaller submunitions; they endanger civilians because they have a wide area effect and because a large number of submunitions fail to detonate on impact, becoming de facto anti-personnel landmines. At the first Oslo Process meeting in February 2007, states adopted the *Oslo Declaration*,[28] in which they committed to concluding a legally binding instrument that would not only ban cluster munitions but also

> establish a framework for cooperation and assistance that ensures adequate provision of care and rehabilitation to survivors and their communities, clearance of contaminated areas, risk education and destruction of stockpiles of prohibited cluster munitions.[29]

The Lima Discussion Text, released at the second Oslo Process meeting, already included separate articles on clearance and victim assistance.[30]

Over the course of subsequent negotiations, the clearance provisions in the *CCM* became more detailed in ways that advanced the Convention's humanitarian aim. The Lima Discussion Text's article on clearance had followed the *Anti-Personnel Landmines Convention*'s basic structure of an overarching obligation to clear within ten years, a list of implementation duties, and rules regarding requests for extensions.[31] Later texts expanded the scope of the article from unexploded submunitions to a broad range of cluster munition remnants and lengthened the list of required steps for the implementation of clearance.[32]

27 The Oslo Process followed the Ottawa Process model of independent negotiations outside of the UN: Human Rights Watch, *Meeting the Challenge: Protecting Civilians through the Convention on Cluster Munitions* (November 2010) 120.

28 Oslo Conference on Cluster Munitions, *Oslo Declaration* (Declaration, 23 February 2007) [1], reprinted in Gro Nystuen and Stuart Casey-Maslen (eds), *The Convention on Cluster Munitions: A Commentary* (Oxford University Press, 2010) annex 2, 631.

29 Ibid.

30 *Lima Discussion Text* (Chair's Discussion Text, 23–25 May 2007) arts 4–6, reprinted in Gro Nystuen and Stuart Casey-Maslen (eds), *The Convention on Cluster Munitions: A Commentary* (Oxford University Press, 2010) annex 3, 632.

31 Ibid., arts 4(1)–(3).

32 For a discussion of the evolution of the cluster munition remnants definition, see Bonnie Docherty et al., 'Article 2: Definitions' in Gro Nystuen and Stuart Casey-Maslen (eds), *The Convention on Cluster Munitions: A Commentary* (Oxford University Press, 2010) 144, 224–6 [2.194]–[2.196]. The final treaty defined cluster munition remnants as 'failed cluster munitions, abandoned cluster munitions, unexploded submunitions and unexploded bomblets': *CCM* (n 2) art 2(7). For evidence of the expanding list of implementation steps, see *Vienna Discussion Text* (Chair's Discussion Text, 14 November 2007) art 4(2), and *Draft Cluster Munitions Convention* (Draft Instrument, 21 January 2008) art 4(2), reprinted in Gro Nystuen and Stuart Casey-Maslen (eds), *The Convention on Cluster Munitions: A Commentary* (Oxford University Press, 2010) annexes 4–5, 641, 653.

These texts also made risk reduction education an obligation for affected states parties rather than merely a matter of international cooperation and assistance.[33] The most contentious element related to the proposal to oblige user states parties to assist affected states parties with clearance of remnants that pre-dated the Convention's entry into force. Ultimately, drafters agreed to a political rather than legally binding commitment, that is, a provision 'strongly encourag[ing]' user states parties to provide such support.[34]

Compared to the *Anti-Personnel Landmines Convention*, the clearance provisions in the *CCM* contain additional obligations and greater detail regarding implementation. The preamble of the *CCM*, like that of its predecessor, emphasises the importance of clearing cluster munition remnants in an efficient and coordinated manner.[35] Also drawing from the *Anti-Personnel Landmines Convention*, art 6 obliges states parties 'in a position to do so' to assist with clearance in a range of ways, and art 7 requires reporting on the status and progress of clearance efforts. The *CCM* goes further, however. Article 4(4) creates the above-mentioned political commitment on user state responsibility, and art 4(2)(e) mandates risk reduction education 'to ensure awareness among civilians'. While the *Anti-Personnel Landmines Convention* obliges states parties to mark, monitor, and clear contaminated areas, states parties to the *CCM* have additional obligations. They are required to assess the threat; prioritise needs, including for the protection of civilians; adopt a national plan; and post warning signs.[36]

The *CCM* sharpened its predecessor's clearance provisions, but it represented a sea change in the law of victim assistance. Responding to pressure from survivors and the Cluster Munition Coalition ('CMC'), a global civil society campaign, states agreed at only the second Oslo Process meeting that 'victim assistance should be a core provision of the new treaty contained in a separate Article'.[37] The so-called Vienna Consensus that emerged from the third meeting presented victim assistance as 'a key legal obligation of the same quality as the other main building blocks of the future treaty'.[38] That meeting's discussion text obliged affected states parties to provide for 'medical care and rehabilitation, psychological support and social and economic inclusion'.[39] During final negotiations in Dublin, participants added even more detail, including steps for implementation that were designed to make progress easier to measure

33 *Vienna Discussion Text* (n 32), art 6(8); *Draft Cluster Munitions Convention* (n 32) art 4(2)(e).
34 John Borrie, *Unacceptable Harm: A History of How the Treaty to Ban Cluster Munitions Was Won* (UNIDIR, 2009) 302–3 ('*Unacceptable Harm*'); *CCM* (n 2) art 4(4)(a).
35 *CCM* (n 2) preamble 5.
36 *CCM* (n 2) art 4(2).
37 Markus Reiterer and Tirza Leibowitz, 'Article 5: Victim Assistance' in Gro Nystuen and Stuart Casey-Maslen (eds), *The Convention on Cluster Munitions: A Commentary* (Oxford University Press, 2010) 328, 330–1 [5.2], 335–6 [5.14].
38 Docherty et al., 'Article 2' (n 32) 151 [2.7] citing Ambassador Wolfgang Petritsch (Closing Remarks, Vienna Conference, 7 December 2007).
39 *Vienna Discussion Text* (n 32) art 5(1).

and monitor.[40] The adopted text further specified that victim assistance should show sensitivity to age and gender, be integrated into frameworks related to disabilities, development, and human rights, and incorporate the principle of non-discrimination among cluster munition victims or between them.[41]

As with clearance, a proposal to impose user state responsibility became a point of contention, but it was set aside to avoid 'undue politicization of the debate'.[42] Participants also held substantial discussions about whether the treaty should define the term 'cluster munition victim' and how broad the definition should be.[43] Despite having many elements to consider, negotiators collaborated in good faith to refine the victim assistance provisions over the course of the Oslo Process.

As adopted, the *CCM* revolutionised the law surrounding victim assistance in five key ways.[44] It defines 'cluster munition victim', incorporating families and communities as well as directly affected individuals.[45] It dedicates an entire article to victim assistance obligations: art 5 obliges affected states parties to provide assistance to victims in their territory and enumerates specific steps for implementation. The Convention creates a new requirement to report on the status and progress of victim assistance programmes. It also makes all of its victim assistance measures obligatory by using the word 'shall'.[46] Finally, it invokes international human rights law in the preamble and in art 5, which requires states to provide victim assistance 'in accordance with applicable international humanitarian and human rights law'.[47] Ken Rutherford, co-founder of Landmine Survivors Network and a leader of the CMC's victim assistance advocacy, said '[t]his is a huge[ly] positive development that set the bar so high', and predicted that the treaty's victim assistance provisions would become the standard for future instruments.[48]

C Treaty on the Prohibition of Nuclear Weapons

The *TPNW*, like its humanitarian disarmament predecessors, not only banned the use of a class of weapons but also included positive obligations. States had hitherto approached the elimination of nuclear weapons primarily from a national security perspective, focusing on 'deterrence, self-defence and the role of

40 Reiterer and Leibowitz (n 37) 364–5 [5.89] quoting Survivor Corps, 'Improving Language on Victim Assistance in the Cluster Munitions Treaty' (May 2008).
41 *CCM* (n 2) art 5.
42 Reiterer and Leibowitz (n 37) 345 [5.35]–[5.36].
43 Docherty et al. 'Article 2' (n 32) 150–7 [2.5]–[2.22].
44 Bonnie Docherty, 'Breaking New Ground: The Convention on Cluster Munitions and the Evolution of International Humanitarian Law' (2009) 31(4) *Human Rights Quarterly* 934, 949–52 ('Breaking New Ground').
45 *CCM* (n 2) art 2(1).
46 Ibid., arts 5, 6(7), 7(1)(k).
47 Ibid., preamble paras 6, 9–10, art 5(1).
48 Docherty 'Breaking New Ground' (n 44) 952 quoting interview with Kenneth R Rutherford (Bonnie Docherty, 24 June 2008). Landmine Survivors Network later became Survivor Corps.

nuclear weapons in military doctrine more generally'.[49] Building on the success of the *Anti-Personnel Landmines Convention* and the *CCM*, however, advocates for a prohibition on nuclear weapons began to reframe the issue as a matter of humanitarian concern.[50] In 2010, ICRC President Jakob Kellenberger declared that the 'debate must ultimately be about human beings'.[51] In 2013 and 2014, states convened for a series of independent conferences, which were part of the Humanitarian Initiative, to consider the human and environmental consequences of nuclear weapons.[52] Following those meetings, the International Campaign to Abolish Nuclear Weapons ('ICAN'), a coalition of more than 570 non-governmental organisations from more than 100 states, declared that positive obligations should be a pillar of a future treaty.[53] The UN General Assembly voted in December 2016 to negotiate a 'legally binding instrument to prohibit nuclear weapons' the following year.[54] Consistent with its overarching humanitarian purpose, the final document included provisions on victim assistance and environmental remediation (the latter being analogous to the clearance of other remnants of war).[55]

The *TPNW* negotiations considered victim assistance and environmental remediation together. The first draft of the treaty, released in May 2017, contained an article entitled 'Assistance' that incorporated provisions on both of these subjects. The victim assistance paragraph drew heavily from art 5(1) of the *CCM*, with a key qualification: it required affected states parties to provide assistance only if they were 'in a position to do so'.[56] The much weaker environmental remediation paragraph did not establish any obligations. It simply gave affected

49 Vincent Bernard, 'A Price Too High: Rethinking Nuclear Weapons in Light of Their Human Cost' (2015) 97 *International Review of the Red Cross* 499, 504.

50 Elizabeth Minor, 'Changing the Discourse on Nuclear Weapons: The Humanitarian Initiative' (2015) 97 *International Review of the Red Cross* 711, 721–2.

51 Jakob Kellenberger, 'Bringing the Era of Nuclear Weapons to an End' (2015) 97 *International Review of the Red Cross* 883, 883.

52 See generally Alexander Kmentt, 'The Development of the International Initiative on the Humanitarian Impact of Nuclear Weapons and Its Effects on the Nuclear Weapons Debate' (2015) 97 *International Review of the Red Cross* 681.

53 ICAN, *Principles of a Treaty Banning Nuclear Weapons* (Report, April 2015) (Web Page) <http://www.icanw.org/wp-content/uploads/2015/04/principles-2.pdf>. The Humanitarian Pledge produced by Austria at the end of the Humanitarian Initiative recognised that 'the rights and needs of victims have not yet been adequately addressed' and acknowledged environmental harm, although it did not specifically call for a new treaty to include obligations to address those problems: Government of Austria, *Humanitarian Pledge* (Pledge, March 2015) (Web Page) <http://www.icanw.org/wp-content/uploads/2015/03/HINW14vienna_Pledge_Document.pdf>.

54 *Taking forward multilateral nuclear disarmament negotiations*, GA Res 71/258, UN GAOR, 71st sess, 68th plen mtg, Agenda Item 98, Supp No 49, UN Doc A/Res/71/258 (23 December 2016) para 8; 'UN General Assembly approves historic resolution', *ICAN* (Web Page, 23 December 2016) <http://www.icanw.org/campaign-news/un-general-assembly-approves-historic-resolution/>.

55 *TPNW* (n 2) arts 6(1)–(2).

56 *Draft Convention on the Prohibition of Nuclear Weapons*, UN Doc A/CONF.229/2017/CRP.1 (22 May 2017) art 6(1).

states parties the right to seek and receive assistance for remediation of contaminated areas.[57] Co-ordinated civil society advocacy at the initial negotiating conference in March and in the weeks that followed contributed to the inclusion of these provisions in the May draft text.[58] Significant improvements were needed, however, to bring them in line with humanitarian disarmament precedent.

During the June–July 2017 negotiating sessions, proponents of the positive obligations succeeded in strengthening them. Progress was initially slow. Despite state support for several amendments, the second draft included only superficial changes, such as reorganising paragraphs and changing the article title to 'Victim Assistance and Environmental Remediation'.[59] The third draft removed the 'in a position to do so' caveat and created a clear obligation to remediate the environment.[60] States disagreed, however, on who should bear responsibility for these measures. Some states wanted states that had used or tested nuclear weapons to be held responsible because they caused the harm.[61] Other states along with ICAN and the ICRC argued that affected states parties should bear primary responsibility because they have a duty under international human rights law to care for their own people, the arrangement protects their sovereignty, and their proximity to the problem puts them in the best place to assess needs and render assistance.[62] To ensure that affected states would not bear an undue burden, proponents of this approach called for other states parties to help affected states parties meet their obligations.[63] This framework of shared responsibility reflected a humanitarian disarmament approach borrowed from the *CCM*.

The often-heated debate continued until the close of the negotiations.[64] In the end, the *TPNW*, like the *CCM*, combined affected state responsibility with international cooperation and assistance obligations. As a result of pressure from many states in the Global South, however, the *TPNW* went a step further and included a paragraph in art 7 explicitly placing legal responsibility on using or testing states parties to 'provide adequate assistance to affected States Parties, for the purpose of victim assistance and environmental remediation'.[65]

The positive obligations in the *TPNW*'s final text follow the general structure of their predecessors while addressing different types of harm. Framing the issue

57 Ibid., art 6(2).

58 Author's observations of this advocacy and the *TPNW* negotiations.

59 *Draft Treaty on the Prohibition of Nuclear Weapons*, UN Doc A/CONF.229/2017/CRP.1/Rev.1 (27 June 2017) arts 7–8.

60 *Draft Treaty on the Prohibition of Nuclear Weapons*, Agenda Item 9, UN Doc A/CONF.229/2017/L.3 (3 July 2017) art 6.

61 See, eg, statements by Cuba, Egypt, Iran, Malaysia, and Vietnam, in author's notes from *TPNW* negotiations, 20 June 2017.

62 See, eg, statements by Ecuador, Ghana, the Holy See, Ireland, Sweden, Switzerland, and ICRC, in author's notes from *TPNW* negotiations, 20 June 2017. See also Molly Doggett and Alice Osman, 'Responsibility for Victim Assistance and Environmental Remediation' (2017) 2(7) *Nuclear Ban Daily* 2.

63 Ibid.

64 Author's notes and observations from *TPNW* negotiations.

65 *TPNW* (n 2) art 7(6).

as a humanitarian one, the preamble recognises the 'unacceptable suffering of and harm caused to the victims' of the use and testing of nuclear weapons.[66] Article 6(1), which closely parallels art 5(1) of the *CCM*, imposes a clear obligation on affected states parties to provide victim assistance. Article 6(2), the equivalent of earlier clearance provisions, requires affected states parties to 'take necessary and appropriate measures towards the environmental remediation of [contaminated] areas'. Article 7 lays out requirements for other states parties, including user states, to help affected states parties meet their obligations.[67] While including the key remedial measures of the *Anti-Personnel Landmines Convention* and the *CCM*, the *TPNW* extends the application of the provisions. It establishes for the first time positive obligations that deal with the ongoing impacts of nuclear weapons and with toxic, rather than explosive, remnants of war.[68] The *TPNW* thus reinforces the precedent of humanitarian disarmament while expanding its scope.

III Challenges to the positive obligations

As far back as the 1996 *Ottawa Declaration*, states recognised that the humanitarian approach to disarmament required remedial as well as preventive measures.[69] Translating this general understanding into specific legal provisions on clearance and victim assistance, however, was not always easy. Some states were reluctant to break new ground, concerned about the feasibility of implementing the positive obligations, and resistant to assuming additional responsibilities.

A Reluctance to break new ground

In entering into the treaty negotiations, participants demonstrated a commitment to certain elements of humanitarian disarmament. They embraced the approach's humanitarian purpose and agreed to engage in a distinctive process to achieve it. When it came to drafting specific provisions, however, their hesitancy to move beyond the traditional parameters of disarmament posed a challenge to the development of the positive obligations in the three treaties.

States supported adopting clearance provisions in the *Anti-Personnel Landmines Convention* and the *CCM* because the provisions built on legal precedent,

66 Ibid., preamble para 6. The preamble also recognises the disproportionate impact on women, girls, and indigenous peoples and the 'grave implications' for the environment: at paras 4, 7.

67 Although the provisions are less detailed in some places than those in the *Anti-Personnel Landmines Convention* and *CCM*, states parties can look to the provisions and practices associated with the earlier treaties for guidance on implementation.

68 Docherty 'A "Light for All Humanity"' (n 3) 184–5. A toxic remnant of war is '[a]ny toxic or radiological substance resulting from military activities that forms a hazard to humans or ecosystems': Aneaka Kellay, *Pollution Politics: Power, Accountability and Toxic Remnants of War* (Report, 24 November 2014) 30 (Web Page) <https://ceobs.org/wp-content/uploads/2018/01/WEB_READY-TRW_Pollution_Politics_Report.pdf>.

69 *Ottawa Declaration* (n 11) [4]–[5].

but they were slow to include the less familiar environmental remediation obligation in the later *TPNW*. The 1996 *Amended Protocol II to the CCW*,[70] which dealt with mines and booby-traps, required the removal of minefields after hostilities, thus providing a starting point for negotiating clearance provisions in the earlier humanitarian disarmament treaties.[71] At the time of the *TPNW* negotiations, by contrast, environmental remediation appeared to be a novelty in disarmament law. Instead of focusing on a physical remnant of war, environmental remediation involves containing or removing amorphous contamination spread through the air, ground, and water. To overcome resistance to requiring environmental remediation, proponents presented it as a different type of clearance and argued that it was essential to achieving the underlying humanitarian aim of the negotiations.[72]

A reluctance to create new paradigms also impeded the evolution of victim assistance provisions. Even though states participating in the Ottawa Process endorsed the concept of victim assistance in their initial declaration, they could not reach agreement on a provision once the drafting of the *Anti-Personnel Landmines Convention* began. During the final negotiations, civil society campaigners supplemented their long-standing calls to reduce human suffering with arguments that an obligation to assist anti-personnel mine victims was consistent with other areas of international humanitarian law.[73] The campaigners' shift from moral to legal reasoning suggested that they realised the importance of citing precedent to their advocacy. States ultimately incorporated a provision in the *Anti-Personnel Landmines Convention*, but it came only in the form of an international cooperation and assistance obligation. States were more amenable to victim assistance measures during the negotiations of the *CCM* and the *TPNW*, in large part, because the emergence of a humanitarian disarmament framework of law and practice provided precedent.

B Concerns about feasibility

Feasibility concerns presented a second challenge to the inclusion and evolution of positive obligations. In particular, states were hesitant to adopt obligations when fulfilment would be costly, difficult to measure, and perhaps unachievable.

The question of the feasibility of clearance arose primarily with regard to toxic rather than explosive remnants of war. Clearance of landmines and cluster munitions is a realistic, albeit sometimes daunting, endeavour because it is a quantifiable activity that can be completed according to measurable, international

70 *Amended Protocol on Prohibitions or Restrictions on the Use of Mines, Booby-Traps and Other Devices*, opened for signature 31 May 1995, 35 ILM 1206 (entered into force 3 December 1998) ('*Amended Protocol II*').

71 See, eg, Maslen '*Anti-Personnel Landmines Convention Commentary*' (n 11) 178–9 [5.29].

72 Article 36 and International Human Rights Clinic (Harvard Law School), 'Environmental Remediation in the Nuclear Weapon Ban Treaty: A Comprehensive and Detailed Approach' (June 2017) 6–7 (Web Page) <http://www.article36.org/wp-content/uploads/2017/06/ER-ban-treaty-full-1.pdf>.

73 White and Rutherford (n 19) 113–4.

standards.[74] Therefore, states were willing from early in the Ottawa and Oslo Processes to agree to clearance requirements provided there were extensions to deadlines in cases of heavy contamination.[75] In the *TPNW* negotiations, by contrast, states did not agree to the obligation to remediate the environment until much later. The delay was likely attributable not only to its legal novelty but also to a recognition that returning an area affected by nuclear fallout to its original state is rarely, if ever, possible. In the end, art 6(2) of the *TPNW* obliged states parties to engage in remediation, but it presented remediation as a goal to work towards rather than to complete.

With regard to victim assistance, concerns about feasibility emerged during the negotiations of the *Anti-Personnel Landmines Convention*. Such assistance can entail providing a wide range of support over the lifetime of an individual and can be hard to quantify and assess because it is often incorporated into general healthcare funding. Reportedly concerned about 'financial ramifications', donor states — that is, non-affected states that would provide international cooperation and assistance — wanted to limit assistance to rehabilitation, a concrete form of support, which encompassed medical treatment and the provision of prostheses.[76] Other states, especially from Africa, and the ICBL, however, called for measures to promote social and economic reintegration, a broader and less tangible concept that could encompass, *inter alia*, education, vocational training, legislation, and steps to minimise discrimination.[77] The latter approach prevailed, but only late in the negotiations.[78]

C Resistance to responsibility

The question of responsibility presented a third hurdle to adopting the positive obligations. States generally supported including international cooperation and assistance provisions, despite having divergent views about the details, and such obligations appear in all three of the humanitarian disarmament treaties discussed here. At different times, however, affected states and user states resisted the imposition of more specific responsibility.

Early in the Ottawa Process, drafters agreed that the clearance of landmines required a joint effort by affected and non-affected states parties,[79] but efforts to assign responsibility for the more novel and far-reaching concept of victim

74 'Clearance Requirements' (International Mine Action Standard 09.10, 2nd ed, 1 January 2003, as amended June 2015) 1–2.

75 *Anti-Personnel Landmines Convention* (n 1) art 5(3); *Lima Discussion Text* (n 30) art 4.

76 Maslen '*Anti-Personnel Landmines Convention Commentary*' (n 11) 190 [6.9].

77 Ibid., 57–8 [0.111], 196–7 [6.23].

78 The *Anti-Personnel Landmines Convention* itself was the first text to reference social and economic reintegration: *Anti-Personnel Landmines Convention* (n 1) art 6(3).

79 The second draft of the *Anti-Personnel Landmines Convention* explicitly imposed clearance-related obligations on both affected states parties and other states parties in a position to do so: *Convention on the Prohibition of the Use, Stockpiling, Production and Transfer of Anti-Personnel Mines and on Their Destruction (Second Austrian Draft Text)*, arts 5–6, 7(3), reprinted in Maslen '*Anti-Personnel Landmines Convention Commentary*' (n 11) appendix 4, 431.

assistance encountered obstacles. States from Africa, a widely affected continent, were adamant that a victim assistance obligation was imperative, and they succeeded in securing its inclusion.[80] The provision, however, places responsibility to provide assistance on states parties 'in a position to do so' and does not assign primary responsibility to any particular state, even if it has victims under its jurisdiction or control.[81] The fact that key proponents of victim assistance in the *Anti-Personnel Landmines Convention* were affected states may have contributed to negotiators' decision to address it exclusively through international cooperation and assistance.

By the time of the *CCM* negotiations, the debate over responsibility centred on user states. One of the most contentious issues related to whether a state that had used cluster munitions before the treaty entered into force should be required to assist affected states with clearance. The issue was only resolved in the final moments of the negotiations with a provision that 'strongly encouraged' user states to provide technical, financial, material, or human resources support for clearance activities.[82] Meanwhile, the conference President recommended that the victim assistance working group not address the question of user state responsibility because it could politicise the group's discussions.[83] The *CCM* did not place a specific obligation on user states parties to support victim assistance efforts.

Resistance to responsibility for both victim assistance and environmental remediation presented a challenge during the *TPNW* negotiations. The first draft obliged only affected states 'in a position to do so' to assist victims, and although the draft mentioned the right of affected states to request help for environmental remediation, it did not place an obligation on any state to implement it.[84] Some states recommended adopting the humanitarian disarmament model of having affected states take the lead on these positive obligations.[85] Others argued that nuclear armed states should be held responsible for any harm caused by use and testing and noted that affected states often lack resources to address the impacts of nuclear weapons.[86] States eventually reached a compromise by placing primary responsibility on affected states and requiring states parties that used and tested nuclear weapons to provide 'adequate assistance to

80 Maslen '*Anti-Personnel Landmines Convention Commentary*' (n 11) 32 [0.60], 38 [0.78].
81 *Anti-Personnel Landmines Convention* (n 1) art 6(3).
82 Borrie '*Unacceptable Harm*' (n 34) 302–3; Virgil Wiebe, John Borrie and Declan Smyth, 'Introduction' in Gro Nystuen and Stuart Casey-Maslen (eds), *The Convention on Cluster Munitions: A Commentary* (Oxford University Press, 2010) 1, 35–6 [0.74]–[0.76].
83 Reiterer and Leibowitz (n 37) 345 [5.35]–[5.36], 352 [5.53].
84 *Draft Convention on the Prohibition of Nuclear Weapons*, UN Doc A/CONF.229/2017/CRP.1 (22 May 2017) art 6.
85 See, eg, statements by Brazil, the Holy See, Ghana, Ireland, Mozambique, and the Philippines, reported in Tamara L Patton, 'News in Brief' (2017) 2(5) *Nuclear Ban Daily* 5. See also author's notes from *TPNW* negotiations, 20 June 2017.
86 See, eg, statements by Cuba, Ecuador, Egypt, Iran, Nigeria, and Vietnam, reported in Patton (n 85). See also author's notes from *TPNW* negotiations, 20 June 2017.

affected states parties, for the purpose of victim assistance and environmental remediation'.[87]

IV Countering the challenges

While reluctance to break new ground, concerns about feasibility, and resistance to responsibility posed significant challenges to the development of the three treaties discussed in this chapter, key features of humanitarian disarmament helped overcome such obstacles. A humanitarian purpose paved the way for incorporating remedial measures. An inclusive negotiating process increased awareness of the obligations' importance and influenced their shape and successful adoption. A framework of law and practice provided precedent for the provisions while allowing for their adaptation to new circumstances.

A Humanitarian purpose

The humanitarian disarmament treaties discussed in this chapter share a common purpose to protect people, particularly civilians, from the harm inflicted by indiscriminate and inhumane weapons. The *Anti-Personnel Landmines Convention* opens by articulating a determination 'to put an end to the suffering and casualties caused by anti-personnel mines'.[88] In its second preambular paragraph, the *CCM* calls for 'an end for all time to the suffering and casualties caused by cluster munitions'. The *TPNW*'s preamble expresses deep concern 'about the catastrophic humanitarian consequences' associated with nuclear weapons and recognises 'the consequent need to completely eliminate such weapons'.[89] The common humanitarian aim of these instruments set the stage for coupling preventive measures with remedial ones, which was essential to addressing fully the humanitarian impact of the banned weapons.

The humanitarian motivations behind the *Anti-Personnel Landmines Convention* put clearance and victim assistance provisions on the table and ultimately prevailed over any reluctance to break new ground in disarmament law. Participants in the Ottawa Process recognised that prohibitions alone could not achieve the goal of ending civilian suffering, and their desire for a more comprehensive solution inspired proposed positive obligations.[90] After the initial Ottawa Conference, the ICRC expressed 'confidence that the unspeakable suffering of mine victims has finally touched the conscience of leaders of governments', and

87 *TPNW* (n 2) art 7(6).
88 *Anti-Personnel Landmines Convention* (n 1) preamble para 1.
89 *TPNW* (n 2) preamble para 2.
90 *Global Plan of Action: Towards a Global Ban on Anti-Personnel Mines* (Chairman's agenda, 7 October 1996), reprinted in Louis Maresca and Stuart Maslen (eds), *The Banning of Anti-Personnel Landmines: The Legal Contribution of the International Committee of the Red Cross* (Cambridge University Press, 2000) 481: 'This Agenda for Action reflects the interrelationship of the global ban, mine clearance and victim assistance agendas'.

optimism about plans to complement a ban on anti-personnel landmines with increased resources for clearance and victim assistance.[91] The text adopted 11 months later showed that the ICRC's faith in the power of a humanitarian purpose to make legal change had been well placed.

Humanitarian concerns similarly led to the inclusion of remedial measures in the *CCM*. In the *Oslo Declaration*, states expressed their aim to 'effectively address the humanitarian problems caused by cluster munitions' and recognised the weapons' 'grave consequences'.[92] To address this 'unacceptable harm', they committed to negotiating a treaty that not only banned cluster munitions but also ensured clearance of contaminated areas and assistance to victims.[93]

Humanitarian aims again inspired a paradigm shift in the *TPNW*. Remedial measures had never appeared in a treaty on nuclear weapons. Some states and even certain members of civil society initially felt that such provisions would distract from efforts to adopt a ban on nuclear weapons.[94] Proponents of the positive obligations, many of whom were humanitarian disarmament veterans, countered by harking back to the concerns that had brought states to the negotiating table.[95] In a statement during the UN treaty process, for example, ICAN's Elizabeth Minor argued that victim assistance and environmental remediation obligations were necessary to 'reflect the humanitarian underpinnings of the treaty'.[96]

B Inclusive processes

The inclusive nature of humanitarian disarmament's negotiating processes also facilitated the development of clearance and victim assistance provisions. In an analysis of disarmament processes, Patrick McCarthy writes that in traditional disarmament negotiations, '[c]ivil society groups, to the extent that they were involved at all, were typically viewed with suspicion and considered to be outsiders whose activities were to be monitored and, when necessary, curtailed'.[97] The Ottawa Process, in which civil society actors partnered with like-minded states and international organisations to drive disarmament progress, changed

91 'Ottawa Mine Conference: The Beginning of the End' (Press Release, International Committee of the Red Cross, 6 October 1996), reprinted in Louis Maresca and Stuart Maslen (eds), *The Banning of Anti-Personnel Landmines: The Legal Contribution of the International Committee of the Red Cross* (Cambridge University Press, 2000) 487, 488.

92 *Oslo Declaration* (n 28) chapeau.

93 Ibid., [1].

94 Author's conversations with state and civil society representatives during the course of the *TPNW* negotiations, 2017.

95 See, eg, Bonnie Docherty, 'Advancing Humanitarian Disarmament through the Ban Treaty' (2017) 1(3) *Nuclear Ban Daily* 5.

96 Elizabeth Minor, 'Cluster 4: Positive Obligations' (Statement, *TPNW* Negotiating Conference, New York, 20 June 2017) (Web Page) <http://www.reachingcriticalwill.org/images/documents/Disarmament-fora/nuclear-weapon-ban/statements/20June_ICAN.pdf>.

97 McCarthy (n 2) 56.

that perception.[98] With the advent of 'citizen diplomacy', disarmament negotiations became 'more inclusive and more open to viewing civil society groups as the possessors and purveyors of expertise, field experience and energy potentially beneficial to multilateral negotiating processes'.[99] This inclusiveness brought to the negotiating process the voices of those with an interest in remedial measures.

The effectiveness of ICAN's team of positive obligation advocates exemplified the importance of civil society participation. During the first week of the *TPNW* negotiations in March 2017, the positive obligations team made the case that complementing prohibitions on nuclear weapons with measures to address the ongoing harm of past use and testing was essential to achieving the *TPNW*'s humanitarian purpose.[100] Many states responded by calling for victim assistance and environmental remediation provisions, and the topic was added to the agenda of the June-July negotiations.[101] Recognising the need to maintain humanitarian disarmament's high standard, the ICAN team, along with the ICRC and supportive states, then worked to strengthen the relatively weak language in the early treaty drafts.[102] Through presentations, publications, plenary interventions, and behind-the-scenes conversations, these advocates allayed concerns related to the provisions' novelty, feasibility of implementation, and state responsibility.[103]

Humanitarian disarmament's inclusive processes also allowed for greater input from those who could speak with authority about the real-world problems weapons posed. In an assessment of the humanitarian approach to disarmament after the *Anti-Personnel Landmines Convention*'s adoption, John Borrie of the UN Institute for Disarmament Research ('UNIDIR') emphasised the importance of 'field-based perspectives' brought by non-governmental organisations, international agencies, and other humanitarian actors in shaping the direction of

98 Williams and Goose (n 4).

99 Ibid.; McCarthy (n 2) 57. In addition to bringing substantive expertise, non-governmental organisations can mobilise public opinion, generate media attention, and influence governments.

100 See, eg, Elizabeth Minor, 'Statement for Topic 2' (Statement, *TPNW* Negotiating Conference, New York, 29 March 2017) (Web Page) <http://www.reachingcriticalwill.org/images/documents/Disarmament-fora/nuclear-weapon-ban/statements/29March_A36.pdf>.

101 Author's notes from *TPNW* negotiations, March 2017; Article 36 and International Human Rights Clinic (Harvard Law School), 'Environmental Remediation in the Nuclear Weapon Ban Treaty' (n 72) 1; *Indicative Timetable for the Meetings of the Conference*, Agenda Item 5, UN Doc A/CONF.229/2017/3/Add.1/Rev.1 (12 June 2017).

102 See, eg, Lan Mei, 'Recalling the Humanitarian Agenda: The Need to Strengthen Positive Obligations' (2017) 2(10) *Nuclear Ban Daily* 2; 'Comments of the International Committee of the Red Cross on Key Provisions of the Draft Convention on the Prohibition of Nuclear Weapons', A/CONF/229/2017/WP.7, 5–7.

103 See, eg, Article 36 and International Human Rights Clinic (Harvard Law School), 'Environmental Remediation in the Nuclear Weapon Ban Treaty' (n 72); Article 36 and International Human Rights Clinic (Harvard Law School), 'Victim Assistance in the Nuclear Weapon Ban Treaty: A Comprehensive and Detailed Approach' (June 2017); ICAN, *Victim Rights and Victim Assistance in a Treaty Prohibiting Nuclear Weapons: A Humanitarian Imperative*, UN Doc A/CONF.229/2017/NGO/WP.14 (31 March 2017).

disarmament.[104] During the Ottawa Process, for example, the first-hand expertise of healthcare workers, de-miners, and mine victims

> made them compelling spokespersons who could not be easily dismissed by politicians, diplomats or military personnel. Anti-mine campaigners could consistently trump military experts by pointing to the clear disjuncture between mine warfare theory and practice.[105]

In addition to highlighting the urgency of the problem, proponents of remedial measures could provide practical input on ways to address it. The ICRC, for example, drew from its staff's on-the-ground experiences to argue for the feasibility of clearance deadlines and to make specific proposals for victim assistance measures.[106] Field reporting and expertise played a similar role in the processes to create the *CCM* and the *TPNW*.[107]

Survivors, who have the deepest understanding of the unacceptable harm caused by certain weapons, were especially strong advocates for humanitarian disarmament and its remedial measures. During the Oslo Process, for example, Handicap International (now Humanity & Inclusion) created the Ban Advocates project, which brought cluster munition survivors from around the world to lobby on their own behalf. Those survivors included civilian bystanders, military de-miners, directly affected individuals, and relatives of those killed or injured. The participation of survivors gave the negotiations 'a human face' and ensured that the *CCM* 'would work on concretely improving the lives of people whose suffering has been caused by cluster munitions'.[108] Their advocacy on victim assistance in particular 'helped bring the issue to the fore and garner almost universal support'.[109] The Ban Advocates persuaded affected states and donor states to accept responsibility for the *CCM*'s provisions on clearance and victim assistance, which are the strongest and most detailed in a humanitarian disarmament treaty.

104 John Borrie, 'Rethinking Multilateral Negotiations: Disarmament as Humanitarian Action' in John Borrie and Vanessa Martin Randin (eds), *Alternative Approaches in Multilateral Decision Making: Disarmament as Humanitarian Action* (UNIDIR, 2005) 7, 25.

105 Ibid., quoting Don Hubert, 'The Landmine Ban: A Case Study in Humanitarian Advocacy' (Occasional Paper, No 42, Thomas J Watson Jr Institute for International Studies, 2000) 31.

106 See, eg, Chris Giannou, 'The Provision of Assistance to Mine Victims' (19 May 1997), reprinted in Louis Maresca and Stuart Maslen (eds), *The Banning of Anti-Personnel Landmines: The Legal Contribution of the International Committee of the Red Cross* (Cambridge University Press, 2000) 527, 533–4.

107 See, eg, Human Rights Watch, *Fatally Flawed: Cluster Bombs and Their Use by the United States in Afghanistan* (Report, Vol 14 No 7, December 2002); Kmentt (n 52) 691–2 citing John Borrie and Tim Caughley, *An Illusion of Safety: Challenges of Nuclear Weapon Detonations for United Nations Coordination and Response* (UNIDIR, 2014).

108 'Ban Advocates', *Handicap International* (Web Page) <https://www.handicapinternational.be/nl/en/banadvocates> archived at <https://perma.cc/S3Z5-XGZC>.

109 Reiterer and Leibowitz (n 37) 331 [5.2].

The inclusiveness of the humanitarian disarmament process applied to states as well as international and non-governmental organisations. More than two dozen affected states along with more than half of the world's cluster munition stockpilers and two-thirds of its users and producers participated in the Oslo Process.[110] Lebanon demonstrated an affected state's potential for influence through its engagement in one of the most contentious elements of the *CCM*.[111] In partnership with the CMC, Lebanon spearheaded efforts to require user states to help affected states with clearance. While user and possessor states, such as the United Kingdom, France, and Italy, objected to the creation of a retroactive legal obligation, Lebanon and its supporters made moral and practical arguments for including it.[112] The debate continued through to the end of the negotiations. The proposed legally binding language of a user states party ('shall provide ... assistance [to affected states parties]') had been replaced with 'is encouraged to provide ... assistance' in the clearance working group.[113] Just before the treaty was adopted, however, the President of the negotiations, acting under pressure from Lebanon, amended the text to 'strongly encouraged'.[114]

C Framework of law and practice

While a humanitarian purpose and inclusive process overcame states' initial concerns about including groundbreaking remedial measures, the emergence of an established body of law and practice helped address challenges to the positive obligations' ongoing evolution. This framework created precedent that provided a model for clearance and victim assistance provisions yet was adaptable to specific circumstances.

The remedial measures in the *CCM* built on norms that grew out of the *Anti-Personnel Landmines Convention*. The latter's clearance provisions were relatively general, but their implementation sparked the development of more detailed standards. For example, the *Nairobi Action Plan*, produced at the *Anti-Personnel Landmines Convention*'s First Review Conference in 2004, called on affected states parties to take specific actions, including several that were not mentioned in the treaty's article on clearance.[115] The *Nairobi Action Plan*

110 Human Rights Watch, *Meeting the Challenge: Protecting Civilians through the Convention on Cluster Munitions* (November 2010) 121–2.

111 For a discussion of the use of cluster munitions in Lebanon, see Human Rights Watch, *Flooding South Lebanon: Israel's Use of Cluster Munitions in Lebanon in July and August 2006* (Report, Vol 20 No 2(E), February 2008) 3.

112 This account derives in part from the observations of the author, who participated in the negotiations and the clearance working group. See also Borrie '*Unacceptable Harm*' (n 34) 302–3.

113 *Draft Cluster Munitions Convention*, above n 28, art 4(4) proposing 'shall'.

114 Borrie '*Unacceptable Harm*' (n 34) 302–3; Wiebe, Borrie and Smyth (n 82) 35–6 [0.74]–[0.76].

115 *Final Report*, First Review Conference of the States Parties to the Convention on the Prohibition of the Use, Stockpiling, Production and Transfer of Anti-Personnel Mines and on Their Destruction, UN Doc APLC/CONF/2004/5 (9 February 2005) Part II ('Ending the

committed those states parties to 'urgently develop and implement national plans' and to 'ensure that mine risk education programs are made available in all communities at risk'.[116] Drafters in the Oslo Process looked closely at these more developed standards of practice. The clearance article in the *CCM* would transform political commitments into legally binding obligations.[117]

The strengthening of victim assistance provisions between the *Anti-Personnel Landmines Convention* and the *CCM* was even more dramatic than the increase in clearance responsibilities. Although the *Anti-Personnel Landmines Convention* only required assistance for victims from states parties 'in a position to' provide it, the *Maputo Declaration*,[118] released at the First Meeting of States Parties in 1999, stated that victim assistance 'must be accorded the highest political importance and practical commitment by States Parties and all those in the international community who care about this issue'.[119] Articulating a detailed scheme for victim assistance, the *Nairobi Action Plan* made it clear that affected states parties 'have the greatest responsibility to act' even though other states parties must assist them.[120] It also called on states parties, *inter alia*, to develop laws and policies that 'effectively address the needs and fundamental human rights of mine victims', to respond to victims' psychological as well as physical harm, to improve data gathering, and to make assistance age and gender sensitive.[121] Drafters of the *CCM* drew heavily on *Nairobi Action Plan*, and art 5 reflected its elements.[122] On the 20th anniversary of the *Anti-Personnel Landmines Convention*, the President of the Meeting of States Parties noted that its 'innovative provisions on victim assistance have set a new standard for other legal instruments'.[123]

Suffering Caused by Anti-Personnel Mines: Nairobi Action Plan 2005–2009') para 4 ('*Nairobi Action Plan*'); *Anti-Personnel Landmines Convention* (n 1) art 5.

116 *Nairobi Action Plan* (n 115) actions 19, 21.

117 Stuart Casey-Maslen, 'Article 4: Clearance and Destruction of Cluster Munition Remnants and Risk Reduction Education' in Gro Nystuen and Stuart Casey-Maslen (eds), *The Convention on Cluster Munitions: A Commentary* (Oxford University Press, 2010) 275, 282 [4.7]: '[T]he drafting of Article 4 … was strongly influenced by both the framing of the obligation in [the *Anti-Personnel Landmines Convention*] and subsequent experience in its implementation'.

118 *Maputo Declaration*, Meeting of the States Parties to the Convention on the Prohibition of the Use, Stockpiling, Production and Transfer of Anti-Personnel Mines and on Their Destruction, Agenda Item 17, UN Doc APLC/MSP.1/1999/L.6* (6 May 1999) ('*Maputo Declaration*').

119 *Maputo Declaration* (n 118) [14].

120 *Nairobi Action Plan* (n 115) [5].

121 Ibid., actions 31–5.

122 Reiterer and Leibowitz (n 37) 352 [5.54] noting the convention's 'victim assistance package is not a radically new invention … it can be seen as the logical consequence — if not codification — of the work undertaken and lessons learned in implementing the victim assistance provision of the [*Anti-Personnel Landmines Convention*]'.

123 *President's Final Declaration*, UN Doc APLC/MSP.16/2017/WP.1 (28 December 2017) 1 [3]. The drafters of the *CCM* also applied principles of the 2006 *Convention on the Rights of Persons with Disabilities* ('*CRPD*'), treating survivors as 'subjects of the law' rather than 'objects of charity' and requiring states parties to involve survivors in decisions that affect their

Humanitarian disarmament law and practice also provided precedent that overcame the challenges to including positive obligations in the *TPNW*.[124] Like the *Anti-Personnel Landmines Convention* and the *CCM*, the *TPNW* sought to address harms caused by remnants of banned weapons, in this case, nuclear contamination. Past humanitarian disarmament treaties thus became a source of model language for the *TPNW* drafters. Article 6(1) of the *TPNW* on victim assistance and art 7 of the *TPNW* on international cooperation and assistance closely mirror their counterparts in the *CCM*.

While humanitarian disarmament looked to previous law and practice to bolster the positive obligations, it also adapted that precedent to fit specific situations. For example, the clearance deadlines in the *Anti-Personnel Landmines Convention* and the *CCM* were critical to ensuring progress. The *TPNW*, however, simply required 'necessary and appropriate measures towards … environmental remediation' because the territorial and temporal scope of nuclear weapons contamination made it more difficult to impose a deadline.[125] In addition, although the *TPNW*'s art 7 on international cooperation and assistance drew much of its language from the *CCM*, it added a paragraph requiring states parties that used or tested nuclear weapons to assist affected states parties with victim assistance and environmental remediation.[126] These changes increased the feasibility of the positive obligations in the *TPNW* and made them acceptable to more negotiating states.

V Fulfilling the promise

Over the past two decades, the humanitarian approach to disarmament has inspired the adoption of positive obligations and countered challenges to their evolution. In turn, the clearance and victim assistance provisions have strengthened the impact of humanitarian disarmament.

The positive obligations have made humanitarian disarmament a more complete and powerful legal response to arms-inflicted harm. Consistent inclusion in adopted treaties has established the remedial measures as realistic and important complements to the prohibitions of modern disarmament law. Through their breadth of application, the positive obligations have pushed humanitarian disarmament to address adverse effects attributable to conventional weapons,

---

lives: *Convention on the Rights of Persons with Disabilities*, opened for signature 30 March 2007, 2515 UNTS 3 (entered into force 3 May 2008); Reiterer and Leibowitz (n 37) 334 [5.10]; *CCM* (n 2) art 5(2)(f).

124 The President of the conference, Ambassador Elayne Whyte Gomez, opened the discussion of the positive obligations on 20 June 2017 by noting that the victim assistance proposal was based on existing rules in the *CCM* and *Anti-Personnel Landmines Convention*: author's notes from *TPNW* negotiations, 20 June 2017; Patton (n 85) 5.

125 Article 36 and International Human Rights Clinic (Harvard Law School), 'Environmental Remediation in the Nuclear Weapon Ban Treaty' (n 72) 2–3, 13; *TPNW* (n 2) art 6(2).

126 *TPNW* (n 2) art 7(6).

weapons of mass destruction, and explosive and toxic remnants of war. By spreading responsibility for clearance and victim assistance across states parties, the provisions have enhanced the humanitarian approach's effectiveness and fairness. Finally, the positive obligations and their implementation have led to the emergence of widely accepted standards that provide practical guidelines for clearing contaminated areas and assisting victims.

The remedial measures in the *Anti-Personnel Landmines Convention* and the *CCM*, which have both entered into force, have also enabled humanitarian disarmament to have a real-world impact on the ground. States parties have achieved noteworthy progress in clearance and victim assistance.[127] According to the *Landmine and Cluster Munition Monitor*, clearance of contaminated areas had been completed by 29 states parties to the *Anti-Personnel Landmines Convention* as of November 2018, and by eight states parties to the *CCM* as of August 2019.[128] Many states have developed national victim assistance plans and consulted victims on co-ordination activities.[129] The resources available to survivors, especially medical care and rehabilitation services, have increased and even benefited persons with disabilities unrelated to arms and armed conflict.[130] From 2007 to 2017, donor and affected states contributed US$5.2 billion to mine action, which encompasses clearance and victim assistance activities for landmines and explosive remnants of war.[131]

The positive obligations have the potential to achieve much more if they are adapted to different contexts and better implemented in existing ones. To extend their legal impact, clearance and victim assistance provisions should be pillars of other humanitarian disarmament initiatives, including those that involve different kinds of instruments, not only formal treaties. For example, states and civil society proponents should push for robust victim assistance in a new political declaration that would commit states to cease using explosive weapons with wide

127 The *Landmine and Cluster Munition Monitor* is an annual ICBL-CMC publication that has become the '*de facto* monitoring regime for the [*Anti-Personnel Landmines Convention*] and the Convention on Cluster Munitions': 'What Is the Landmine and Cluster Munition Monitor?', *Landmine and Cluster Munition Monitor* (Web Page, September 2019) <http://www.the-monitor.org/en-gb/the-issues/faqs/most-common/what-is-the-landmine-and-cluster-munition-monitor.aspx>.

128 IBCL-CMC, *Landmine Monitor 2018* (Annual Report, November 2018) 3 (Web Page) <http://www.the-monitor.org/media/2918780/Landmine-Monitor-2018_final.pdf> ('*Landmine Monitor 2018*'); IBCL-CMC, *Cluster Munitions Monitor 2019* (Annual Report, August 2019) (Web Page) <http://www.the-monitor.org/media/3047840/Cluster-Munition-Monitor-2019_online.pdf> ('*Cluster Munitions Monitor 2019*').

129 *Landmine Monitor 2018* (n 128) 61–3; *Cluster Munition Monitor 2019* (n 128) 51–2.

130 The *Cluster Munition Monitor 2018* reported that humanitarian disarmament 'has contributed to making more resources available to survivors as well as people with similar needs': IBCL-CMC, *Cluster Munition Monitor 2018* (Annual Report, August 2018) (Web Page) <http://www.the-monitor.org/media/2907293/Cluster-Munition-Monitor-2018_web_revised4Sep.pdf> 108, 111 ('*Cluster Munition Monitor 2018*').

131 *Landmine Monitor 2018* (n 128) 74. Some assistance is provided by states not party to the *Anti-Personnel Landmines Convention* and the *CCM*.

area effects in populated areas.[132] From a practical perspective, the positive obligations that have already been adopted demand more timely and complete implementation. To achieve this end, states should increase to assess contamination and expedite clearance in order to avoid the need for extension requests.[133] They should significantly expand victim assistance in the areas of psycho-social support and economic inclusion, and make survivor input a more important factor in decision-making.[134] Donor states should maintain and augment funding for mine action, which, though significant, has generally been inadequate, especially for victim assistance.[135]

The development of clearance and victim assistance provisions has already revolutionised disarmament law and reduced civilian suffering from armed conflict. Applied to other arms-related issues and more fully implemented, the positive obligations can ensure that humanitarian disarmament fulfils its promise in both law and practice.

132 'Explosive Weapons in Populated Areas: Key Questions and Answers' (Background Paper, International Network on Explosive Weapons, September 2019) 2.

133 As of November 2018, 12 states parties had requested extensions to their *Anti-Personnel Landmines Convention* obligations, and another 13 states parties did not appear to be on track to meet their deadlines: *Landmine Monitor 2018* (n 130) 31. Although signatories to the *CCM* have had a better track record than non-signatories, more than half of the 26 affected states, including both groups, did not know the full extent of cluster munition contamination by August 2018: *Cluster Munition Monitor 2018* (n 130) 60, 76. Two states parties, Germany and Lao PDR, submitted extension requests to the 2019 Meeting of States Parties to the *CCM*: *Cluster Munition Monitor 2019* (n 128) 38.

134 *Landmine Monitor 2018* (n 128) 4, 63, 66; *Cluster Munition Monitor 2019* (n 128) 51, 54.

135 While limited funding affected both clearance and victim assistance programmes, in 2018, victim assistance programmes received only two percent of mine action funding: *Landmine Monitor 2018* (n 128) 83. See also *Cluster Munition Monitor 2019* (n 128) 2, 51.

5 Human rights-humanitarianism in disarmament law

Anna Crowe

I Introduction

The concept of humanitarian disarmament — disarmament aimed more at reducing human suffering than fulfilling national security objectives[1] — has had a growing influence on the development of disarmament law over the last two decades. However, the relationship between the humanitarian imperative that has prompted the prohibition or regulation of particular weapons and human rights law — an intuitively connected field — is relatively understudied.[2] As concepts and language drawn from human rights law are pulled into disarmament law through humanitarian disarmament, increased interplay between the two fields appears inevitable. But the results of this interaction are not clear at present and could take multiple forms in the future.

This chapter shows that while humanitarian disarmament and human rights law are largely complementary, the way the relationship between the two plays out, specifically in the concept of victim assistance, is complex. The chapter uses the term 'human rights-humanitarianism' to capture this dynamic, in which human rights law contributes legal content to humanitarian disarmament while humanitarianism provides the underlying frame of ending or reducing human suffering. After defining key terms in Part II, the chapter maps out the extent to which disarmament law and human rights law share similar goals and outlines the ways humanitarian disarmament treaties have formally incorporated human rights law in Part III. This mapping shows that the motivations behind disarmament law and human rights law overlap, providing the initial scaffolding on which the human rights-humanitarian dynamic is built. The chapter then turns in Part IV to consider humanitarianism in disarmament law, before examining in Part V the growing role of human rights

1 See the definition provided in Part II below.

2 For examples of scholarship that does address the two together, see Daniel Rietiker, *Humanization of Arms Control: Paving the Way for a World Free of Nuclear Weapons* (Routledge, 2017); Michael Schoiswohl, 'Human Rights and Disarmament – A Blind Date or a Shotgun Marriage' (2013) 15(1) *Austrian Review of International and European Law* 109.

in humanitarianism. These Parts illustrate how concepts and ideas have flowed between the various fields.

Finally, Part VI focuses on how the relationship between human rights and humanitarianism plays out in the context of victim assistance. Victim assistance is a legal concept that straddles humanitarianism and human rights, but the human rights-humanitarianism dynamic produces a thinner engagement with human rights than textual references to human rights law in humanitarian disarmament treaties would suggest. While the humanitarian goal of reducing suffering is suggested by the very words 'victim assistance', the obligation itself is given content through human rights law. It is, however, only a partial borrowing. The result is an uneasy alliance of humanitarian and human rights ideas, particularly around the right to a remedy.

The chapter views human rights law and disarmament law from an international perspective, and it follows a largely textual approach, drawing on the language of the disarmament instruments themselves. It focuses on the three 'core' humanitarian disarmament treaties: the 1997 *Anti-Personnel Landmines Convention*;[3] the 2008 *Convention on Cluster Munitions* ('*CCM*');[4] and the 2017 *Treaty on the Prohibition of Nuclear Weapons* ('*TPNW*').[5] The chapter's aim is to illustrate the legal complications that human rights-humanitarianism produces, rather than present a critique of victim assistance as it is understood and implemented in the realm of practice.

II Definitions

Traditionally, the concept of 'disarmament' referred to measures that quantitatively reduce weapons, leading to their elimination, but the term has taken on a broader meaning over time (albeit not one that is universally recognised) that encompasses the fields of arms control and non-proliferation.[6] The term 'disarmament law', however, does not have a meaning that is intuitively understood in legal or academic settings; it is a field whose content, scope, and boundaries (or indeed, existence as a separate field of legal enquiry) are not well established. This book itself is an attempt to fill in some of the gaps in this field, and provide an initial definition of 'disarmament law'.[7]

3 *Convention on the Prohibition of the Use, Stockpiling, Production and Transfer of Anti-Personnel Mines and on Their Destruction*, opened for signature 3 December 1997, 2056 UNTS 211 (entered into force 1 March 1999) ('*Anti-Personnel Landmines Convention*').

4 *Convention on Cluster Munitions*, opened for signature 3 December 2008, 2688 UNTS 39 (entered into force 1 August 2010) ('*CCM*').

5 *Treaty on the Prohibition of Nuclear Weapons*, opened for signature 20 September 2017 (not yet in force) ('*TPNW*').

6 See, eg, John Kierulf, *Disarmament under International Law* (McGill-Queen's University Press, 2017) 5.

7 See Dunworth and Hood, 'Chatper 1'.

In contrast to disarmament law, international human rights law is a clearly defined field whose corpus is subject to intense scholarly and legal debate. Its modern legal genesis[8] lies in the *Universal Declaration of Human Rights* ('*UDHR*'),[9] which together with the subsequent *International Covenant on Civil and Political Rights*[10] and the *International Covenant on Economic, Social and Cultural Rights*,[11] as well as aspects of the *Charter of the United Nations*, comprise an 'International Bill of Rights'. The field includes a range of treaties and jurisprudence from numerous courts and international bodies, and has multiple communities of practitioners.[12]

Humanitarianism, meanwhile, is a cross-disciplinary concept that derives from international humanitarian law (the law that applies during times of armed conflict) but is not bounded by it.[13] While there is no accepted definition of humanitarianism, understandings often align with a set of values associated with 'humanitarian action' or 'humanitarian assistance' — traditionally, the delivery of aid during armed conflict or other large-scale crises. The main goal of humanitarian action is to alleviate human suffering[14] and the principles of humanity, impartiality, neutrality, and independence govern how action is undertaken.[15]

8 See Samuel Moyn, *The Last Utopia: Human Rights in History* (Harvard University Press, 2010). Cf Lena Halldenius, 'On the Use and Abuse of History in Philosophy of Human Rights' in Karen-Margrethe Simonsen and Jonas Ross Kjærgård (eds), *Discursive Framings of Human Rights: Negotiating Agency and Victimhood* (Routledge, 2017).

9 *Universal Declaration of Human Rights*, GA Res 217(A) III, UN GAOR, 3rd sess, 183rd plen mtg, UN Doc A/810 (10 December 1948) ('*UDHR*').

10 *International Covenant on Civil and Political Rights*, opened for signature 16 December 1966, 999 UNTS 171 (entered into force 23 March 1976) ('*ICCPR*').

11 *International Covenant on Economic, Social and Cultural Rights*, opened for signature 16 December 1966, 993 UNTS 3 (entered into force 3 January 1976) ('*ICESCR*').

12 As noted in, for example, *Max Planck Encyclopedia of Public International Law* (at March 2007), Thomas Buergenthal, 'Human Rights'.

13 As Hilhorst has noted,

> [t]he dominant story that humanitarian aid has told about itself for decades is rooted in the experience of Henri Dunant at the Battlefield of Solferino in 1859. This set into motion the evolution of International Humanitarian Law and the definition and organization of modern humanitarianism as a principled endeavour:

Dorothea Hilhorst, 'Classical Humanitarianism and Resilience Humanitarianism: Making Sense of Two Brands of Humanitarian Action' (2018) 3 *Journal of International Humanitarian Action* 1, 3.

14 See International Federation of Red Cross and Red Crescent Societies and the International Committee of the Red Cross, *Code of Conduct for the International Red Cross and Red Crescent Movement and Non-Governmental Organisations (NGOs) in Disaster Relief* (September 1994) ('Code of Conduct') [1].

15 See *Strengthening of the Coordination of Humanitarian Emergency Assistance of the United Nations*, GA Res 46/182, UN GAOR, 46th sess, 78th plen mtg, Supp No 49, UN Doc A/RES/46/182 (19 December 1991) annex [2]; *Strengthening of the Coordination of Emergency Humanitarian Assistance of the United Nations*, GA Res 58/114, UN GAOR, 58th sess, 75th plen mtg, Supp No 49, UN Doc A/RES/58/114 (5 February 2004) preamble para 4. The list of humanitarian principles developed by the Red Cross and Red Crescent Movement adds

Humanitarian disarmament is a legal space or approach that brings together concepts from humanitarianism, human rights, and disarmament law.[16] Instruments reflecting this approach ban weapons outright and/or contain other obligations aimed specifically at reducing human suffering (such as post-conflict remedial measures). As noted in the Introduction to this chapter, three treaties are typically labelled as the core examples of humanitarian disarmament: the 1997 *Anti-Personnel Landmines Convention*, the 2008 *CCM*, and the 2017 *TPNW*.[17]

III Human rights law and disarmament law

Although all measures requiring disarmament might be said to implicate human rights in some way or another, as Schoiswohl has observed, disarmament and human rights 'have ignored each other ... since their institutional birth as part of the UN framework'.[18] This observation depends in part on the frame of reference however: practitioners and instruments focused on traditional bilateral disarmament certainly have paid less attention to human rights than they might have, but human rights discourse is well established in other areas of disarmament, particularly in the realm of small arms and light weapons.[19] Likewise, the argument that expenditure on weapons and other military activities has detracted from states' realisation of social, economic, and cultural rights is long-standing.[20] What is notable is that while human rights arguments have

voluntary service, unity, and universality: 'The Humanitarian Ethos in Action' (2015) 97(897–8) *International Review of the Red Cross* 7, 18.

16 Docherty defines it as 'a groundbreaking approach to disarmament that makes ending civilian suffering its core objective': Bonnie Docherty, 'Ending Civilian Suffering: The Purpose, Provisions, and Promise of Humanitarian Disarmament Law' (2013) 15(1) *Austrian Review of International and European Law* 7, 7.

17 Markus Reiterer and Cornelia Kratochvil, 'Introduction to the Agora on Humanitarian Disarmament' (2013) 15(1) *Austrian Review of International and European Law* 3, noting that the *Anti-Personnel Landmines Convention* and *CCM* were (at the time) the only 'true' humanitarian disarmament treaties: at 4. See also Bonnie Docherty, 'A "Light for All Humanity": The Treaty on the Prohibition of Nuclear Weapons and the Progress of Humanitarian Disarmament' (2018) 30(2) *Global Change, Peace & Security* 163, 163–4.

18 Schoiswohl (n 2) 119. At an institutional level, human rights bodies have infrequently considered the relationship of disarmament treaties to the realisation of human rights. Although see Human Rights Committee, *Concluding Observations on the Seventh Periodic Report of Colombia*, UN Doc CCPR/C/COL/CO/7 (17 November 2016) [22]–[23]; Rietiker, *Humanization of Arms Control* (n 2) 92–103.

19 See, eg, Barbara Frey, Special Rapporteur, *Prevention of Human Rights Violations Committed with Small Arms and Light Weapons*, 58th sess, UN Doc A/HRC/Sub.1/58/27 (27 July 2006); Amnesty International, 'Human Rights Abuses with Small Arms: Illustrative cases from Amnesty International Reports 2000–01' (Research Paper POL 34/007/2001, 8 July 2001); Susan Waltz, 'Arms Transfers and the Human Rights Agenda' in George Andreopoulos and Zehra F Kabasakal Arat (eds), *The Uses and Misuses of Human Rights* (Palgrave Macmillan, 2014) 147.

20 See the discussion in Giles Giacca and Tahmina Karimova, 'Implications for Arms Acquisitions of Economic, Social, and Cultural Rights' in Stuart Casey-Maslen (ed), *Weapons Under*

been present in disarmament circles, direct operative references to human rights law itself appear in only two disarmament treaties – the *CCM* and the *TPNW*.

At first glance, it is evident that human rights law and disarmament law share similar goals, rooted in the foundations of the international order built following the Second World War. Although both fields can rightly claim more ancient origins, the bulk of their legal development has occurred over the last 70 years. At a highly abstracted level, disarmament law builds towards a larger objective of enabling peace and security. This goal is articulated in the *Charter of the United Nations*, which sets out the power of the General Assembly to 'consider the general principles of co-operation in the maintenance of international peace and security, including the principles governing disarmament and the regulation of armaments'.[21]

Similarly, the *Charter of the United Nations*, whose focus is international peace and security (and whose revolutionary contribution to international law was to recast the resort to armed force as an exceptional measure), speaks of 'faith in fundamental human rights, in the dignity and worth of the human person' in its preamble.[22] The *UDHR* explicitly makes the link between dignity and peace in its preamble, recognising that 'the inherent dignity [and] the equal and inalienable rights of all members of the human family is the foundation of freedom, justice and peace in the world'.[23]

At a lesser level of abstraction, the motivations of the two fields diverge. While human rights law has been consistently animated by a concern for human dignity,[24] disarmament law has served a spectrum of interests. At one end of the spectrum, there are instruments that serve primarily national security (state sovereignty-driven) interests.[25] At the other, are instruments whose core

International Human Rights Law (Cambridge University Press, 2014) 472. The Human Rights Committee has expressed similar concerns in relation to weapons of mass destruction in particular: Human Rights Committee, *General Comment No 14: Article 6 (Right to Life) Nuclear Weapons and the Right to Life*, 23rd sess, UN Doc HRI/GEN/1/Rev.9 (Vol. I) [3]; Human Rights Committee, *General Comment No 36 (2018) on article 6 of the International Covenant on Civil and Political Rights, on the right to life*, 124th sess, UN Doc CCPR/C/GC/36 (30 October 2018) [66].

21 *Charter of the United Nations* art 11(1). Similar language also appears at art 47.

22 Ibid., preamble para 1.

23 *UDHR* (n 9) preamble para 1.

24 See Paolo G Carozza, 'Human Dignity' in Dinah Shelton (ed), *The Oxford Handbook of International Human Rights Law* (Oxford University Press, 2013) 345.

25 See the examples in the following paragraph. This chapter does not address the concept of human security, although it is strongly connected to human rights and peace, and it notably influenced the development and text of the *TPNW*. In one of its most commonly cited formulations, through a 2012 UN General Assembly Resolution, human security is defined as a notion that includes '[t]he right of people to live in freedom and dignity, free from poverty and despair … with an equal opportunity to enjoy all their rights and fully develop their human potential' and that 'recognizes the interlinkages between peace, development and human rights, and equally considers civil, political, economic, social and cultural rights': *Follow-up to paragraph 143 on human security of the 2005 World Summit Outcome*, GA Res 66/290, UN GAOR, 66th

objective is humanitarian — to reduce human suffering.[26] These goals find explicit expression in the language of instruments depending on where they fall on this spectrum.[27]

Instruments that reduce numbers of weapons, or otherwise provide limits short of absolute prohibition (those typically given the labels of arms control or non-proliferation) perhaps unsurprisingly tend to fall closest to the national security end of the spectrum. For example, the preamble to the multilateral 1990 *Treaty on Conventional Armed Forces in Europe*[28] speaks of the 'common responsibility which [states parties] all have for seeking to achieve greater stability and security in Europe', and records that the parties aim for 'a new pattern of security relations'.[29]

At the humanitarian disarmament end of the spectrum, the two fields of human rights law and disarmament law meet formally. For example, the *CCM*'s preamble directly records the determination of states 'to ensure the full realisation of the rights of all cluster munition victims and recognis[e] their inherent dignity'.[30] Article 5, which is titled simply 'victim assistance', gives expression to that recognition: it requires states parties to 'adequately provide age- and gender- sensitive assistance' to cluster munition victims 'in areas under its jurisdiction or control ... in accordance with applicable international humanitarian and human rights law' and without discrimination 'among cluster munition victims, or between cluster munition victims and those who have suffered injuries or disabilities from other causes'.[31]

Another example is the *TPNW* which also includes a victim assistance obligation and references human rights law directly. It requires states parties to provide assistance to victims, without discrimination, 'in accordance with applicable international humanitarian and human rights law'.[32] Additionally, its preamble contains a more general reference to 'the need for all states at all times to comply with applicable international law, including international humanitarian law and international human rights law'.[33] Although human rights arguments, particularly around the right to life, have long been present in nuclear disarmament discussions,[34] the *TPNW* was the first treaty to make a textual link between human rights law and nuclear disarmament.

---

sess, 127th plen mtg, Agenda Items 14 and 117, Supp No 49, UN Doc A/RES/66/290 (25 October 2012) paras 3(a), 3(c).

26 The *CCM* (n 4), the *Anti-Personnel Landmines Convention* (n 3), and the *TPNW* (n 5).

27 For an analysis of 'how security and/or humanitarian interests shape [disarmament treaties'] underlying purposes and textual provisions', see Docherty, 'Ending Civilian Suffering' (n 16) 10.

28 *Treaty on Conventional Armed Forces in Europe*, signed 19 November 1990, 30 ILM 1 (entered into force 17 July 1992).

29 Ibid., preamble para 5.

30 *CCM* (n 4) preamble para 6.

31 Ibid., arts 5(1), 5(2)(e).

32 *TPNW* (n 5) art 6(1).

33 Ibid., preamble para 8.

34 See, eg, Human Rights Committee, *General Comment No 14: Article 6 (Right to Life) Nuclear Weapons and the Right to Life*, 23rd sess, UN Doc HRI/GEN/1/Rev.9 (Vol. I); *Legality of the*

IV Disarmament law and humanitarianism

Humanitarianism's influence is strongest in humanitarian disarmament, but it also finds expression in disarmament law instruments that are motivated by national security goals. References to international humanitarian law appear in the *Convention on Certain Conventional Weapons*,[35] for example, and even the bilateral national security focused 2010 *New Strategic Arms Reduction Treaty*[36] between Russia and the United States contains an oblique reference to reducing human suffering, with the preamble noting 'the historic goal of freeing humanity from the nuclear threat'.[37]

The unique aspect of humanitarian disarmament treaties is the degree to which humanitarian motivations drive their development and ultimate content. Textually, all three core humanitarian disarmament treaties draw on the Martens Clause (an historical commitment to ensuring individuals' protection from suffering even if no specific legal rule covers a situation that arises in an armed conflict)[38] and contain a nearly identical clause in their preambles:[39] states parties '[stress] the role of public conscience in furthering the principles of humanity as evidenced by [the call for a ban on the weapon in question]'.[40] Each treaty also references 'suffering' that the banned weapons have caused as a motivation for the treaty.[41]

Threat or Use of Nuclear Weapons (Advisory Opinion) [1996] ICJ Rep 226, 239–40 [24]–[25].

35 *Convention on Prohibitions or Restrictions on the Use of Certain Conventional Weapons Which May Be Deemed to be Excessively Injurious or to Have Indiscriminate Effects (with Protocols I, II and III)*, opened for signature 10 April 1981, 1342 UNTS 137 (entered into force 2 December 1983) ('*CCW*').

36 *Treaty between the United States of America and the Russian Federation on Measures for the Further Reduction and Limitation of Strategic Offensive Arms*, signed 8 April 2010, 50 ILM 340 (entered into force 5 February 2011) ('*New Strategic Arms Reduction Treaty*').

37 Ibid., preamble para 3.

38 For a discussion on the 'Martens Clause', which appeared in the *1899 Hague Convention (II) with Respect to the Laws and Customs of War on Land*, signed 29 July 1999, 32 Stat 1803 (entered into force 4 September 1990) preamble, see Rupert Ticehurst, 'The Martens Clause and the Laws of Armed Conflict' (1997) 37 *International Review of the Red Cross* 125. The Martens Clause, as it appears in the *1899 Hague Convention*, reads:

> Until a more complete code of the laws of war is issued, the High Contracting Parties think it right to declare that in cases not included in the Regulations adopted by them, populations and belligerents remain under the protection and empire of the principles of international law, as they result from the usages established between civilized nations, from the laws of humanity and the requirements of the public conscience.

39 A version of the clause is also contained in the *CCW* (n 35). Docherty refers to the *CCW* and its protocols as 'the classic instruments of hybrid disarmament', representing 'a blend of elements characteristic of security disarmament and humanitarian disarmament': Docherty, 'Ending Civilian Suffering' (n 16) 13–4.

40 *Anti-Personnel Landmines Convention* (n 3) preamble para 8; *CCM* (n 4) preamble para 17; *TPNW* (n 5) preamble para 24.

41 *Anti-Personnel Landmines Convention* (n 3) preamble para 1: 'Determined to put an end to the suffering and casualties caused by anti-personnel mines'. *CCM* (n 4) preamble para 2: 'Determined to put an end for all time to the suffering and casualties caused by cluster munitions at

In the main, humanitarian disarmament treaties arguably draw more on principles of humanitarian action than strictly international humanitarian law, an approach that is reflected in the United Nations Institute for Disarmament Research's alternative framing of humanitarian disarmament as 'disarmament as humanitarian action'[42] or 'humanitarian approaches to disarmament'.[43] While in international humanitarian law the principle of humanity must sit alongside the principle of military necessity,[44] in humanitarian action it assumes an absolute character. For humanitarian organisations,[45] the principle of humanity requires that '[h]uman suffering must be addressed wherever it is found. The purpose of humanitarian action is to protect life and health and ensure respect for human beings'.[46] Humanitarian disarmament treaties import this absolute character: human suffering demands the prohibition of a particular weapon regardless of military utility. Likewise, in contrast to international humanitarian law, which applies in times of armed conflict, humanitarian disarmament treaties apply in all circumstances (as human rights law does).[47]

V Human rights and humanitarianism

At the same time as humanitarian approaches have been making inroads into disarmament law, human rights discourse has increasingly entered the humanitarian space. The emergence of the human rights-humanitarian dynamic in disarmament law itself illustrates this trend. From a historical perspective, Moyn has described 'the slow amalgamation of humanitarian concern for suffering with human rights' and noted the 'almost universal tendency [to] conflate the two categories'.[48] On the legal side, the infusion of human rights law

---

the time of their use'. *TPNW* (n 5) preamble para 6: 'Mindful of the unacceptable suffering of and harm caused to the victims of the use of nuclear weapons (hibakusha), as well as of those affected by the testing of nuclear weapons'.

42 John Borrie and Vanessa Martin Randin (eds), *Alternative Approaches in Multilateral Decision Making: Disarmament as Humanitarian Action* (UNIDIR, 2005) 3.

43 'Fact Sheet: Humanitarian Approaches to Disarmament', *United Nations Office of Disarmament Affairs* (Web page) <https://www.un.org/disarmament/factsheets>.

44 *Max Planck Encyclopedia of Public International Law* (at July 2013), Geoffrey S Corn, 'Principle of Humanity'.

45 Here understood to mean those organisations that adhere to the Red Cross 'Code of Conduct' (n 14).

46 'Humanitarian Principles' *United Nations Office for the Coordination of Humanitarian Affairs* (Web page, June 2012) <https://www.unocha.org/sites/dms/Documents/OOM-humanitarianprinciples_eng_June12.pdf>; Robin Coupland, 'Humanity: What Is It and How Does It Influence International Law?' (2001) 83(844) *International Review of the Red Cross* (2001) 969, 973.

47 Article 1 of each treaty states that '[e]ach State Party undertakes never under any circumstances to [carry out banned activities]': *Anti-Personnel Landmines Convention* art 1; *CCM* (n 4) art 1; *TPNW* (n 5) art 1.

48 Moyn, *The Last Utopia* (n 8) 220; Samuel Moyn, 'Theses on Humanitarianism and Human Rights', *Humanity* (Blog Post, 23 September 2016) (Web Page) <http://humanityjournal.org/blog/theses-on-humanitarianism-and-human-rights>.

into the legal framework governing armed conflict is a well-known phenomenon and part of what Meron has labelled the 'humanization' of international humanitarian law.[49]

While humanitarianism and human rights may be two sides of the same coin, they imply different philosophical starting points. Human rights law is centred on human dignity, a concept that does not allow for easy definition.[50] Nonetheless, it is apparent that promoting dignity is not the same thing as preventing or reducing suffering. For example, in the disarmament context, a suffering-focused approach would emphasise thinking about a weapon in terms of its potential to cause harm (because, under humanitarianism, identifying harm is the starting point for reducing suffering); meanwhile, a dignity-focused approach would start by considering how people relate to the weapon more broadly (because dignity is a more holistic concept). Viewed this way, preventing suffering is a narrower concept than ensuring dignity. So conceived, humanitarian goals in disarmament law could be subsumed within the more encompassing framework of human rights. Indeed, from Moyn's perspective, 'human rights and humanitarianism are fused enterprises, with the former incorporating the latter and the latter justified in terms of the former'.[51]

At the level of practice, Hilhorst and Jansen speak of the 'twinning' of human rights and humanitarianism. They observe that

> [w]hereas humanitarian workers originally found legitimation and guidance for their work in the humanitarian principles of neutrality and impartiality that were derived from international humanitarian law and refugee law, since the 1990s they increasingly adopt rights-based frameworks that are grounded in human rights declarations and conventions.[52]

As a result, '[h]uman rights-speak has rapidly turned into one of the constituent elements of humanitarian action'.[53] It remains to be seen how this trend might

49 In a seminal article, Meron described the principle of humanity as 'the common denominator' of both human rights law and international humanitarian law. Theodor Meron, 'The Humanization of Humanitarian Law' (2000) 94(2) *American Journal of International Law* 239, 245. This chapter does not address the formal relationship between international humanitarian law and human rights law, however.

50 Carozza (n 24) 345–6.

51 Moyn, *The Last Utopia* (n 8) 221. See also Michael N Barnett, 'Humanitarianism and Human Rights' in Chris Brown and Robyn Eckersley (eds), *The Oxford Handbook of International Political Theory* (Oxford University Press, 2018) 289.

52 Dorothea Hilhorst and Bram J Jansen, 'Constructing Rights and Wrongs in Humanitarian Action: Contributions from a Sociology of Praxis' (2012) 46(5) *Sociology* 891, 892, 899.

53 Ibid., 902. See also Joost Herman, 'International Law and Humanitarian Space in the Twenty-First Century: Challenged Relationships' in Andrej Zwitter et al. (eds), *Humanitarian Action: Global, Regional, and Domestic Legal Responses* (Cambridge University Press, 2014) 11, 16: 'At the core of the human rights-based approach to humanitarianism is the conviction that human beings both in circumstances of peace and of conflict are in need of having, and are entitled to have, their human dignity protected'.

be affected by changes in the priority accorded to human rights discourse in international affairs.[54]

In this context, it is not surprising that leading diplomatic proponents of humanitarian disarmament have listed 'a strong and direct link to international human rights law' among the measures that give a treaty a humanitarian character.[55] In other words, using language from human rights law affirms a disarmament treaty's humanitarian character, at least in part because of the prevalence of rights-speak in the practice of humanitarianism, but also as a result of the broader 'fusion' that Moyn has described.[56]

VI Victim assistance and human rights law

All of these threads come together in the concept of victim assistance, which pairs humanitarian motivations with human rights law. This part looks at the victim assistance provisions in the three humanitarian disarmament treaties and argues that, in this context, human rights-humanitarianism produces a compromise that promises a deeper engagement with human rights law than it delivers.

The part begins in section A by setting out the way that the relationship between victim assistance and human rights has evolved across the three humanitarian treaties. It then turns in section B to describe how 'assistance' is, primarily, a humanitarian concept: although it must be provided 'in accordance with' human rights law, textually, it retains a humanitarian framing, complicating its human rights legal implications, a point developed in section C. In section D, it shows that the humanitarian disarmament idea of 'victim' draws on human rights law but incompletely so: whereas a human rights violation entails a right to a remedy, using a weapon banned by a humanitarian disarmament treaty or carrying out another banned activity does not generate an obligation on the user to repair harm to victims (although victim assistance can have remedial elements). This part concludes by exploring the implications of territorial-based jurisdiction for victim assistance. It makes the argument that such jurisdiction reflects the state-centric nature of disarmament law and reinforces the disconnect between victim and remedy.

54 Whereas once human rights might have been considered 'a universal ideology, an international standard of legitimacy for sovereign power, [and] a common vernacular of justice for global civil society', the power the field exerts in international affairs may be diminishing, although it is too early to make normative predictions: David Kennedy, 'The International Human Rights Regime: Still Part of the Problem?' in Rob Dickinson et al., (eds), *Examining Critical Perspective on Human Rights* (Cambridge University Press, 2012) 19, 20.

55 Reiterer and Kratochvil (n 17) 5. Both authors participated in the negotiations for the *CCM* as part of the Austrian delegation; Austria was a member of the 'core group' of states that led the process for that treaty.

56 See David Luban, 'Human Rights Thinking and the Laws of War' in Jens David Ohlin (ed), *Theoretical Boundaries of Armed Conflict and Human Rights* (Cambridge University Press, 2016) 45.

It is important to note that none of this analysis is to deny the practical benefits of victim assistance: establishing a concrete legal obligation to provide victim assistance was ground-breaking and has served as a foundation for advocates and practitioners to advance the rights of victims in a variety of contexts.[57] Rather, this is an observation on how human rights-humanitarianism has manifested in this legal context.

A *The evolution of the relationship between victim assistance and human rights*[58]

The *Anti-Personnel Landmines Convention* was the first disarmament treaty to incorporate the concept of victim assistance, providing 'an essential hook for human rights to finally enter the disarmament arena'.[59] In a textual sense though, it was the barest of hooks — states parties 'in a position to do so' were required to 'provide assistance for the care and rehabilitation, and social and economic reintegration, of mine victims'.[60] While there was no direct reference to human rights law, the establishment of an obligation to victims — human beings harmed by landmines — provided an entry point for human rights discourse.

The *CCM* established a stronger and more specific victim assistance provision: art 5 required states parties with cluster munitions victims in their territories ('affected states') to provide victim assistance. This was separate from the obligation in art 6 on all states parties 'in a position to do so' to provide international assistance — financial or otherwise — to affected states. The *CCM* also set out a list of actions affected states must take under the rubric of victim assistance, including developing national plans and budgets, designating focal points, and '[c]losely consult[ing] with and actively involv[ing] cluster munition victims and their representative organisations'.[61] Additionally, as already noted, the *CCM* included a direct requirement for affected states to provide victim assistance 'in accordance with applicable international ... human rights law' and without discrimination.[62]

At least three factors influenced the development of art 5's textual connection to human rights and the expanded scope of victim assistance in the *CCM* as compared to the *Anti-Personnel Landmines Convention.* First, human

57 See, eg, International Campaign to Ban Landmines – Cluster Munition Coalition (ICBL-CMC), *2018–19 Operational Plan* (2018) 8.

58 This chapter does not attempt to document the history of victim assistance. See Docherty, Chapter 4 in this book for a more in-depth discussion of this topic.

59 Schoiswohl (n 2) 122.

60 *Anti-Personnel Landmines Convention* (n 3) art 6(3). The 2003 Protocol on Explosive Remnants of War (Protocol V to the *CCW*) contains a limited victim assistance provision that closely resembles the *Anti-Personnel Landmines Convention's* formulation: *Protocol on Explosive Remnants of War to the Convention on Prohibitions or Restrictions on the Use of Certain Conventional Weapons Which May Be Deemed to Be Excessively Injurious or to Have Indiscriminate Effects (Protocol V),* adopted 28 November 2003, 2399 UNTS 100 (entered into force 12 November 2006) art 8.

61 *CCM* (n 4) art 5(2).

62 Ibid., arts 5(1), 5(2)(e).

rights arguments around cluster munition use were part of the general advocacy background that informed the treaty's negotiations. These arguments included that the use of cluster munitions (and the problem of unexploded submunitions) could violate the right to life and the right not to be subjected to cruel or inhuman treatment, and have implications for social, cultural, and children's rights.[63] A second factor that influenced this development was that a practitioner-understanding had developed in the implementation of the *Anti-Personnel Landmines Convention* that the treaty's victim assistance obligations and states' more general human rights obligations were strongly linked.[64] The third influence was the conclusion of the *Convention on the Rights of Persons with Disabilities*.[65] This treaty had been negotiated only a couple of years prior to the *CCM* and its advocates played an important role in shaping the *CCM*'s victim assistance obligations and bringing in human rights language.[66]

The path to victim assistance was not so straightforward in the *TPNW*, the first draft of which placed a relatively weak obligation on affected states.[67] The eventual victim assistance provision in the *TPNW*, art 6, remained fairly bare, reflecting the drafters' general preference for brevity in the treaty text as a whole. Unlike the *CCM*, the *TPNW* victim assistance provision did not contain a list of actions to guide victim assistance implementation but, like the *CCM*, it separated out the responsibility of all affected states to provide victim assistance (in art 6) from the responsibility of all states parties 'in a position to do so' to provide international assistance (in art 7). Article 7, however, also required, without qualification, any state party 'that has used or tested nuclear weapons' (the 'user state') to 'provide adequate assistance to affected states parties, for the purpose of victim assistance'.[68]

63 See Alexander Breitegger, *Cluster Munitions and International Law: Disarmament with a Human Face?* (Routledge, 2012) 90–124.

64 In particular, the 2004 *Nairobi Action Plan 2005–2009*, adopted at the *Anti-Personnel Landmines Convention*'s First Review Conference, laid the groundwork for the elements of victim assistance that found expression in the text of the *CCM* itself: *Final Report*, First Review Conference of the States Parties to the Convention on the Prohibition of the Use, Stockpiling, Production and Transfer of Anti-Personnel Mines and on Their Destruction, UN Doc APLC/CONF/2004/5 (9 February 2005) Part II ('Ending the Suffering Caused by Anti-Personnel Mines: Nairobi Action Plan 2005–2009') ('*Nairobi Action Plan*'). See Docherty, Chapter 4 in this book for a detailed description of the evolution of victim assistance obligations.

65 *Convention on the Rights of Persons with Disabilities*, opened for signature 30 March 2007, 2515 UNTS 3 (entered into force 3 May 2008) ('*CRPD*').

66 See, eg, Markus Reiterer and Tirza Leibowitz, 'Article 5: Victim Assistance' in Gro Nystuen and Stuart Casey-Maslen (eds), *The Convention on Cluster Munitions: A Commentary* (Oxford University Press, 2010) 328, 331 [5.2]. It is notable that the *CCM* directly references the *CRPD* in its preamble, para 9.

67 *Draft Convention on the Prohibition of Nuclear Weapons*, UN Doc A/CONF.229/2017/CRP.1 (22 May 2017) art 6. Rietiker, for example, labelled the *TPNW*'s inclusion of a victim assistance and environmental remediation provision 'unexpected': Daniel Rietiker, 'New Hope for Nuclear Disarmament or "Much Ado About Nothing?": Legal Assessment of the New "Treaty on the Prohibition of Nuclear Weapons" and the Joint Statement by the USA, UK, and France Following Its Adoption' (2017) 59 *Harvard International Law Journal Online Journal* 22, 29.

68 *TPNW* (n 5) art 7(6).

B The concept of assistance and humanitarianism

In humanitarian disarmament, the term 'assistance' in 'victim assistance' is firmly rooted in humanitarianism rather than human rights. 'Humanitarian assistance' is a familiar term in the field of humanitarian action and, as noted in Part II, refers to the delivery of aid in situations of conflict or large-scale crisis. For example, it appears in the 1993 *Convention on the Prohibition of the Development, Production, Stockpiling and Use of Chemical Weapons and on Their Destruction* ('*CWC*') as a potential precursor to the concept of victim assistance.[69] Article 10(9) of the *CWC* says that states parties can request 'emergency assistance' if chemical weapons are used and 'humanitarian assistance' if there is a threat of use.[70]

At a conceptual level, 'assistance' is something that is provided to individuals, rather than a right they may claim, and has charitable connotations.[71] In the *Anti-Personnel Landmines Convention* — the first clear articulation of a victim assistance obligation — only states 'in a position to do so' are required to provide victim assistance, invoking a concept of charity, rather than obligation.[72] The treaty's description of 'care and rehabilitation' as a form of assistance — albeit including 'social and economic reintegration'[73] — also suggests a humanitarian framing, focused on the alleviation of suffering more than the vindication of rights.[74]

This conclusion is reinforced by early interpretations of victim assistance that focused largely (although not exclusively) on medical needs: in 2003, the

69 *Convention on the Prohibition of the Development, Production, Stockpiling and Use of Chemical Weapons and on Their Destruction*, opened for signature 13 January 1993, 1974 UNTS 45 (entered into force 29 April 1997).

70 In cases where 'there are victims of use of chemical weapons and immediate action is indispensable', a designated treaty official 'shall take emergency measures of assistance, using [resources already set aside for the purpose]': Ibid., art 10(11). See also art 8(39)(b) by which a body established under that treaty is charged with 'coordinat[ing] the establishment and maintenance of permanent stockpiles of emergency and humanitarian assistance by States parties'.

71 Barnett (n 51) 301:

> Humanitarianism demands that we give to those in need — that is, we express feelings of charity and benevolence. I give to suffering others not because they are "entitled" and I "owe" them, but rather because of my generosity. Human rights, on the other hand, demands that we intervene to end violations and punish violators. By tackling these violations, rights agencies are attempting to make the world right and whole; the goal is empowerment, justice, and prosperity.

72 The *Commentary* to the *Anti-Personnel Landmines Convention* notes that there is no 'absolute legal obligation' to provide assistance: Stuart Maslen, *Commentaries on Arms Control Treaties Volume 1: The Convention on the Prohibition of the Use, Stockpiling, Production, and Transfer of Anti-Personnel Mines and on Their Destruction* (Oxford University Press, 2nd ed, 2005) 195 [6.20] ('*Anti-Personnel Landmines Convention Commentary*').

73 The preamble situates 'social and economic reintegration' as a type of 'care and rehabilitation': *Anti-Personnel Landmines Convention* (n 3) preamble para 3; whereas art 6 appears to consider them as separate types of assistance: at art 6(3).

74 The word 'care' possibly derives from the context of humanitarian assistance to refugees in situations of protracted displacement, where 'care and maintenance' is established terminology.

International Mine Action Standards,[75] for example, defined assistance to mine victims as referring to

> all aid, relief, comfort and support provided to victims (including survivors)[76] with the purpose of reducing the immediate and long-term medical and psychological implications of their trauma.[77]

While the *CCM* explicitly drew on human rights law, it maintained the *Anti-Personnel Landmines Convention*'s framing of assistance, with 'medical care, rehabilitation and psychological support' given as the first examples of 'assistance', in the text of art 5,[78] followed by 'social and economic inclusion' — the latter more a nod than a direct reference to human rights.[79] The *TPNW* maintained the same structure and language as the *CCM* in this respect.

C Delivering assistance 'in accordance with' human rights law

As noted above in Part VI(A), in the *CCM* and the *TPNW*, the humanitarian concept of assistance meets human rights law. States parties are explicitly required to provide assistance 'in accordance with' human rights law (as well as international humanitarian law, if the context is an armed conflict). The *Commentary* to the *CCM* notes:[80]

> In principle, all norms established within the realm of international human rights law may be relevant for victim assistance; this includes norms promoting equality and non-discrimination, economic, social, and cultural rights, and civil and political rights, as well as those protecting the rights of marginalized groups, such as persons with disabilities, women, and children.[81]

75 *International Mine Action Standards* (04.10, 2nd ed, January 2003).

76 For a description of the distinction drawn between the two terms 'victim' and 'survivor', see Elke Hottentot, 'Victim Assistance in the Context of Mines and Explosive Remnants of War' (Policy Brief No 11, Handicap International, July 2014) (Web Page) <https://handicap-international.ch/sites/ch/files/documents/files/assistance-victimes-mines-reg_anglais.pdf>.

77 *International Mine Action Standards* (04.10, 2nd ed, January 2003) standard 3.226, cited in Maslen, *Anti-Personnel Landmines Convention Commentary* (n 72) 196 [6.24]. The *Commentary* also notes the more expansive definition used by the International Campaign to Ban Landmines: at 196 [6.24].

78 In the sense that these are the terms used with the word 'assistance' within the text of art 5(1): 'Each State Party ... shall ... adequately provide age- and gender-sensitive assistance, including medical care, rehabilitation and psychological support, as well as provide for their social and economic inclusion'.

79 Although victim advocates' themselves emphasise the realisation of rights as the key element to victim assistance. See, eg, Handicap International, 'The Way Forward on Victim Assistance' (Briefing Paper, June 2014).

80 Reiterer and Leibowitz (n 66) 358 [5.70].

81 In practice, the victim assistance obligation has been interpreted as responding in a targeted fashion to the specific harms suffered by those affected by the weapon, with the larger goal of

Arguably, as a result, the disarmament law obligation of victim assistance is subsumed under human rights law. The primacy given to human rights law is reinforced by the human rights obligation of non-discrimination, which is the only specific human right referenced in the *CCM* (art 5) and the *TPNW* (art 6).[82] In practice, non-discrimination means, for example, that services provided to a cluster munition victim with a particular need must be equally available to someone with the same need.

There is a conceptual tension between viewing victim assistance as a distinct disarmament law obligation while at the same time imbuing its content with the vast corpus of human rights law. On this interpretation, rather than establishing a separate legal regime, victim assistance provisions inform how an affected state should implement its human rights obligations in cases where a person or community (living in that state) have been harmed by a banned weapon. The less an individual or community's impairment of rights stems from direct physical or psychological harm caused by a banned weapon, the harder it is to pinpoint the added value of the disarmament law obligation: the measures required to fulfil the requirement to provide victim assistance become essentially indistinguishable from those human rights law already requires. And the closer the provision of assistance hems to responding to direct harm caused by banned weapons, the more it looks like a classic humanitarian response focused primarily on addressing medical need.

Although the provision of assistance to victims 'in accordance with' human rights law can support the fulfilment of victims' human rights (and organisations working the field explicitly adopt a rights-based approach),[83] the two things are not the same from a legal perspective. Victim assistance puts a gloss on affected states' pre-existing human rights obligations to their own populations; provides a guarantee that services will be delivered without discrimination; and names a set of discrete activities that affected states should undertake to address aspects of the harm victims suffered, which could also advance human rights objectives. These are not trivial accomplishments (and the practical effect of victim assistance obligations has undoubtedly been significant),[84] but the engagement with

social (re)integration or inclusion in mind. See, eg, International Human Rights Clinic, *Victim Assistance under the Treaty on the Prohibition of Nuclear Weapons*, Harvard Law School (April 2018) (Web Page) <http://hrp.law.harvard.edu/wp-content/uploads/2018/04/Victim-assistance-short-4-8-18-final.pdf>.

82 See, eg, *ICESCR* (n 11) art 2(2).

83 See, eg, Handicap International (n 79). According to Reiterer, 'The [*CCM*] embodies a rights-based approach to victim assistance, i.e. an approach that takes as a reference point not only the needs of victims, but also their rights': Markus A. Reiterer, 'Assistance to Cluster Munition Victims: A Major Step Toward Humanitarian Disarmament' (2010) 1 *Disarmament Forum* 25, 30.

84 See, eg, the sections on 'Casualties' and 'Victim Assistance' for each state party in the *Landmine Monitor and Cluster Munition Monitor*, annual publications that monitor progress in the implementation of the *Anti-Personnel Landmines Convention* and *CCM* respectively: *Landmine and Cluster Munition Monitor* (Web Page) <http://www.the-monitor.org>.

human rights law is limited: a concept of assistance meaningfully imbued with concepts from human rights law would require more than a textual reference to the field and the significance of non-discrimination.

D The concept of a victim and the right to a remedy

While 'assistance' is rooted in humanitarianism, 'victim' crosses both human rights law and humanitarianism. In general human rights law, 'victim' is an established term that refers to someone whose human rights have been violated, and who has a corresponding right to a remedy for that violation.[85] It is strongly connected with legal or quasi-legal contexts, particularly litigation; in non-legal human rights settings, the language of 'survivor' or 'affected person' is often preferred because it better recognises the agency of the person whose rights have been violated.[86]

The concept of victim assistance borrows from human rights law in its understanding of who comprises a victim. In its definitions section, art 2, the *CCM* defines 'cluster munition victims' broadly as including 'all persons who have … suffered … substantial impairment of the realisation of their rights caused by the use of cluster munitions'.[87] To craft this definition, the drafters of the *CCM* consciously drew on the established meaning of 'victim' in the *Anti-Personnel Landmines Convention* context[88] as well as the definition of 'victim' in the 2005 *Basic Principles and Guidelines on the Right to a Remedy and Reparation for Victims of Gross Violations of International Human Rights Law and Serious Violations*

85 See, eg, the *Convention for the Protection of Human Rights and Fundamental Freedoms*, opened for signature 4 November 1950, 213 UNTS 221 (entered into force 3 September 1953), as amended by *Protocol No 11 to the Convention for the Protection of Human Rights and Fundamental Freedoms*, opened for signature 11 May 1994, ETS No 155 (entered into force 1 November 1998) arts 5(5) and 34 ('*European Convention on Human Rights*'); *International Convention for the Protection of All Persons from Enforced Disappearance*, opened for signature 6 February 2007, 2716 UNTS 3 (entered into force 23 December 2010) arts 8, 15, 24.

86 See also Fiona McKay, 'What Outcomes for Victims?' in Dinah Shelton (ed), *The Oxford Handbook of International Human Rights Law* (Oxford University Press, 2013) 921, 954. In victim assistance circles, 'survivor' takes on the meaning of a person directly harmed by a weapon, whereas 'victim' includes wider groups of people affected by the weapon: Hottentot (n 76).

87 *CCM* (n 3) art 2(1). The full definition reads:

> "Cluster munition victims" means all persons who have been killed or suffered physical or psychological injury, economic loss, social marginalisation or substantial impairment of the realisation of their rights caused by the use of cluster munitions. They include those persons directly impacted by cluster munitions as well as their affected families and communities.

88 See the final report of the first review conference (the 2004 Nairobi conference) of the *Anti-Personnel Landmines Convention*. 'It is now generally accepted that *victims* include those who either individually or collectively have suffered physical or psychological injury, economic loss or substantial impairment of their fundamental rights through acts or omission': *Nairobi Action Plan* (n 64) Part II, [64] (emphasis in original).

of International Humanitarian Law, soft law human rights guidance.[89] In the *TPNW*, the term 'victim' is used in the preamble and title of art 6 ('[v]ictim assistance and environmental remediation'), but it is not defined, except by implication in art 6(1), which refers to 'individuals … who are affected by the use or testing of nuclear weapons'. Likewise, the *Anti-Personnel Landmines Convention* leaves the term 'mine victim' undefined.

Despite references to victims' rights (and in the *CCM*'s case 'the full realisation of [victims'] rights'), none of the humanitarian disarmament treaties identifies the act of using banned weapons or carrying out other banned activities as producing a corresponding duty on the user to remedy harm to individuals.[90] As such, although who comprises a victim is defined at least partly in terms of human rights, when the term 'victim' is used in disarmament law, it is decoupled from its opposite identity: the perpetrator.[91] In disarmament law, an individual or group is harmed *by a weapon*, rather than *by a state or non-state actor.*

While humanitarian disarmament law does not require those who caused harm to remedy it, the right to a remedy is a core element of human rights law (even if — particularly in the extraterritorial context — this right is not always fulfilled in practice).[92] Although the word remedy connotes judicial or other adjudication, the right is not limited to judicial concerns. As leading human rights jurist M Cherif Bassiouni has noted:

> A victim's right to remedies for violations of international human rights encompasses three overarching rights. The first is equal and effective access to justice. The second is the right to adequate, effective and prompt reparation for the harm suffered. The third is the right to truth.[93]

89 Docherty et al., 'Definitions' in Gro Nystuen and Stuart Casey-Maslen (eds), *The Convention on Cluster Munitions: A Commentary* (Oxford University Press, 2010) 144, 152 [2.9]. See also *Declaration of Basic Principles of Justice for Victims of Crime and Abuse of Power*, GA Res 40/34, UN GAOR, 40th sess, 96th plen mtg, UN Doc A/RES/40/34 (29 November 1985). For a discussion on the *Basic Principles and Guidelines* and their relationship with established human rights law, see M Cherif Bassiouni, 'International Recognition of Victims' Rights' (2006) 6(2) *Human Rights Law Review* 203.

90 An argument could potentially be made that the requirement that states parties provide assistance 'in accordance with' human rights law could import the concept of remedy (for affected states who caused harm to victims in their territory), but this would be a challenging argument to sustain. The ordinary meaning of the word 'assistance' and the context in which it appears militates against this interpretation: *Vienna Convention on the Law of Treaties*, opened for signature 23 May 1969, 1155 UNTS 331 (entered into force 27 January 1980) art 31. It would also contravene the drafters' intentions: Reiterer and Leibowitz (n 66) 336–7 [5.16].

91 See discussion in Kay Schaffer and Sidonie Smith, *Human Rights and Narrated Lives* (Palgrave Macmillan, 2004) 232, on the contentious identities of 'victim' and 'perpetrator' in human rights discourse.

92 See, eg, *ICCPR* (n 10) art 3; *UDHR* (n 9) art 8; *African Charter on Human and Peoples' Rights*, adopted 1 June 1981, 1520 UNTS 217 (entered into force 21 October 1986) art 7; *American Convention on Human Rights*, opened for signature 22 November 1969, 1144 UNTS 123 (entered into force 18 July 1978) art 25; *European Convention on Human Rights* art 13.

93 Bassiouni (n 89) 260.

Similarly, the Human Rights Committee — the official body created by the *ICCPR* to monitor its implementation — has observed that reparation can involve a number of different measures such as 'restitution, rehabilitation and measures of satisfaction, such as public apologies, public memorials, guarantees of non-repetition and changes in relevant laws and practices, as well as bringing to justice the perpetrators of human rights violations'.[94]

Absent a clear connection to a remedy or to the idea of a perpetrator, the term 'victim' in disarmament law becomes divorced from its human rights origins. In any context 'victim' suggests passivity or helplessness, rather than agency, and in the disarmament law context this impression is reinforced by its coupling with the term 'assistance' and not, for example, 'rights' or 'empowerment'.[95] In other words, although victims include people who have suffered a substantial impairment of their rights because of a weapon's use, the harm they suffered is delinked from the causal act's instigator, who is not required to remedy that harm. None of this analysis is to deny that aspects of victim assistance can serve remedial purposes (for example, through rehabilitation), but rather to highlight a gap in accountability for harm.

In essence, humanitarian disarmament does not establish a right to a remedy for weapons victims even though it condemns the act of using a banned weapon as morally repugnant and unlawful. This choice is not accidental: it stems directly from a humanitarian framing that presents addressing suffering as an apolitical endeavour. During the *CCM* negotiations, for example, a state proposal to require user states to provide assistance to affected states for victim assistance was deflected because, the *Commentary* records, 'discussion of user responsibility could have [led] to an undue politicization of the debate on a topic [victim assistance] that had hitherto profited from its predominantly humanitarian character'.[96] While the *TPNW* went one step further than the *CCM* and assigned user states 'a responsibility to provide adequate assistance to affected States Parties,

94 Human Rights Committee, *General Comment No 31: The Nature of the General Legal Obligation Imposed on States Parties to the Covenant*, 80th sess, UN Doc CCPR/C/21/Rev.1/Add.13 (26 May 2004) [16].

95 A disconnect that practitioners in the field of victim assistance themselves find uncomfortable. Humanity & Inclusion (previously Handicap International), a non-governmental organisation active in the disability sector, has noted that the term 'victim' reflects an 'outdated understanding' and its use in the *CCM* 'risks promoting a disempowering image and presenting disability as a charitable issue'. Humanity & Inclusion suggests:

> [T]o overcome language barriers in a context where terminology matters much, [victim assistance] stakeholders must stress the fact that there is now a common understanding of the social and rights based model of disability and that the CRPD is the overarching framework to realize the human rights of persons with disabilities, including those impaired by [mines or other explosive remnants of war].

Handicap International (n 79) 5

96 Reiterer and Leibowitz (n 66) 345 [5.36]. However, the *CCM* does 'strongly encourag[e]' user states to provide assistance to affected states for clearance, destruction of cluster munition remnants, and risk reduction education: *CCM* (n 3) art 4(4)(a).

for the purpose of victim assistance',[97] this obligation to provide assistance to *affected states* was not coupled with an obligation to victims themselves.[98]

The meshing of human rights language into disarmament law obscures the intentional gap between victim and remedy. While victim assistance provisions can establish or bolster a limited remedial framework within a state (and in the case of the *TPNW*, a direct remedial duty on user states towards affected states), references to human rights law, victims' human rights, rehabilitation, and social and economic reintegration suggest a complete framework to address harm. However, disarmament law does not require the elements of remedy that require user state involvement, such as acknowledgement of harm as part of reparation.

Fundamentally, the difference between human rights law and humanitarian disarmament is that humanitarian disarmament treaties do not challenge the primacy disarmament law accords to the principle of state sovereignty (nor the realist conception of states as the central actors in international affairs),[99] whereas one of the most transformative aspects of human rights law was its disruption of traditional narratives of state sovereignty: states' internal affairs were no longer their exclusive domain; individuals had rights vis-à-vis the state at an international level.[100] Humanitarian disarmament treaties, like all disarmament treaties, are not about the relationship between states and individuals. They give state sovereignty primacy: they are conventional international treaties in the sense that they are about how states relate to each other, and are not focused on the obligations states owe to human beings. A violation of their provisions is a wrong vis-à-vis other states, and not a wrong vis-à-vis an individual harmed by that treaty breach. From a legal perspective, victim assistance provisions only somewhat shift the dial in this respect.

E Territorial limitations to victim assistance

The territorial limitations on victim assistance further illustrate humanitarian disarmament's state-centric orientation. The *CCM* and *TPNW* place responsibility for providing victim assistance exclusively on affected states. The *CCM* victim

97 *TPNW* (n 5) art 7(6).

98 See Camins, Chapter 6 in this book on the potential for individual reparations for violations of disarmament law. This chapter assumes that such a right does not exist under the law as it stands and that, if it did, reparations that might be available would not necessarily align with the human rights concept of reparation. Whether an individual harmed by a weapon might be owed reparation outside the framework of the *CCM*, or another humanitarian disarmament treaty, is a separate question.

99 However, the humanitarian disarmament approach arguably does depart significantly from other tenets of classical realism, such as the idea that states act only in self-interest. This chapter does not explore international relations theory.

100 Although the implementation of this legal vision is another matter. See, eg, Mark Philip Bradley, 'Approaching the Universal Declaration of Human Rights' in Akira Iriye, Petra Goedde and William I Hitchcock (eds), *The Human Rights Revolution: An International History* (Oxford University Press, 2012) 327; see also Moyn, *The Last Utopia*, (n 8) 176–211.

assistance obligation applies only to victims 'in areas under [the state party's] jurisdiction or control'. The *TPNW* uses more expansive language in its victim assistance provision, referring to 'affected individuals under [a state party's] jurisdiction', but this apparent expansion beyond the *CCM* does not seem to have been intentional;[101] a territorial-based understanding of jurisdiction is likely to emerge as the preferred interpretation.[102]

Consequently, user states owe no obligations directly to the people they harm, unless the user states happen to use banned weapons on their own territory. Like the absence of a right to a remedy, territorial-based jurisdiction aligns more with a state — than a human — centric orientation: the obligation to provide assistance to an individual or community does not follow the weapon or the person harmed by the weapon, but attaches to the state in which the harmed person finds themselves.

In practical terms, the territorial state makes sense as the entity with responsibility for the types of activities the *CCM* envisages as victim assistance — for example, assessing the needs of victims, developing a national plan and budget — just as the primary responsibility for protecting an individual or group's human rights lies with the government of the state in which they live, or which exercises jurisdiction over them. The difference is that in human rights law, states also owe obligations to individuals outside their territory in some circumstances;[103] in humanitarian disarmament law, they never do. The practical reality that many victim assistance measures are appropriately in the hands of the territorial state distracts from the idea that had a disarmament treaty ***additionally*** assigned user states the duty to make reparation, for example, that approach would have better aligned humanitarian disarmament with human rights law.[104]

The challenge in seeing this disjunction stems from the rubric of 'assistance' and the activities the *CCM* describes. Saying that a user state should provide victim assistance implies that the user state should interfere in matters that are clearly better dealt with by the affected state, such as developing a national victim assistance plan or new domestic laws and policies.[105] This fear is valid, but

101 At the negotiations for the *TPNW*, which the author attended as a civil society representative, it appeared that the desire for brevity across the treaty resulted in textual compromises, such as this one, that were not intended to disrupt accepted understandings.

102 In theory, 'under its jurisdiction' could include individuals outside a state's territory, such as affected state citizens living abroad.

103 According the Human Rights Committee, a state's obligation to protect the right to life includes an obligation to 'persons located outside any territory effectively controlled by the State, whose right to life is nonetheless impacted by its military or other activities in a direct and reasonably foreseeable manner': Human Rights Committee, *General Comment No 36 (2018) on article 6 of the International Covenant on Civil and Political Rights, on the right to life*, 124th sess, UN Doc CCPR/C/GC/36 (30 October 2018) [63].

104 Reparation could include, for example, a public apology. The political feasibility of such an approach is an entirely different question. This conclusion is a commentary on the legal situation.

105 Such an approach would open up humanitarian disarmament to similar criticisms to those humanitarianism has faced in relation to humanitarian intervention (by which, in its strongest articulation, a state uses armed force against another state in an effort to alleviate intense

at cross purposes with the concept of remedy. Requiring a user state to directly provide victim assistance in the forms the *CCM* describes would put the user state in the driver's seat, whereas establishing that victims have the right to claim a remedy for the wrong they suffered (and providing a forum in which to exercise that right) would give agency to victims themselves. Such an approach would not, legally speaking, detract from an affected state's obligations to fulfil its human rights obligations to those in its territory, including through holding primary responsibility for victim assistance measures.[106]

The absence of extraterritorial obligations to individuals in humanitarian disarmament is not merely a theoretical gap. Although human rights law can apply extraterritorially,[107] its underlying factual assumption — while not typically articulated this way — is that it is the territorial state that poses the greatest risk to the human rights of the people living within it and so domestic measures to ensure the protection of human rights are of paramount importance.[108] However, in the disarmament context, the same assumption does not necessarily hold true in relation to the states that perpetrate harm through banned weapon use: historically, it has often (although certainly not always) been non-territorial states that have posed the greatest risk of causing individuals harm through the use of cluster munitions, nuclear weapons, or antipersonnel mines.

Reducing suffering caused by non-territorial states is at the core, not the periphery, of humanitarian disarmament's purpose. And yet when states use banned weapons outside their own territory they create victims to whom they owe no obligations pursuant to the texts of humanitarian disarmament treaties. This accountability gap has not gone unnoticed,[109] but its appearance in the understudied field of disarmament law has left it largely unexamined by practitioners and scholars. A consequence of drawing human rights law into disarmament law, however, is to open up that field to analysis informed by human rights law.

---

human suffering): John Tirman, 'The New Humanitarianism: How Military Intervention Became the Norm', *Boston Review* (online, 1 December 2003) (Web Page) <http://bostonreview.net/world/john-tirman-new-humanitarianism>.

106 In other words, on the whole, the realisation of rights would not become dependent on user state participation in the treaty.

107 See Human Rights Committee, *General Comment No 31: The Nature of the General Legal Obligation Imposed on States Parties to the Covenant*, 80th sess, UN Doc CCPR/C/21/Rev.1/Add.13 (26 May 2004) [10]; Human Rights Committee, *Views: Communication No 52/1979*, 13th sess, UN Doc CCPR/C/OP/1 (29 July 1981) [12.3] ('*Lopez v Uruguay*'); see generally Marco Milanovic, *Extraterritorial Application of Human Rights Treaties: Law, Principles, and Policy* (Oxford University Press, 2011).

108 As reflected in the *ICCPR* (n 10) art 2(2).

109 Although delegates at the negotiating conferences for the *CCM* and *TPNW* framed their concerns largely around user state responsibility to affected states, rather than individual victims: Reiterer and Leibowitz (n 66) 345 [5.36]. In the *TPNW* context, see Stuart Casey-Maslen, *The Treaty on the Prohibition of Nuclear Weapons: A Commentary* (Oxford University Press, 2019) 7.05. See also the statement made by Egypt (supported by eight states) in the plenary session held on 5 July 2017: Allison Pytlak 'News in Brief' (2017) 2(13) *Nuclear Ban Daily* 5, 7–8.

In the human rights field, the extraterritorial application of human rights treaties is the subject of rigorous scholarly and judicial debate.[110]

VII Conclusion

Human rights-humanitarianism, as described in this chapter, is a shorthand way to understand a series of interactions, rather than a prediction of how the subset of disarmament law that most draws from humanitarianism might develop in the future. The concept of victim assistance illustrates the key interaction to date, particularly through the *CCM*. In essence, victim assistance provisions direct states to think about and plan for the needs of weapons victims as they implement their human rights obligations. But the core of the victim assistance obligation is humanitarian and situated within a state-centric frame. As the dynamic of human rights-humanitarianism evolves in disarmament law, whether such legal disjunctions can be maintained remains to be seen. Regardless, the possibilities in this space are diverse and rich: the challenge now is to creatively explore the different paths the dynamic could take, and engage purposefully with their potential implications.

110 See Milanovic (n 107). The European Court of Human Rights in particular has grappled with the extraterritorial application of the *European Convention on Human Rights* in a number of cases. In the context of armed conflict, see, eg, *Banković v Belgium* [2001] XII Eur Court HR 333; *Issa v Turkey* (2004) 41 EHRR 567; *Al-Skeini v United Kingdom* (2011) 53 EHRR 18.

6 Addressing victim suffering under disarmament law

Rights, reparations and humanising trends in international law

Emily Camins[*]

I Introduction

Recent years have borne witness to growing demands for international law to address the suffering of victims of mass violence, reflecting a broader shift in the focus of international law from primarily state-centred to increasingly individual-centred.[1] In disarmament law,[2] this humanising trend has manifested in, and been driven by, humanitarian considerations being placed at the forefront of disarmament movements.[3] This has shaped disarmament law through, among other things, the insertion of victim assistance provisions in treaties, including the *Convention on Cluster Munitions*[4] ('*CCM*') and the *Treaty on the Prohibition*

* I wish to acknowledge the input of Holly Cullen, Philipp Kastner and Dale Stephens, as well as the constructive feedback given by the editors of this volume and participants at the Auckland Law School conference in June 2018. Any errors remain mine alone.

1 See, eg, Theodor Meron, *The Humanization of International Law* (Martinus Nijhoff Publishers, 2006).

2 In this chapter 'disarmament law' encompasses the rules and norms of international law that apply to disarmament, arms control and non-proliferation, including rules regulating testing, production, storage, transfer, deployment, use, clearance and destruction of weapons: see, eg, John Kierulf, *Disarmament under International Law* (McGill–Queen's University Press, 2016) 6. As it is beyond the scope of this chapter to cover the field of disarmament law obligations, I will focus on the obligations which will tend to have a more direct effect on individuals, such as use and clearance.

3 The *Oxford English Dictionary* defines humanise as 'make (something) more humane or civilized'. Humane, in turn, means 'having or showing compassion or benevolence … inflicting the minimum of pain'. Humanitarian means 'concerned with or seeking to promote human welfare': *Oxford English Dictionary* (Oxford University Press, 2nd ed, 2003) *'humanise' (v), 'humane' (adj), 'humanitarian' (n and adj)'*. On the humanisation of disarmament law, see Bonnie Docherty, 'Ending Civilian Suffering: The Purpose, Provisions, and Promise of Humanitarian Disarmament Law' (2010) 15(1) *Austrian Review of International and European Law Online* 7; Daniel Rietiker, *Humanization of Arms Control: Paving the Way for a World Free of Nuclear Weapons* (Routledge, 2017).

4 *Convention on Cluster Munitions*, opened for signature 3 December 2008, 2688 UNTS 39 (entered into force 1 August 2010) art 5 ('*CCM*').

of Nuclear Weapons ('*TPNW*').[5] Efforts to humanise international law also frequently involve moves to confer or recognise individual rights to reparations, including compensation, with some suggestions that considerations of humanity demand such rights.[6] In the disarmament context, individuals have sought compensation from states and other actors for injuries arising out of the use of or failure to clear certain weapons.[7] These claims have generally been brought on the basis of national legislation or human rights agreements, leaving unresolved the narrower question of whether disarmament treaties themselves give rise to individual rights to compensation.

Precisely how the humanisation of international law is best achieved is by no means settled.[8] Prompted by this consideration, as well as by questions surrounding the status of individual rights in disarmament law, this chapter seeks to do two things: first, to further understanding as to how disarmament law treaties deal with victim suffering; and second, to address the broader implications of the various approaches.

By way of background, Part II sets out the legal framework around individual primary and secondary rights. While the law on this issue is complex and not definitively settled, the chapter identifies points of consensus and contention and seeks to adopt a workable legal framework. Applying the framework set out in Part II, Part III analyses whether two disarmament treaties – the *Chemical Weapons Convention*[9] ('*CWC*') and the *CCM* – recognise or confer individual primary and secondary rights. In order to undertake this analysis, Part III provides some background to each treaty, and an overview of how each treaty approaches individuals, including through victim assistance measures. Applying the framework from Part II, it then considers whether either treaty gives rise to individual primary or secondary rights. It argues that neither the *CWC* nor the *CCM* can be said to confer individual primary or secondary rights directly enforceable under international law. In light of the findings in Part III, Part IV looks to the future humanisation of disarmament

5 *Treaty on the Prohibition of Nuclear Weapons*, opened for signature 20 September 2017 (not yet in force) art 6 ('*TPNW*').

6 For an example of an international effort to strengthen international rights to reparations, see *Basic Principles and Guidelines on the Right to a Remedy and Reparation for Victims of Gross Violations of International Human Rights Law and Serious Violations of International Humanitarian Law*, GA Res 60/147, UN GAOR, 3rd Comm, 60th sess, 64th mtg, Agenda Item 71(a), Supp No 49, UN Doc A/RES/60/147 (21 March 2006, adopted 16 December 2005) art 3(d) ('*UN Basic Principles*'). On the notion that considerations of humanity demand individual rights, see, eg, *Jurisdictional Immunities of the State (Italy vs Germany: Greece Intervening) (Judgment)* [2012] ICJ Rep 99 ('*Jurisdictional Immunities*') (Judge Cançado Trindade). Cf David Luban, 'Human Rights Thinking and the Laws of War' in Jens Ohlin (ed), *Theoretical Boundaries of Armed Conflict and Human Rights* (Cambridge University Press, 2016) 48–50.

7 See below Part III(a)(iii) and Part III(b)(iii).

8 See generally Luban (n 6).

9 *Convention on the Prohibition of the Development, Production, Stockpiling and Use of Chemical Weapons and on Their Destruction*, opened for signature 13 January 1993, 1974 UNTS 45 (entered into force 29 April 1997) ('*CWC*').

law. It argues that while disarmament law's emerging response to victim suffering may take a different tack from rights-based approaches to victims, it is by no means less valuable, and may even guide development in cognate areas of law.

II Individual rights and reparations: the legal framework

The responsibility of states to make full reparations to another state for injuries caused by internationally wrongful acts is well established in international law.[10] Under the *Articles on the Responsibility of States for Internationally Wrongful Acts* ('*ARSIWA*'), this (secondary) responsibility arises as an obligation of the violating state ensuing from the breach of the primary rule.[11] States are the traditional beneficiaries of the obligation to make reparations.[12] However, in some instances, an obligation of reparation which exists towards a state may accrue to the benefit of another (non-state) actor.[13] Art 33(2) of the *ARSIWA* recognises this possibility, providing that '[t]his part is without prejudice to any right, arising from the international responsibility of a State, which may accrue directly to any person or entity other than a State'.[14] The *ARSIWA* do not define the circumstances in which a non-state actor will be entitled to invoke responsibility directly.[15]

By explicitly conferring individual rights and procedures for invoking such rights, some human rights treaties provide a clear example of a situation in which an obligation of reparation accrues to the individual.[16] However, most rules of international law are less straightforward, and opinions differ as to the appropriate test for determining both the existence and enforceability of individual

10 See, eg, *Factory at Chorzów (Germany v Poland) (Jurisdiction)* [1927] PCIJ (ser A) No 9, 21; *Responsibility of States for Internationally Wrongful Acts,* GA Res 56/83, UN GAOR, 56th sess, 85th plen mtg, Supp No 49, UN Doc A/RES/56/83 (28 January 2002, adopted 12 December 2001) annex art 31 ('*ARSIWA*').

11 *ARSIWA* (n 10) art 31. See 'Draft Articles on Responsibility of States for Internationally Wrongful Acts, with Commentaries' [2001] II(2) *Yearbook of the International Law Commission* 31, 91 ('Draft Articles Commentary'); see especially 91[4].

12 See, eg, *ARSIWA* (n 10) art 33(1).

13 'Draft Articles Commentary' (n 11) 95.

14 *Responsibility of States for Internationally Wrongful Acts,* GA Res 62/61, UN GOAR, 62nd sess, Agenda Item 78, UN Doc A/RES/62/61 (8 January 2008) art 33(2).

15 See 'Commentary on the Articles on the Responsibility of States for Internationally Wrongful Acts' (International Law Commission, 2001) 13, 95.

16 See, eg, *Convention for the Protection of Human Rights and Fundamental Freedom,* opened for signature 4 November 1950, 213 UNTS 221 (entered into force 3 September 1953) art 5(5) ('*European Convention on Human Rights*'); *Convention against Torture and Other Cruel, Inhuman or Degrading Treatment or Punishment,* opened for signature 10 December 1984, 1465 UNTS 85 (entered into force 26 June 1987) arts 13–14; *Optional Protocol to the International Covenant on Civil and Political Rights,* opened for signature 16 December 1966, 999 UNTS 171 (entered into force 23 March 1976) arts 2(3), 9(5), 14(6). See further *Rome Statute of the International Criminal Court,* opened for signature 17 July 1998, 2187 UNTS 90 (entered into force 1 July 2002) art 75 ('*Rome Statute*').

rights.[17] Some argue by analogy with human rights law that other areas of international law do, or should, confer similar rights and remedies.[18] This position is reflected in the *UN Basic Principles*[19] and invoked in claims for individual reparations under other branches of international law.

The jurisprudence from the International Court of Justice ('ICJ' or 'the Court') on the question of individual rights is inconclusive, though the cases clearly anticipate the possibility of individual rights under international law. Cases such as *LaGrand*[20] and *Avena*[21] confirm that individuals might hold primary rights under international law (in both cases under the *Vienna Convention on Consular Relations*).[22] It is, moreover, apparent from the *Israeli Wall Advisory Opinion* that individuals may be the beneficiaries of an obligation to compensate under international law.[23] The Court was of the view that Israel had an obligation to compensate 'in accordance with the applicable rules of international law, all natural or legal persons having suffered any form of material damage as a result of the wall's construction'.[24] More recently, in the *Jurisdictional Immunities* case, the ICJ found that there is no *jus cogens* rule requiring payment of full compensation to individual victims of war, but considered it unnecessary to decide whether such victims are entitled to a directly enforceable right to claim compensation under international law.[25]

These cases confirm that the applicable rules of international law may confer on individuals primary rights, and impose on states secondary obligations to compensate for breaches of such rights. They do not, however, comprehensively set out the circumstances in which such rights and obligations exist. There is, accordingly, some debate as to the circumstances in which: (a) such rights arise under a treaty; and (b) such rights give rise to a corresponding, enforceable

17 See Roland Portmann, *Legal Personality in International Law* (Cambridge University Press, 2010). See further Gabriela Echeverria, 'The UN Principles and Guidelines on Reparation: Is There an Enforceable Right to Reparation for Victims of Human Rights and International Humanitarian Law Violations?' (Doctor in Philosophy Thesis, University of Essex, 2017) 35.

18 See, eg, Paola Gaeta, 'Are Victims of Serious Violations of International Humanitarian Law Entitled to Compensation?' in Orna Ben-Naftali (ed), *International Humanitarian Law and International Human Rights Law* (Oxford University Press, 2011) 305.

19 *UN Basic Principles* (n 6).

20 *LaGrand (Germany v United States of America) (Judgment)* [2001] ICJ Rep 466, 494 [77].

21 *Avena and Other Mexican Nationals (Mexico v. USA) (Judgment)* (2004) ICJ Rep 12, 35 [40], 65 [140].

22 *Vienna Convention on Consular Relations*, opened for signature 24 April 1963, 596 UNTS 261 (entered into force 19 March 1967) ('*Vienna Convention on Consular Relations*').

23 *Legal Consequences of the Construction of a Wall in the Occupied Palestinian Territory (Advisory Opinion)* [2004] ICJ Rep 136 ('*Israeli Wall Advisory Opinion*'), 198 [153].

24 Ibid., 198 [153]. Cf *Application of the Convention on the Prevention and Punishment of the Crime of Genocide Case (Bosnia and Herzegovina v Serbia and Montenegro) (Judgment, Merits)* [2007] ICJ Rep 43, discussed in Christine Evans, *The Right to Reparation in International Law for Victims of Armed Conflict* (Cambridge University Press, 2012) 30.

25 *Jurisdictional Immunities* (n 6) 140 [94]. Cf at 145 [108].

right to reparation as a matter of general international law.[26] These matters are addressed in turn.

A Primary rights

The source of individual rights is contested.[27] The preferable view appears to be that individual rights will exist where a treaty confers such rights.[28] Individual rights are readily recognised in human rights treaties due to both the terms and the singular object and purpose of such treaties.[29] They have also been recognised in other contexts. In *LaGrand*, for example, the ICJ found that art 36(1) of the *Vienna Convention on Consular Relations* created individual rights which may be invoked by the national state of the detained person.[30] Whether they exist in other contexts is, however, controversial, particularly when treaties are silent on the question of individual rights. In such situations, the principles of treaty interpretation may be persuasive in determining their existence.[31] In interpreting a treaty, regard must be had to the ordinary meaning of a term in its context and in light of its object and purpose, with regard being had to supplementary means of interpretation where the interpretation is ambiguous or obscure.[32] The idea behind these interpretative rules is that 'the various elements ... would be thrown into the crucible, and their interaction would give the legally relevant interpretation'.[33]

B Secondary rights and procedural mechanisms

Whether, and if so in what circumstances, primary rights give rise to enforceable secondary rights to reparations is a matter of debate.[34] Some argue that the

26 See further Echeverria (n 17) 35–6.

27 See generally Portmann (n 17). On the varying legal relationships sometimes described as 'rights', see René Provost, *International Human Rights and Humanitarian Law* (Cambridge University Press, 2002) 17–8; Wesley Hohfeld, 'Fundamental Legal Conceptions as Applied in Judicial Reasoning' (1913) 23(1) *Yale Law Journal* 16.

28 See, eg, Portmann (n 17) 278; see further 'Draft Articles Commentary' (n 13) 95.

29 See above n 16. See further Antônio Augusto Cançado Trindade, *International Law for Humankind: Towards a New Jus Gentium* (Martinus Nijhoff Publishers, 2nd ed, 2013) 430; 'Draft Articles Commentary' (n 13) 95, noting the status of individuals as 'the ultimate beneficiaries and ... holders of the relevant rights' under human rights treaties.

30 *LaGrand* (n 20) 494 [77]. See further *Appeal from a Judgment of the Hungaro/Czechoslovak Mixed Arbitral Tribunal (Peter Pázmány University v Czechoslovakia) (Judgment)* [1933] PCIJ (ser A/B) No 61, 231, noting that 'the capacity to possess civil rights does not necessarily imply the capacity to exercise those rights oneself'.

31 See, eg, Portmann (n 17) 276–8.

32 *Vienna Convention on the Law of Treaties*, opened for signature 23 May 1969, 1155 UNTS 331 (entered into force 27 January 1980) ('*VCLT*') arts 31–32.

33 'Draft Articles on the Law of Treaties with Commentaries' [1966] II *Yearbook of the International Law Commission* 187, 219–20; see the discussion in Richard Gardiner, *Treaty Interpretation* (Oxford University Press, 2008) 9. See further International Law Commission, *Draft Conclusions on Subsequent Agreements and Subsequent Practice in Relation to the Interpretation of Treaties*, UN Doc A/73/10 (8 August 2018) [51] conclusion 2(5).

34 See, eg, Echeverria (n 17) 35–6.

existence of an individual primary right gives rise to a corollary secondary right to reparations, of which the individual is the beneficiary.[35] This view is reflected in such soft law instruments as the *UN Basic Principles*.[36]

However, this view is not clear from state practice or *opinio juris* in respect of international law generally.[37] Rather, the dominant view seems to be that even if an individual holds primary rights, this does not automatically confer secondary rights to reparations that would be directly enforceable by the individual vis-à-vis the offending state.[38] As Clapham succinctly notes, 'individuals can have international law rights without remedies'.[39] Thus, absent a conferral by treaty of a directly actionable remedy,[40] individuals are largely reliant on their state exercising diplomatic protection to assert their rights on the international stage.[41] Accordingly, in determining whether disarmament law treaties confer individual rights to compensation, one must ascertain first whether an individual holds a primary right under international law, and second, whether as a matter of interpretation, the treaty confers a directly actionable right to a remedy.

35 See, eg, *Jurisdictional Immunities* (n 6) 204–8 [68]–[73] (Judge Cançado Trindade); Echeverria (n 17) 35–6. Cf Rainer Hofmann and Frank Riemann, *Compensation for Victims of War* (Background Report, International Law Association Committee on Compensation for Victims of War, 17 March 2004) 31.

36 *UN Basic Principles* (n 6). See also International Law Association, *Declaration of International Law Principles on Reparation for Victims of Armed Conflict (Substantive Issues)*, Res 2/2010, 74th Conf (15–20 August 2010) ('*ILA Declaration (Substantive Issues)*'). Cf Christian Tomuschat, 'Individuals' in James Crawford et al. (eds), *The Law of International Responsibility* (Oxford University Press, 2010) 985, 988 on the unrealised pursuit of perfect equality between injured states and injured individuals.

37 See, eg, Andrew Clapham, 'The Role of the Individual in International Law' (2010) 21(1) *European Journal of International Law* 25, 27. In the context of international humanitarian law, see, eg, Provost (n 27) 47–9; Christian Tomuschat, 'State Responsibility and the Individual Right to Compensation Before National Courts' in Andrew Clapham et al. (eds), *The Oxford Handbook of International Law in Armed Conflict* (Oxford University Press, 2014) 811 ('Tomuschat on Compensation'); Ilaria Bottigliero, *Redress for Victims of Crimes Under International Law* (Martinus Nijhoff Publishers, 2004) 84.

38 See, eg, Portmann (n 17) 275–6; Hofmann and Riemann (n 35) 31 noting that, in the absence of a customary right, individual claims often fail due to a lack of express treaty provisions for a right of action; International Law Association, Committee on Reparation for Victims of Armed Conflict, *Reparation for Victims of Armed Conflict (Procedural Issues)* (Sofia Conference Final Report, 2012) 2; Provost (n 27) 43–56; Tomuschat 'Individuals' (n 36) 986; Bottigliero (n 37) 84. Cf Evans (n 24) 43.

39 Clapham (n 37) 29; 'Draft Articles on Diplomatic Protection with Commentaries' [2006] II(2) *Yearbook of the International Law Commission* 26, 27.

40 For a secondary right to a remedy to be directly actionable it may require a procedural mechanism. Whether this is required will generally be a matter of treaty interpretation. For treaty examples see above n 16; see further Dinah Shelton, *Remedies in International Human Rights Law* (Oxford University Press, 2005) 113–43.

41 See 'Draft Articles on Diplomatic Protection with Commentaries' (n 39) 27; see further Giorgio Gaja, 'The Position of Individuals in International Law: An ILC Perspective' (2010) 21(1) *European Journal of International Law* 11. Other potential avenues for individual claims, which also depend on state action or consent, include national legislation and claims commissions.

III Individual rights to reparations under disarmament law

Humanitarian considerations, alongside security considerations, have long been drivers in the development of disarmament law.[42] In recent years, the attention devoted to victims in disarmament treaties has grown.[43] This increased willingness of states to address victim suffering following weapons use, together with the emergence of individual legal claims arising out of injuries from regulated weapons,[44] leads us to consider whether victims can claim and enforce rights, including a right to reparations, directly under disarmament law (as opposed to via the framework of human rights conventions or favourable national legislation).[45] While humanising elements are by no means synonymous with individual rights, the former generally precedes and often coexists with the latter.

Applying the approach set out in Part II, Part III considers the question of individual rights, particularly rights to reparations, under the *CWC* and the *CCM*. These treaties have been selected as they raise divergent considerations, due in part to the weapons they regulate and in part to the considerations which influenced their adoption.[46] They have, moreover, the benefit of longevity, meaning that regard can be had to the practical application of these treaties. As such, these conventions offer an opportunity to address several of the issues that arise in determining the existence of an individual right to reparations. They provide a focal point not only for identifying humanising trends in victim assistance, but also for considering whether, as a matter of international law, such developments manifest in individual rights.

A The Chemical Weapons Convention

1 Treaty overview

The *CWC* built on earlier efforts to outlaw chemical weapons. The *Declaration on Asphyxiating Gases* adopted in 1899[47] and *Geneva Protocol 1925*[48] failed

42 See Geoffrey Best, *Humanity in Warfare: The Modern History of the International Law of Armed Conflict* (Weidenfeld and Nicolson, 1980) 160.

43 See, eg, Rietiker (n 3); Docherty (n 3); Alexander Breitegger, *Cluster Munitions and International Law: Disarmament with a Human Face?* (Taylor and Francis, 2011); Trindade (n 29) ch XVII; Meron (n 1) 78–85 on the impact of humanitarian considerations in the development of some disarmament treaties.

44 See, eg, *Behrami v France* [2007] 45 EHRR SE10; *Santo Domigo Massacre v Columbia* (Judgement) (Inter-American Court of Human Rights, Series C No 259, 30 November 2012).

45 For a thorough overview of such cases, see Rietiker (n 3).

46 See, eg, Docherty (n 3).

47 *Declaration (IV, 2) Concerning Asphyxiating Gases 1899* reproduced in James Brown Scott (ed), *Hague Conventions and Declarations of 1899 and 1907* (Oxford University Press, 2nd ed, 1915).

48 *Protocol for the Prohibition of the Use in War of Asphyxiating, Poisonous or Other Gases, and of Bacteriological Methods of Warfare*, opened for signature 17 June 1925, (1929) XCIV LNTS 65–74 (entered into force 8 February 1928).

to withstand the 'pressure of military expedience',[49] with several instances of chemical weapons use between the First World War and the late 1980s.[50] Negotiated through the height of the Cold War, the *CWC* regime sought to address the security threat posed by chemical weapons.[51] The *CWC* was heralded as a revolution in disarmament law, being the first 'comprehensively verifiable multilateral treaty to completely ban an entire class of weapons, and firmly limit and monitor activities that may contribute to the production of those weapons'.[52]

The treaty preamble sets out the determination of the parties to '[achieve] effective progress towards general and complete disarmament under strict and effective international control, including the prohibition and elimination of all types of weapons of mass destruction'.[53] Article I of the *CWC* sets out the obligation of states to refrain under any circumstances from developing, acquiring, stockpiling, transferring or using chemical weapons.[54] States undertake, moreover, to destroy any chemical weapons they own or possess, along with chemical weapons they have abandoned on the territory of another state party.[55] In subsequent provisions, the *CWC* establishes the Organisation for the Prohibition of Chemical Weapons ('OPCW'), whose goal is to achieve the object and purpose of the *CWC*, ensure implementation and provide a forum for the cooperation of states parties.[56] Other provisions provide an extensive regime of declarations, verification and destruction, designed to ensure the effectiveness of the key treaty requirements.[57]

Having provided a broad overview of the CWC, the next section turns to consider the place of victims in the treaty framework.

2 Victims under the Chemical Weapons Convention

Victims receive limited explicit consideration in the *CWC*. Article X provides for assistance and protection against chemical weapons, but this is clearly intended to operate on an inter-state basis. The very definition of assistance ties its provisions to states parties:

> 'Assistance' means the coordination and delivery *to States Parties* of protection against chemical weapons, including, inter alia, the following: detection equipment and alarm systems; protective equipment; decontamination

49 Robert J Mathews and Timothy L H McCormack, 'The Influence of Humanitarian Principles in the Negotiation of Arms Control Treaties' (1999) 81(834) *International Review of the Red Cross* 331, 333.

50 See Robert J Mathews, 'Chemical and Biological Weapons' in Rain Liivoja and Tim McCormack (eds), *Routledge Handbook of the Law of Armed Conflict* (Routledge, 2016) 212, noting eight authenticated uses of chemical weapons between 1925 and 1988.

51 Docherty (n 3) 13.

52 Mathews (n 50) 219.

53 *CWC* (n 9) preamble para 1.

54 Ibid., art 1(1).

55 Ibid., art 1(2)–1(3).

56 Ibid., art 8.

57 See especially ibid., arts 3–6.

> equipment and decontaminants; medical antidotes and treatments; and advice on any of these protective measures.[58]

Article X(8) confers on states parties a 'right to request and, subject to the procedures set forth in paragraphs 9, 10 and 11, to receive assistance and protection against the use or threat of use of chemical weapons' against them.[59] This request triggers the dispatch of emergency and humanitarian assistance,[60] followed by an investigation. Article X(11) goes on:

> If the information available from the ongoing investigation or other reliable sources would give sufficient proof that there are victims of use of chemical weapons and immediate action is indispensable, the Director-General shall notify all States Parties and shall take emergency measures of assistance, using the resources the Conference has placed at his [sic] disposal for such contingencies.[61]

The right to request such assistance is thus prima facie available only to states.[62] However, art X(11) does allow for some input by non-state agents, with the reference to information from 'other reliable sources' being the basis for taking emergency measures. Thus, the reports of the OPCW Fact-Finding Mission and other reputable organisations could potentially suffice to ground emergency assistance measures for individuals even in the absence of a state-led request. This is an important measure given that a state using chemical weapons against its own nationals is unlikely to request assistance.[63] Of course, it is acknowledged that assistance measures under the *CWC* are of an entirely different nature than compensation, representing primary, rather than secondary obligations.[64]

Another provision in the treaty dealing with the needs of victims is art XII, which addresses measures to redress a situation where chemical weapons have

58 Ibid., art 5(1) (emphasis added).
59 Ibid., art 5(8).
60 Ibid., art 5(9).
61 Ibid., art 10(11).
62 Ibid., art 5(8). See further 'Request for Assistance', *Organisation for the Prohibition of Chemical Weapons* (Web Page) <https://www.opcw.org/our-work/assistance-protection/assistance-against-chemical-weapons/requests-for-assistance/>.
63 On the political vulnerability of this system, see Edmond Mulet, 'How the Security Council Failed the Syria Chemical Weapons Investigators and Victims', *New York Times* (online, 29 December 2017) (Web Page) <https://www.nytimes.com/2017/12/29/opinion/syria-chemical-weapons-united-nations-security-council.html>.
64 See, eg, Alan Rosas, 'Reactions to Non-Compliance with the Chemical Weapons Convention' in Michael Bothe, Natalino Ronzitti and Allan Rosas (eds), *The New Chemical Weapons Convention – Implementation and Prospects* (Interactive Factory, 1999) 430.

been used and to ensure compliance.[65] Article XII(1) provides that the Conference of the States Parties ('the Conference') 'shall take the necessary measures ... to ensure compliance with this Convention and to redress and remedy any situation which contravenes the provisions of this Convention'.[66] In some respects, art XII resembles art 91 of the *Additional Protocol I to the Geneva Conventions*,[67] which some have suggested may permit individual compensation claims.[68] It is also the case that the use of the word 'remedy' is often invoked in the context of providing redress for victims under human rights law.[69] However, it appears from references elsewhere in the *CWC*, including subsequent sub-paragraphs in art XII, that the reference to 'redress and remedy' is better understood as referring to ensuring treaty compliance and restoring security, rather than to compensation (whether to states or individuals).[70] This view is supported by the fact that the provision does not impose on violating states a strict obligation to compensate, but rather requires the Conference to take measures to ensure compliance and redress the situation. The focus on compliance is apparent given that, according to Dekker, the phrase 'redress and remedy' was used instead of the term 'sanctions' in order to complement but not infringe upon the prerogatives of the United Nations Security Council.[71] There is no reported practice of art XII being invoked.[72]

65 *CWC* (n 9) art XII is titled 'Measures to Redress a Situation and to Ensure Compliance, including Sanctions'.

66 See also ibid., art 8(21)(k) which empowers the Conference of the States Parties to '[t]ake the necessary measures to ensure compliance with this Convention and to redress and remedy any situation which contravenes the provisions of this Convention, in accordance with Article XII'.

67 *Protocol Additional to the Geneva Conventions of 12 August 1949, and Relating to the Protection of Victims of International Armed Conflicts*, opened for signature 12 December 1977, 1125 UNTS 3 (entered into force 7 December 1978) ('*Additional Protocol I to the Geneva Conventions*').

68 See, eg, *Jurisdictional Immunities* (n 6) 296 [19] (Judge Yusuf), 204–6 [68]–[70] (Judge Cançado Trindade); cf Yves Sandoz, Christophe Swinarski and Bruno Zimmermann (eds), *Commentary on the Additional Protocols of 8 June 1977 to the Geneva Conventions of 12 August 1949* (ICRC/Martinus Nijhoff Publishers, 1987) 1056–7.

69 See, eg, *International Covenant on Civil and Political Rights*, opened for signature 16 December 1966, 999 UNTS 171 (entered into force 23 March 1976) art 2(3). See generally Shelton (n 40).

70 *CWC* (n 9) art 7(2)–7(4). This view is bolstered by the fact that the only 'situation' requiring 'redressing' in the OPCW's official records related to the need to increase initial declaration activities of states: Guido den Dekker, 'Article XII: Measures to Redress a Situation and to Ensure Compliance, Including Sanctions' in Walter Krutzsch, Eric Myjer and Ralf Trapp (eds), *The Chemical Weapons Convention: A Commentary* (OUP, 2014) 364, 375.

71 Dekker (n 70) 367. See further Thomas Bernauer, *Projected Chemical Weapons Convention: A Guide to the Negotiations in the Conference on Disarmament* (United Nations, 1990) 181–3, noting the 'delicate' nature of the sanctions question. The Reports of the Conference on Disarmament shed little light on the meaning of the phrase.

72 Ralf Trapp, 'Compliance Management under the Chemical Weapons Convention' in United Nations Institute for Disarmament Research, *WMD Compliance and Enforcement: Lessons Learned from across WMD Treaties* (UNIDIR, 2019).

Despite the relatively limited attention given to victims in the *CWC*, in 2011 the Conference established a Trust Fund for the International Support Network for Victims of Chemical Weapons ('Trust Fund').[73] The decision establishing the Trust Fund, which relies solely on voluntary contributions, encourages states parties to contribute financially to the fund, to provide medical treatment to victims of chemical weapons and to facilitate materials and equipment-related assistance to states parties to assist and support the victims of the use of chemical weapons.[74] The decision refers to the obligation of the Conference to act to further the object and purpose of the *CWC*,[75] with no mention of its obligation to take measures to redress and remedy contraventions,[76] suggesting that victim assistance (as opposed to rights-based compensation) is a key focus.

3 *Analysis: does the* Chemical Weapons Convention *confer individual primary or secondary rights?*

At first glance then, the provisions of the *CWC* do not appear to confer rights on individuals. The key provisions of the treaty prohibiting use of chemical weapons and requiring destruction of abandoned chemical weapons are phrased in terms of obligations owed by states, with no reference to the nature or identity of any victims of those weapons. However, in recent years, there has been an increased focus on the humanitarian aspects of the *CWC*. The Director-General of the OPCW has, for example, described the treaty as '[reinforcing] the sanctity of humanitarian ideals over warfare'.[77] The importance of victims was likewise emphasised with the Conference's decision to establish the Trust Fund.[78] Such statements and developments suggest an effort to humanise the *CWC*. With the *CWC* silent on the question of who its key provisions seek to protect, can it be said that, given the treaty context, object and purpose and supplementary means of interpretation, it should be interpreted now as protecting – and conferring rights on – individuals?

While this question has not been authoritatively tested, a plausible argument in favour of individual rights might proceed as follows: one of the purposes of the *CWC* is to benefit all of humankind, with goals which exceed the interests of individual states. The opening paragraph of the preamble, for example, acknowledges the determination of states 'to act with a view to achieving effective

73 Conference of the States Parties to the Chemical Weapons Convention, *Decision on the Establishment of the International Support Network for Victims of Chemical Weapons and the Establishment of a Voluntary Trust Fund for This Purpose*, Sixteenth Session C-16/DEC.13, 28 November–2 December 2011) para 1 ('*Voluntary Trust Fund Decision*').

74 Ibid., para 4.

75 Ibid., preamble.

76 As set out in *CWC* (n 9) art 8(21)(k).

77 Ambassador Ahmet Üzümcü, 'The Chemical Weapons Convention: An Instrument for Peace' (Speech, University of Rome Tor Vergata, 28 May 2018) (Web Page) < https://www.opcw.org/sites/default/files/documents/ODG/uzumcu/180528.VS.ODG.Speech_Tor_Vergata.pdf>.

78 *Voluntary Trust Fund Decision* (n 73).

progress towards general and complete disarmament ... of all types of weapons of mass destruction'.[79] The preamble further sets out the desire of states parties to 'contribute to the realization of the purposes and principles of the Charter of the United Nations'.[80] A later paragraph expresses determination 'for the sake of all mankind, to exclude completely the possibility of the use of chemical weapons, through the implementation of the provisions of this Convention, thereby complementing the obligations assumed under the Geneva Protocol of 1925'[81] (these latter obligations being motivated by humanitarian concerns).[82]

Read against this backdrop, key provisions of the *CWC* regime, particularly the prohibition on use, implicitly invoke several human rights or humanitarian norms: the right to life (particularly in a law enforcement context);[83] international humanitarian law prohibitions on indiscriminate weapons and those that cause unnecessary suffering;[84] and, due to its potential for mass destruction, the prohibition on acts of aggression.[85]

Other prohibitions, such as those governing the clearance of old and abandoned chemical weapons, arguably resemble, or at the very least complement, human rights obligations to ensure citizens' safety.[86] By imposing absolute obligations on states to destroy weapons within their ownership, possession, jurisdiction or control,[87] the *CWC* protects a state's own nationals, potentially at a cost to the state.[88] As with violations of international humanitarian law and human rights law,[89] the individual is the ultimate victim of the use or misuse of chemical weapons. Indeed, humanitarian considerations – such as the possible lasting effects of chemical weapons on human health – were discussed during the negotiations which preceded the *CWC*.[90] There is, accordingly, some basis

79 *CWC* (n 9) preamble para 1.
80 Ibid., preamble para 2.
81 Ibid., preamble para 6.
82 See, eg, Docherty (n 3) 10–1.
83 See, eg, Michael Crowley and Malcolm Dando, 'The Use of Incapacitating Chemical Agent Weapons in Law Enforcement' (2015) 19(4) *International Journal of Human Rights* 465, 476.
84 See, eg, Jean-Marie Henckaerts and Louise Doswald-Beck, *Customary International Humanitarian Law* (ICRC/Cambridge University Press, 2005) 259–64. See further *Rome Statute* (n 16) art 8(2)(b)(xvii)–8(2)(b)(xviii) which criminalise the use of poisonous weapons or gases. At art 75, victims of crimes within the Court's jurisdiction may seek reparations.
85 Cf Michael N Schmitt and Christopher M Ford, 'Assessing U.S. Justifications for Using Force in Response to Syria's Chemical Attacks: An International Law Perspective' (2018) 9 *Journal of National Security Law and Policy* 283, 291. While *jus ad bellum* regulates rights and obligations between states, the crime of aggression entails individual criminal responsibility, and potentially a right to reparation for victims, before the International Criminal Court.
86 See, eg, *Universal Declaration of Human Rights*, GA Res 217A (III), UN GAOR, 3rd session, 183 plen mtg, UN Doc A/810 (10 December 1948) art 3.
87 *CWC* (n 9) art 4.
88 Rietiker (n 3) 72 –3 (arguing that the *CWC* protects human rights).
89 See *Jurisdictional Immunities Case* (n 6) (Judge Cançado Trindade), finding that individuals, not states, are the ultimate victims of violations of international humanitarian law: at 266–7 [245].
90 Bernauer (n 71) 15–6.

for arguing that its provisions protect individuals and should be interpreted in accordance with human rights thinking, notwithstanding the treaty's security motivations.[91]

There are, however, compelling counter-arguments. In particular, distinction must be drawn between a treaty obligation which may protect individuals and the question of whether it actually confers individual rights.[92] As noted above, there is nothing explicit either in the text of the treaty or in its drafting history to suggest that the *CWC* confers individual rights.[93] By contrast, security considerations are readily apparent in both the development and text of the *CWC*.[94] Chemical weapons, as weapons of mass destruction, can threaten and harm the security and economic interests of the state. This strategic security consideration has dominated the *CWC*.[95] Thus, while humanitarian and security considerations will often align, it would be erroneous to conflate the two for the purposes of finding that a treaty or norm confers individual rights. Although the *CWC* may benefit individuals, to find that the treaty confers individual rights would require a departure from the ordinary rules of interpretation. In light of this, it is problematic to assert that the *CWC* confers on individuals rights under international law.[96]

It is worth noting that despite this analysis, individuals may nonetheless seek remedies for violations of disarmament law where favourable legislation supports their claims through national courts,[97] or where international agreements

91 On the trend towards viewing security and human protection as complementary, rather than contradictory, goals, see Rietiker (n 3) 12–4; Trindade (n 29) 403 on the concept of human security; Bonnie Docherty, 'The Legal Content and Impact of the Treaty on the Prohibition of Nuclear Weapons' (Seminar Paper, Nobel Peace Prize Legal Seminar, 11 December 2017) (Web Page) <http://hrp.law.harvard.edu/wp-content/uploads/2017/12/Impact-of-TPNW-Nobel-presentation-Dec-2017.pdf>.

92 As discussed in Part II above.

93 For example, with some inconsequential exceptions, during negotiations the phrases 'victim' and 'individual' appear to have referred to 'victim state' or 'individual state' respectively: see Bernauer (n 71) 181.

94 See Docherty (n 3) 18–21, 35, noting the preambular references to the *UN Charter* and to 'general and complete disarmament', as well as the security-oriented verification regime; Mathews and McCormack (n 49) 339, noting that security considerations were the main driver of the development of the *CWC*.

95 See, eg, Ambassador Ahmet Üzümcü (n 77), noting that the *CWC* has 'peace and security at its core'.

96 In the absence of primary rights, one would be hard-pressed to assert individual secondary rights under such provisions as art 7. In any event, there is no explicit conferral of individual rights under art 7, and similar considerations would apply to its interpretation.

97 For discussion of specific schemes addressing chemical weapons injuries, see Jason von Meding, 'Agent Orange, Exposed: How U.S. Chemical Warfare in Vietnam Unleashed a Slow-Moving Disaster' *The Conversation* (Web Page, 4 October 2017)<https://theconversation.com/agent-orange-exposed-how-u-s-chemical-warfare-in-vietnam-unleashed-a-slow-moving-disaster-84572> on the limited compensation scheme available for victims of Agent Orange; Kim Lunman, 'Ottawa Offers Compensation to Test Victims' *The Globe and Mail* (online, 28 March 2017) (Web Page) <https://www.theglobeandmail.com/news/national/ottawa-offers-compensation-to-test-victims/article18259634/>; Jason Rezaian, 'An Ally of Syria, Iran Also Bears Scars from Chemical Weapons Attacks — by Iraq' *The Washington Post* (online, September 12, 2013) (Web Page) <https://www.washingtonpost.com/world/middle_east/an-ally-of-syria-iran-also-bears-scars-from-chemical-weapons-attacks--

provide an appropriate forum. In the case of *X v Japan*,[98] for example, Chinese plaintiffs sought compensation under art 1(1) of the State Redress Act (Act No. 125 of 1947) of Japan,[99] after a 2004 incident in which they opened a blister gas shell which had been abandoned by the Japanese Imperial Armed Forces. The Tokyo District Court held that the Government of Japan had omitted to remove the risk posed by the abandoned weapons, and had an international obligation to destroy the weapons within ten years of the entry into force of the *CWC*.[100] However, as the *CWC* does not directly require the removal of each specific risk, but rather the destruction of abandoned weapons within ten years in principle,[101] the omission was not significantly unreasonable, and therefore not unlawful under art 1(1) of the State Redress Act.[102]

Individuals have also sought remedies before the European Court of Human Rights following the use of chemical agents. In *Finogenov v Russia*, the applicants argued that the use of chemical agents by Russian security forces to bring

---

by-iraq/2013/09/12/2d2eaa6e-1b8b-11e3-80ac-96205cacb45a_story.html?utm_term=.c22348d32868 > on Iranian compensation for injury arising from Iraqi chemical attacks.

98 *X v State of Japan* (Tokyo District Court, Judgment, 16 April 2012), translated in Amuro Wakasa, 'Public International Law Judicial Decisions in Japan' (2014) 57 *Japanese Yearbook of International Law* 487.

99 Art 1(1) requires the state to compensate where a public officer has in the course of his or her duties unlawfully inflicted damage on another person intentionally or negligently.

100 *X v Japan* (n 98) 491–2, referring to Japan's obligations under the *CWC* and the Memorandum of Understanding between Japan and China of July 1999.

101 Ibid., 492.

102 Ibid., 492, 495, finding that the Court should 'take into account general standards and common sense concerning measures to prevent the present-type damage in the disposal operation under the financial, technical, political, diplomatic, and social constraints', as well as other factors including the frequency of past damage, geographical and social considerations: at 492. Similar cases by Chinese nationals have also been unsuccessful, highlighting both the challenges associated with claims arising from abandoned chemical weapons and the consequent need for political solutions: see Masahiko Asada and Trevor Ryan, 'Post-War Reparations between Japan and China and the Waiver of Individual Claims: Japan's Supreme Court Judgments in the *Nishimatsu Construction* Case and the *Second Chinese "Comfort Women"* Case' (2009) 19(1) *The Italian Yearbook of International Law* 205, 208. The ex gratia payment of 300 million yen from Japan to China following a fatal leak of poison gas in 2003 is an example of such a political solution. According to the Chinese embassy, the payment would be distributed to victims and their families: see James Reilly, 'China's History Activism and Sino-Japanese Relations' (2006) 4(2) *China: An International Journal* 189, 203; 'Japan to pay China 300 million yen over mustard gas', Japan Times (online, 20 October 2003) (Web Page) <https://www.japantimes.co.jp/news/2003/10/20/national/japan-topay-china-300-million-yen-over-mustard-gas/#.WguwDVuCzIU>. A private fund has alsobeen established to redress Chinese victims of Japanese chemical weapons: see 'Japan, ChinaEye Foundation for Chemical Weapons Victims: Xinhua', (Tokyo), 2014. See further Congyan Cai, 'International Law in Chinese Courts during the Rise of China' (2016) 110 *American Journal of International Law* 269.

'Japan to pay China 300 million yen over mustard gas', *Japan Times* (online, 20 October 2003) (Web Page) <https://www.japantimes.co.jp/news/2003/10/20/national/japan-to-pay-china-300-million-yen-over-mustard-gas/#.WguwDVuCzIU>. A private fund has also been established to redress Chinese victims of Japanese chemical weapons: see 'Japan, China Eye Foundation for Chemical Weapons Victims: Xinhua', (Tokyo), 2014. See further Congyan Cai, 'International Law in Chinese Courts during the Rise of China' (2016) 110 *American Journal of International Law* 269.

an end to a hostage crisis in a Moscow theatre was a violation of their right to life.[103] The Court held that, in the circumstances, the use of gas was not a disproportionate measure, and, as such, did not breach the right to life provision (art 2) of the *European Convention on Human Rights*.[104]

While these cases indicate potential avenues for individuals to seek redress under human rights agreements or national legislation for injury caused by the use or failure to clear chemical weapons, they do not go to the question of whether individuals have rights directly under the *CWC*. As set out above, it cannot be said that the *CWC* confers on individuals primary rights or secondary rights to reparations against offending states directly under international law.[105] This approach accords with (and may be sustained by) the historical practice of states addressing post-war reparations predominantly through lump sum inter-state reparations, without itemising each specific violation or ground for compensation.[106] As Vattel put it in his 1758 treatise, *The Law of Nations*, '[w]ere the rules of strict and rigid justice to be observed in [a peace treaty], so that each party should precisely receive every thing to which he [sic] has a just

103 *Finogenov v Russia* (European Court of Human Rights, Chamber, Application Nos. 8299/03 and 27311/03, 20 December 2011. See especially [165]–[174].

104 Ibid., [236]. *Convention for the Protection of Human Rights and Fundamental Freedoms*, opened for signature 4 November 1950, 213 UNTS 221 (entered into force 3 September 1953). Cf International Committee of the Red Cross, *"Incapacitating Chemical Agents": Law Enforcement, Human Rights Law and Policy Perspectives* (Expert Meeting Report, January 2013) (Web Page) < https://www.icrc.org/en/doc/assets/files/publications/icrc-002-4121.pdf>. See further Crowley and Dando (n 75), noting the Court's 'inexplicable failure' to discuss the *CWC*: at 476.

105 On the distinct but related question of claims against private actors, see Liesbeth Zegveld, 'Compensation for the Victims of Chemical Warfare in Iraq and Iran' in Carla Ferstman, M Goetz and A Stephens (eds), *Reparations for Victims of Genocide, War Crimes and Crimes against Humanity: Systems in Place and Systems in the Making* (Martinus Nijhoff, 2009); Liesbeth Zegveld, 'Decision that Van Anraat Must Pay Compensation to Victims of Chemical Attacks in Iraq Confirmed' *Liesbeth Zegveld* (online, 7 April 2015) (Web Page) <http://www.liesbethzegveld.com/en/selection-of-cases/decision-that-van-anraat-must-pay-compensation-to-victims-of-chemical-attacks-in-iraq-confirmed/>. Cf Alex Bollfrass, 'Iran-Iraq Chemical Warfare Aftershocks Persist' *Arms Control Association* (online, 1 July 2007) (Web Page) <https://www.armscontrol.org/act/2007_07-08/IranIraq>.

106 Eg Silja Vönery, 'Implementation and Enforcement of International Humanitarian Law' in Dieter Fleck (ed), *The Handbook of International Humanitarian Law* (Oxford University Press, 3rd ed, 2013) 647, 683–4, noting that such payments often neglect to award specific compensation for breaches; Tomuschat 'Individuals' (n 36) 988; see further *X v Japan* (Tokyo District Court, Judgment, 25 February 2015) 61 Shomu Geppo (9) 1737 [2015], translated in Kento Nisugi 'Public International Law Judicial Decisions' (2016) 59 *Japanese Yearbook of International Law* 463–89; Rosas (n 64) 429. The fact of such historical interstate reparations payments can obfuscate questions of state responsibility and individual rights (thanks to Dale Stephens for this point). Several uses of chemical weapons have gone uncompensated: see, eg, 'Iran "Owed Billions for Saddam War"', *BBC News* (online, 18 December 2003) (Web Page) <http://news.bbc.co.uk/2/hi/middle_east/3329671.stm>; 'Kurds ask for Halabja compensation on 30th anniversary', *BBC Monitoring Middle East* (London), 2018.

title, it would be impossible ever to make a peace'.[107] Thus, while reparations for violations of the law might, in theory, be specified in a peace treaty, in reality such agreements were effected with a broad brush, which omitted the minutiae of claims.

Accordingly, while the *CWC*, with its focus on security, leaves limited scope for individuals to claim reparations vis-à-vis offending states, the establishment of the Trust Fund may go some way to assisting victims of chemical weapons exposure. The following section will consider the extent to which a more recent disarmament treaty, the *CCM*, provides avenues for assistance or redress for victims of cluster munitions.

B The Convention on Cluster Munitions

1 Treaty overview

In contrast with the *CWC*, while security considerations were taken into account over the course of the negotiations preceding the *CCM*,[108] that convention was clearly focused on ending human suffering,[109] and widely heralded as a humanitarian disarmament treaty.[110] The opening lines of the treaty preamble express the deep concern of states parties 'that civilian populations and individual civilians continue to bear the brunt of armed conflict', and the determination of states 'to put an end for all time to the suffering and casualties caused by cluster munitions at the time of their use, when they fail to function as intended or when they are abandoned'.[111] Article 1 of the *CCM* sets out the obligation of states parties not to *inter alia* use, develop, produce, stockpile or retain cluster munitions. Article 3 addresses stockpiling and destruction of cluster munitions, requiring states to separate the banned weapons from other munitions retained for operational use, mark them for destruction and destroy such weapons within eight years. Under art 4, each state party agrees 'to clear and destroy, or ensure the clearance and destruction of, cluster munition remnants located in cluster

107 Béla Kapossy and Richard Whatmore (eds), *Emer de Vattel, The Law of Nations 1858* (Liberty Fund, Indianapolis, 2008) (Vol. II), Book IV, Ch II, s 18.

108 Diplomatic Conference for the Adoption of a Convention on Cluster Munitions, *Final Document*, Doc No CCM/58, 19–30 May 2008. See statement of Venezuela, 'International peace and security would be best guaranteed by a total ban on cluster munitions': at 303; statement of Canada, 'Both humanitarian and security considerations had been taken into account in negotiating the Convention': at 286; statement of the United Kingdom, 'The text presented represented the best possible consensus achieved after arduous discussions, balancing humanitarian and security concerns': at 384. A security-oriented paragraph in the draft preamble, which read '*Concerned* that cluster munition remnants can undermine international efforts to build peace and security', did not make its way into the final text: at 39.

109 Breitegger (n 43) 8, noting that wide-ranging participation of civil society ensured that 'normative outcomes adequately reflect[ed] the overarching concern for individuals'.

110 Docherty (n 3) 38; Breitegger (n 43).

111 *CCM* (n 4) preamble paras 1–2.

munition contaminated areas under its jurisdiction or control'. Article 5 requires each state party to provide cluster munitions victims in areas under its jurisdiction or control with adequate assistance. Article 6 addresses international cooperation and assistance measures, authorising affected states to request assistance from other states parties.[112] It further requires states parties 'in a position to do so' to provide technical, material and financial assistance, as well as social and economic inclusion of cluster munitions victims.[113]

2 Victims under the Convention on Cluster Munitions

The victim assistance provision in art 5 is key to understanding the extent to which states might owe obligations to individuals under the *CCM*. The primary obligation under art 5(i) states:

> Each State Party with respect to cluster munition victims in areas under its jurisdiction or control shall, in accordance with applicable international humanitarian and human rights law, adequately provide age- and gender-sensitive assistance, including medical care, rehabilitation and psychological support, as well as provide for their social and economic inclusion.

Article 5 built on experience gained through the victim assistance model set out in the *Anti-Personnel Landmines Convention 1997*[114] and in *Protocol V on Explosive Remnants of War*.[115] In a number of respects, however, it was a significant advance in the extent to which it protected and ensured victims' interests.[116]

First, in contrast with the more discretionary model laid out in the earlier treaties (which obliges states parties 'in a position to do so' to assist),[117] art 5(i) imposes on states with territorial jurisdiction or control over cluster munitions victims an unequivocal obligation of assistance.[118] This said, the term 'adequately'

112 *CCM* (n 4) art 6(1).
113 *CCM* (n 4) art 6(2) and 6(7).
114 *Convention on the Prohibition of the Use, Stockpiling, Production and Transfer of Anti-Personnel Mines and on Their Destruction*, opened for signature 3 December 1997, 2056 UNTS 241 (entered into force 1 March 1999) art 6(3) ('*Anti-Personnel Landmines Convention*').
115 *Protocol on Explosive Remnants of War (Protocol V to the 1980 Convention on Certain Conventional Weapons)*, adopted 28 November 2003, 2399 UNTS 100 (entered into force 12 November 2006) art 8(2) ('*Protocol V on Explosive Remnants of War*').
116 See Markus Reiterer and Tirza Leibowitz, 'Article 5: Victim Assistance' in Gro Nystuen and Stuart Casey-Maslen (eds), *The Convention on Cluster Munitions: A Commentary* (Oxford University Press, 2010) 328, 353 [5.56].
117 *Anti-Personnel Landmines Convention* (n 114) art 6(3); *Protocol V on Explosive Remnants of War* (n 115) art 8(2).
118 Reiterer and Leibowitz (n 116) 353 [5.56]. Article 6 of the *TPNW* is likewise absolute in its obligation, following the deletion of the phrase 'in a position to do so' during negotiations, as recommended by the International Committee of the Red Cross: *Comments of the International Committee of the Red Cross on key provisions of the Draft Convention on the Prohibition of Nuclear Weapons*, UN Doc A/CONF.229/2017/CRP.2 (14 June 2017).

allows for a degree of flexibility in the provision of assistance, allowing for consideration of circumstances and needs.[119]

Another important advance from the earlier treaties is the way in which 'cluster munitions victims' are defined, that is, as:

> all persons who have been killed or suffered physical or psychological injury, economic loss, social marginalisation or substantial impairment of the realisation of their rights caused by the use of cluster munitions. They include those persons directly impacted by cluster munitions as well as their affected families and communities.[120]

Further, and consistent with obligations under human rights law and international humanitarian law, art 5(2)(e) prohibits discrimination against cluster munitions victims, or between cluster munitions victims and those who have suffered due to other causes.

Art 5 particularises the assistance obligation of states with jurisdiction over cluster munitions victims in some detail. States parties must assess the needs of cluster munitions victims and develop, implement and enforce any necessary new laws.[121] States are required to develop a national plan and budget 'with a view to incorporating them within the existing national disability, development and human rights frameworks and mechanisms'.[122] The *Dubrovnik Action Plan*, adopted by states parties to the *CCM* in 2015, encourages states to strengthen national capacity, including through the designation of a focal point within the government to coordinate victim assistance, along with the development of a national disability action plan or a national action plan on victim assistance.[123] The *Action Plan* further requires states to increase the 'economic inclusion' of cluster munitions victims through employment and 'social protection measures', including education, training and providing job opportunities.[124]

Finally, territorial states may request assistance from other states parties, and each state party 'in a position to do so' shall provide technical, material and

119 See Reiterer and Leibowitz (n 116) 354 [5.59].

120 *CCM* (n 4) art 2(1).

121 Ibid., art 5(2)(a)–5(2)(b). For a list of implementing legislation, see Human Rights Watch and Harvard Law School, 'Implementing the Convention on Cluster Munitions: Components of Strong Law and Supporting Examples' (Report, September 2016) (Web Page) <https://www.hrw.org/sites/default/files/supporting_resources/8.2016_legislation_recs_short_form.pdf>, 13–16.

122 *CCM* (n 4) art 5(2)(c).

123 *Dubrovnik Action Plan*, adopted at the First Review Conference of the Convention on Cluster Munitions in September 2015. See further *CCM* (n 4) art 5(2)(g); International Campaign to Ban Landmines ('ICBL') and Cluster Munitions Coalition ('CMC'), *Cluster Munitions Monitor 2017* (Annual Report, August 2017) <http://www.the-monitor.org/media/2582190/Cluster-Munition-Monitor-2017_web4.pdf> 95 ('*Cluster Munitions Monitor*'), noting that by the end of 2016, all states parties except for Guinea-Bissau and Sierra Leone had established government focal points.

124 *Dubrovnik Action Plan* (n 123) action 4.1.

financial assistance.[125] However, both the obligation to clear or destroy cluster munitions and the obligation to provide victim assistance rest primarily on territorial states.[126] There is no additional responsibility on user states.[127]

3 *Analysis: does the* Convention on Cluster Munitions *confer individual primary or secondary rights?*

Those negotiating the *CCM* were clearly motivated by humanitarian considerations. However, that does not in and of itself confer individual rights. Humanitarian considerations should be interpreted in the broader context of the treaty, which includes, among other things, security considerations. Thus, further inquiry is necessary to understand whether the treaty actually confers individual rights directly enforceable under international law. After considering arguments in favour of such rights, the following analysis shows that it cannot be said that the treaty goes this far.

Perhaps the starting point for an argument in favour of individual rights is the general obligation set out in art 1, that is, the prohibition on using cluster munitions. While there is no reference to the intended beneficiary of the provision, an argument in favour of individual rights under this provision would focus on the treaty's victim-centricity, such as the evident intention to end the suffering of civilians caused by cluster munitions,[128] and references elsewhere in the treaty to (individual) rights.[129] An argument might also be made that there is a close relationship between obligations prohibiting use and requiring clearance of cluster munitions on the one hand and human rights obligations in respect of the right to life on the other.[130]

An additional argument in favour of individual rights might be grounded on art 5 (the victim assistance provision) as it explicitly refers to, and benefits, victims. It imposes on states obligations to provide cluster munitions victims

125 *CCM* (n 4) art 6.
126 Ibid., art 4.
127 Cf *TPNW* (n 5) arts 6–7. During negotiations of the *CCM*, the Philippines proposed expanding art 5 to impose a responsibility on the user states to help with providing victim assistance, proposing a new paragraph in art 5:

> When a State Party, before entry into force of the Convention for it, has used or abandoned cluster munitions in areas under the jurisdiction or control of another State Party, the former State Party shall have the responsibility to help the latter State Party in addressing the requirements of victim assistance as delineated in Article 5(1).

Final Document (n 108) 119. Despite supportive statements by Venezuela: at 303, 308; Lao PDR ('Lao'): at 334; Honduras: at 388; and Benin: at 281–2, the proposal was rejected, leaving territorial states to bear the chief burden of victim assistance. The Philippines' proposal was shifted to art 6 discussions but did not make it into the final proceedings: at 351. See further Breitegger (n 43) 200.

128 *CCM* (n 4) preamble paras 1–2.
129 Ibid., art 2(1).
130 Rietiker (n 3) 51.

with 'age- and gender-sensitive assistance, including medical care, rehabilitation and psychological support, as well as provide for their social and economic inclusion'.[131] Indeed, the very definition of cluster munitions victims includes those whose rights have been impaired.[132] It is also notable that states parties are required to legislate to ensure the human rights of cluster munitions victims, and the *Dubrovnik Action Plan* encourages the establishment of a victim assistance focal point to coordinate victim assistance.[133] In this respect, the *CCM* resembles human rights treaties, which rely on states to protect human rights (primarily of those within their jurisdiction) through their domestic legal systems.[134] Statements elsewhere in the *CCM* and preparatory works emphasise the importance of realising victims' human rights. The *CCM* preamble, for instance, expresses the determination of states 'to ensure the full realisation of the rights of all cluster munitions victims and [recognise] their inherent dignity'.[135] Without the ability of individuals to enforce obligations under art 5 directly under international law, they are arguably rendered nugatory.

Do these provisions taken together amount to a conferral of individual rights to assistance? Such a case would be difficult to make under art 1, despite the treaty's focus on human rights and the provision of mechanisms for the granting of assistance. While the intention behind the treaty's key provisions may be to protect or benefit civilians, this should not be conflated with the conferral of individual rights. In this respect, it is noteworthy that while the *CCM* discusses rights in the context of cluster munitions victims and people with disabilities, the language of rights is absent in the context of the general obligations.[136] This suggests a lack of intention on the part of the negotiating states to create individual primary rights under art 1.

Whether the treaty confers individual rights to assistance warrants further consideration. Article 5 does indeed impose human rights-like obligations on states. Nevertheless, it is doubtful that it confers correlative rights on individuals directly enforceable under international law.[137] The *CCM* itself neglects to provide a mechanism for individual claims, but rather relies on states parties to legislate in favour of victims, and in that way (possibly) provide a route for an individual claim. In this respect it resembles art 6 of the *Convention on the Elimination of Racial Discrimination* ('*CERD*'), which imposes reparation

131 *CCM* (n 4) art 5(1).
132 Ibid., art 2(1).
133 *Dubrovnik Action Plan* (n 123) action 4; see further *Cluster Munition Monitor* (n 123).
134 Susan Marks and Fiorentina Azizi, 'Responsibility for Violations of Human Rights Obligations: International Mechanisms' in James Crawford et al. (eds), *The Law of International Responsibility* (Oxford University Press, 2010) 725, 728–9.
135 *CCM* (n 4) preamble para 6.
136 Cf *Vienna Convention on Consular Relations*, as discussed in *LaGrand* [2001] ICJ Rep 466 (n 20).
137 See Reiterer and Leibowitz (n 116) 353 [5.56] n 71.

obligations on states.[138] As Tomuschat observes, '[t]he right to reparation is not conferred on the individual directly under international law in such cases but only indirectly, on the basis of national law'.[139] Under this approach, treaty rights can only be enforced if an individual can point to requisite legislation within a state party.[140]

Any indirect rights that might be read into art 5 are based on primary assistance obligations, rather than secondary compensation obligations. Thus, if there are cluster munitions victims within a state's jurisdiction or control, that state must provide assistance, regardless of whether it was responsible for the use or failure to clear the weapons. However, art 5 does not provide individuals with any right to compensation for violations of the treaty generally.[141] That is, the obligations states undertake in the treaty generally do not give rise to individual claims for compensation or redress: individuals cannot enforce this treaty directly.

In this way, the *CCM* regime effectively circumvents the traditional reluctance of states to confer individual rights for violations of the law based on international responsibility, focusing instead on the primary duties of states with jurisdiction or control over cluster munitions victims.[142] The fact that the *CCM* explicitly prohibits discrimination or preferential treatment on the basis of one's status as a cluster munitions victim[143] further indicates a lack of intention to create secondary compensation rights under the treaty. Based on this analysis, it cannot be said that the *CCM* confers secondary rights to compensation on individual victims for treaty violations.[144]

138 *International Convention on the Elimination of All Forms of Racial Discrimination*, opened for signature 21 December 1965, 660 UNTS 195 (entered into force 4 January 1969) art 6.

139 Tomuschat 'Individuals' (n 36) 986.

140 Legislation enacted to date appears to create primary victim assistance obligations without specifying either individual rights or state liability for failing to meet obligations: see Human Rights Watch and Harvard Law School, 'Staying Strong: Key Components and Positive Precedent for Convention on Cluster Munitions Legislation' (Report, September 2014) (Web Page) <https://www.hrw.org/sites/default/files/reports/cluster0914_ForUpload_0.pdf>, 41–2 outlining the victim assistance legislation of Guatemala and Hungary.

141 See further Breitegger (n 43) 199–200; Reiterer and Leibowitz (n 116) 353 [5.56] n 71.

142 See Reiterer and Leibowitz, above n 116, 353 [5.56]; see further Ursign Hofmann and Pascal Rapillard, 'Post-Conflict Mine Action Environment and Law' in Carsten Stahn, Jens Iverson and Jennifer S Easterday (eds), *Environmental Protection and Transitions from Conflict to Peace: Clarifying Norms, Principles, and Practices* (Oxford University Press, 2017) 396, 410–1. While states preferred to adopt a remedial provision based on duty of care rather than state responsibility, this is not to suggest that arts 5 and 6 of the *CCM* represent a special regime which excludes the application of general principles of responsibility. To this end, it is worth mentioning that Iceland explicitly noted the ongoing application of the usual principles of state responsibility. Injured states could still claim reparations for violations of the *CCM* under general principles of state responsibility: See *Final Document* (n 108) 200, 386.

143 *CCM* (n 4) art 5(2)(e). It was important to negotiating states that victim assistance should not be provided at the expense of other victims of armed conflict: see Reiterer and Leibowitz (n 116) 341–2 [5.26]–[5.27], 355 [5.60]–[5.61].

144 See Breitegger (n 43) 199–200; Hofmann and Rapillard (n 145) 411.

In the absence of national legislation, a claim against an individual's territorial state for injury arising out of cluster munitions use might be possible via a regional human rights court, as has occurred in both the European Court of Human Rights[145] and the Inter-American Court of Human Rights.[146]

IV Where to from here?

The foregoing discussion discloses two key ways in which humanitarian considerations might manifest in disarmament law. The first way is to impose obligations on states to address the needs of victims through medical care, psychological support, and economic and social inclusion assistance measures. The second way in which humanitarian considerations are manifesting in disarmament law involves the imputation or importation of individual rights into disarmament law treaties. This approach is not expressly grounded in disarmament law but could be pursued *de lege ferenda*. Both approaches raise several issues, some of which are touched on below, that warrant further research and reflection.

A An assistance/needs-based approach

A victim assistance regime represents a reasonable response to victim suffering under disarmament law. For example, the *CCM*'s assistance model is conducive to an inclusive and socially sensitive response,[147] due largely to its broad definition of cluster munitions victims and the breadth of assistance obligations imposed on states. In situations involving widespread loss and injury, such as where cluster munitions deprive a community of the opportunity to farm, or leakage from an abandoned weapons cache poisons a water or food source, an inclusive, community-based response will likely be appropriate to address a wide range of victims' needs.

A victim assistance regime is also reasonable because it covers both conflict and non-conflict scenarios, which give rise to divergent needs, demanding a context-sensitive response. Forward-looking approaches, which are based on non-discrimination and aimed at reconciliation, are important for achieving a meaningful response,[148] as an adjunct or alternative to liability- or fault-based measures. By importing a greater degree of flexibility, the victim assistance

145 See, eg, *Behrami v France* (n 44).

146 See, eg, *Santo Domingo Massacre v Colombia* (n 44) [230].

147 On the importance of an inclusive approach to reparations, see *Prosecutor v Thomas Lubanga Dyilo (Decision on Reparations)* (International Criminal Court, Appeals Chamber, Case No ICC-01/04-01/06-3129, 3 March 2015) [215]; see further Emily L Camins, 'Needs or Rights? Exploring the Limitations of Individual Reparations for Violations of International Humanitarian Law' (2016) 10(1) *International Journal of Transitional Justice* 126, 142–4.

148 See *Lubanga (Reparations)* (International Criminal Court, Appeals Chamber, Case No ICC-01/04-01/06-3129, 3 March 2015) [215].

model has the advantage of enabling a broad yet tailored approach to post-war demands.

A *CCM*-type victim assistance regime has the added benefit of efficiency. By requiring states to develop a national plan and budget to be incorporated within existing disability, development and human rights frameworks, obligations to cluster munitions victims are strengthened, without requiring a major overhaul of national legislation and quasi-legal mechanisms.

Finally, the adoption of victim assistance models in recent disarmament treaties indicates that an assistance-based approach is politically palatable to many states. Whereas an individual-rights-based approach challenges notions of state sovereignty on multiple fronts, the incursion presented by victim assistance regimes is qualitatively different, and seemingly more acceptable. In this way, victim assistance may be seen as a conceptual bridge between individualistic and state-centric approaches. The *CCM*, for example, emphasises the duty of territorial states to care for citizens under national law, and requires those states to provide assistance to cluster munitions victims, their families and their communities.[149] While progressive in its recognition of human rights, such an approach is still more legally conservative than a provision conferring individual rights to reparations based on violations.[150] To this end, an assistance-based response also appears to fit comfortably with traditional models of settling conflicts through lump-sum indemnification agreements (which tend not to specify how funds are to be distributed domestically).[151]

Despite these benefits, there are shortcomings with the assistance model. First, many states recovering from conflict lack, and will continue to lack, adequate resources to fulfil the assistance obligations set out in the treaty.[152] In such situations, victims will be left reliant largely on the goodwill and support of other states, and provisions requiring their assistance tend to be much weaker. Second, where the territorial state is also the user state there may be reluctance to enforce the victim assistance provisions, and socio-legal problems with doing so. As Tomuschat observes, '[g]iven that human rights essentially protect individuals against their states of nationality, there is some paradox in the state, a potential violator of human rights, simultaneously protecting them at the international level'.[153] Third, under the assistance model there may be questions of fairness and a lack of accountability where the territorial state is not the user

149 See *CCM* (n 4) art 5(1); see generally above Part III(b)(ii).

150 See Tomuschat 'Tomuschat on Compensation' (n 37) 813.

151 See above n 106. How it accords with national legislation authorising tactical *ex gratia* payments in conflict situations warrants further exploration. See, eg, *Defence Act 1903* (Aus) ss 123H–123J, which authorises 'tactical payments' to victims of armed conflict which are dependent on harm but not liability; see further Scott T Paul, 'The Duty to Make Amends to Victims of Armed Conflict' (2013) *Tulane Journal of International and Comparative Law* 87.

152 See, eg, *Cluster Munition Monitor* (n 123) noting Afghanistan, Bosnia and Herzegovina, Chad, Croatia, Iraq, Lao, Mozambique and Somalia as states parties where funding shortages hindered victim assistance implementation in 2016.

153 Tomuschat 'Individuals' (n 36) 985.

state.[154] This represents a potential source of future tension, between both states and nationals.[155] Finally, a victim assistance regime is limited in the depth of the (financial) compensatory response it can provide, and does not meet demands for enforceable individual rights to a remedy for harms arising under international law. These limitations invite consideration of individual rights to reparations under disarmament law *de lege ferenda.*

B An individual rights-based approach as lex ferenda

If individual rights were to be adopted or recognised under disarmament law *de lege ferenda*, one potential approach would be to borrow from proposals in cognate branches of international law. In 2010, the International Law Association (ILA) published a *Declaration of International Law Principles on Reparation for Victims of Armed Conflict (Substantive Issues)*, which built on existing soft law instruments.[156] The non-binding *Declaration* sought to consolidate emerging principles and develop new law.[157] It is doubtful that it has crystallised into law, but, nevertheless, it has been widely referenced in scholarship and referred to by judges of the ICJ and other tribunals.[158] It therefore provides a useful model for exploring how individual reparations could be imported into disarmament law.

The *Declaration* purports to vest in individuals secondary rights to reparation ensuing from violations of certain primary norms of international law applicable in armed conflict. It proposes the following provision:

> The primary norms the violation of which may give rise to the secondary rights and obligations reflected in the present Declaration are the rules of international law applicable in armed conflict, the object and purpose of which is to protect the victim in the sense of Article 4 [of the *Declaration*].[159]

Article 4 defines 'victim' as 'natural or legal persons who have suffered harm as a result of a violation of the rules of international law applicable in armed

154 Above nn 126–7.

155 See Yukiko Koga, *Inheritance of Loss: China, Japan and the Political Economy of Redemption after Empire* (University of Chicago Press, 2016) epilogue, on the healing effect of inter-state reparations claims. To this end, it is noted that states negotiating the *TPNW* considered it important that user states be held responsible, thus rectifying a significant shortcoming of the *CCM*. See *TPNW* (n 5) arts 6(1), 7(6); Docherty (n 91).

156 See, eg, *UN Basic Principles* (n 6); M Cherif Bassiouni and Daniel Rothenberg, *The Chicago Principles on Post-Conflict Justice* (International Human Rights Law Institute, 2007).

157 International Law Association, 'Report of the International Committee on Reparation for Victims of Armed Conflict and the Declaration of International Law Principles on Reparation for Victims of Armed Conflict (Substantive Issues)' (2010).

158 See, eg, *Jurisdictional Immunities* (n 6) 197 [51] (Judge Cançado Trindade).

159 *ILA Declaration (Substantive Issues)* (n 31) art 3.

conflict'.[160] Under the *Declaration*, victims have a right to reparation, including compensation, from the responsible parties.[161]

The *Declaration* has several positive features for application in the context of disarmament law. First, the *Declaration* implicitly acknowledges that treaty provisions cannot be analysed *en bloc*, and that not all treaty obligations are appropriate candidates for individual rights. Rather, the only provisions which would qualify are those which have as their object and purpose the protection of victims. This would mean that certain disarmament obligations, such as those relating to non-proliferation, would not result in reparations where they are grounded primarily in considerations of security and reciprocity rather than the protection of victims. This is a reasonable outcome. As Happold notes, inter-state reparations tend to apply in cases of injury, including moral or material damage.[162] Breach of certain rules of non-proliferation, such as obligations relating to verification, would not necessarily cause moral or material damage, potentially rendering cessation and non-repetition more relevant than reparations.[163] The same considerations apply, magnified, in the context of individual reparations. However, while some obligations, such as non-proliferation, may fall outside the *Declaration's* formulation, the ILA interpretation is potentially broader than the legal framework set out in Part II. This broader approach might at times result in a more favourable outcome for weapons victims. Second, by allowing for compensation for any financially assessable damage,[164] reparations under the *ILA Declaration* could be responsive to the extent of damage caused by use of weapons. Losses such as property damage and loss of earnings would potentially be compensable, resulting in a more favourable outcome for some victims of conflict or weapons use than existing models. Third, by requiring responsible parties to compensate victims, a rights-based model imposes a degree of accountability and may provide victims with a sense of justice.

Despite the potential benefits of importing individual rights to reparations into disarmament law, there are some limitations. For example, under the ILA *Declaration*, in order to ground an individual right, the victim must have suffered harm *as a result* of a violation of the rules of international law.[165] By focusing on technical legal considerations, such an approach narrows the potential reach of redress regimes as it excludes consideration of the communities of those injured and others indirectly affected. There is, accordingly, a risk of inflaming tensions in already tense scenarios through selective, individualised reparations.

160 Ibid., art 4. This does not prejudice the right of family members to claim on behalf of victims.

161 Ibid., arts 6, 8.

162 Matthew Happold, 'The "Injured State" in the Case of Breach of a Non-Proliferation Treaty and the Legal Consequences of Such a Breach' in Daniel H Joyner and Marco Roscini (eds), *Non-Proliferation Law as a Special Regime: A Contribution to Fragmentation Theory in International Law* (Cambridge University Press, 2012) 175, 191–2.

163 Ibid., 176 and 192; see further Rosas (n 64) 430.

164 *ILA Declaration (Substantive Issues)* (n 31) art 8.

165 Ibid., above n 31, art 4(1). Definition of 'victim': above n 163.

For instance, in some scenarios people injured by lawful weapons may be excluded from compensation, while those injured as a result of unlawful weapons would be entitled to compensation.[166] The ongoing internecine conflict in Syria, punctuated by sporadic chemical weapons use, provides a ready example of suffering resulting from both lawful and unlawful weapons.[167] Unless addressed through additional measures, the fact that individual reparations are rigidly based on technical considerations is potentially damaging to a society seeking to recover from conflict.[168]

Moreover, it may be problematic to speak of individual rights to compensation in situations involving many thousands (if not millions) of victims, for example following extensive damage from weapons of mass destruction. Inter-state conflicts have historically been settled through peace treaty, generally by way of lump sum indemnification payments.[169] Demanding individual compensation payments may hinder the conclusion of peace treaties.[170] Moreover, if peace is reached and inter-state reparations are paid, subsequent individual reparations claims may be economically and practically infeasible. A rights-based approach increases the administrative, evidential and judicial burden of both claiming and awarding reparations, and is financially costly for the responsible state. The burden might be overly onerous not only for the survivors of weapons' attacks, but also for societies and economies rebuilding after conflict.[171]

This discussion leads to broader philosophico-legal questions, including whether reparations are best viewed primarily as a component of the complex ethical and legal principles independently applicable in the aftermath of conflict (sometimes described as *jus post bellum*), or as a component of *jus in bello*.[172] As international lawyers, we tend to be comfortable with notions of compensatory justice arising from violations of *jus in bello*. However, if we focus too narrowly on this aspect of the law, we risk missing important considerations which are critical to achieving long-term peace.[173] As May writes, '[t]he justice of *jus post bellum* is secured not through giving to people what is their due in the short

166 See, eg, Camins (n 149) 139–40.

167 See generally Megan Specia, 'How Syria's Death Toll Is Lost in the Fog of War', *New York Times* (online, 13 April 2018) (Web Page) <https://www.nytimes.com/2018/04/13/world/middleeast/syria-death-toll.html>.

168 See, eg, *Lubanga (Reparations)* (n 151) [215].

169 See above n 106.

170 Tomuschat 'Individuals' (n 36) 988.

171 On the impracticability of individual reparations following widespread destruction, see *Jurisdictional Immunities* (n 6) 170 [18] (Judge Keith).

172 See, eg, Mark Evans, 'At War's End: Time to Turn to Jus Post Bellum?' in Carsten Stahn, Jennifer S Easterday and Jens Iverson (eds), *Jus Post Bellum: Mapping the Normative Foundations* (Oxford University Press, 2014) 26.

173 Larry May, 'Jus Post Bellum, Grotius, and *Meionexia*' in Carsten Stahn, Jennifer S Easterday and Jens Iverson (eds), *Jus Post Bellum: Mapping the Normative Foundations* (Oxford University Press, 1st ed, 2014) 15, 17–8.

run, but in securing what is good for societies that seek to return to a lasting peace'.[174]

Finally, and as a further obstacle to the adoption of a rights-based model, it must be recognised that states have historically been reluctant to take responsibility for compensation post-conflict.[175] As Hofmann and Rapillard put it, 'the international community has, *stricto sensu*, no duty to rebuild or to address damages in post-conflict settings: "You broke it, you own it" does not apply'.[176] This reluctance is often magnified in the context of individual reparations, which may involve states being sued in the courts of foreign states[177] and therefore represents a further incursion into state sovereignty. Absent a significant change in political mood and the politico-legal international structure, to achieve concrete outcomes most injured individuals will likely have to continue to rely on national legislation, ad hoc responses, or the support of their states of nationality vis-à-vis offending states.[178]

V Conclusion

The humanitarian focus of disarmament law, increasingly evident in recent weapons treaties, leads one to query the extent to which individuals might exercise rights, particularly to reparations, under disarmament law. Particularly in the context of human rights abuses and serious violations of international humanitarian law, soft law instruments and some state practice have been pulling towards conferring on individuals a right to compensation.[179] Individual compensation claims, such as those by Chinese nationals in Japan, suggest that disarmament law is not impervious to this trend.

However, the humanising developments evident in disarmament law do not necessarily translate to individual reparations for violations of the law. Despite a welcome increase in focus on victims, it cannot be said that an enforceable individual right to reparations under disarmament law has emerged. To this end, the distinction between humanisation and the individualisation of rights to reparations remains. Humanisation may involve, but does not demand, the individualisation of rights. Rather, humanisation may be said to take place when principles of humanity and the minimising of suffering are commanding motivations of developing law. These principles might include individual rights but might equally involve increased obligations on states based on humanitarian ideals, including the need to limit and address victims' suffering. The victim

174 Ibid., 21.

175 See, eg, Vönery (n 106) 683.

176 Hofmann and Rapillard, (n 145) 411.

177 See Tomuschat 'Tomuschat on Compensation' (n 37) 812–3.

178 See Pierre d'Argent, 'Wrongs of the Past, History of the Future?' (2006) 17(1) *European Journal of International Law* 279, 282. Regional human rights fora might also present opportunities for victims.

179 See, eg, *UN Basic Principles* (n 6); *ILA Declaration (Substantive Issues)* (n 31).

assistance approach in the *CCM*, for example, focuses on strengthening states' duty to care for their own individuals instead of seeking to empower individuals to access reparations at the international level.

Before individual rights to reparations arise, there must (absent customary recognition) be a treaty conferral of both primary and secondary rights on individual victims.[180] In order for individuals to exercise such rights independently under international law (without the need for national legislation or other state-based support), procedural mechanisms for so doing must also be provided, if not by the initial treaty then through an optional protocol or state declaration.[181]

Developments in this area are possible *de lege ferenda*, under either treaty or customary law. However, it appears from recent disarmament law treaties that while instruments of soft international law have been pulling in the direction of empowering victims of armed conflict, hard law is pushing towards reinforcing the duties of states, particularly territorial states, to assist individuals within their jurisdiction. This victim assistance approach adheres to the humanitarian spirit, if not the rights-based letter, of soft law reparations instruments which seek to address victim suffering. While the success of this approach will ultimately lie in effective implementation, it warrants further consideration as a model for cognate areas of international law.

180 See above Part II.
181 See, eg, Tomuschat 'Individuals' (n 36) 986.

Part III

Making disarmament law

7 Article 18 of the *Vienna Convention on the Law of Treaties* obligations and the *Comprehensive Nuclear-Test-Ban Treaty*

Masahiko Asada

I Introduction

The *Comprehensive Nuclear-Test-Ban Treaty* ('*CTBT*' or the 'Treaty'),[1] labelled by United States ('US') President Bill Clinton as the 'longest-sought, hardest-fought prize in arms control history',[2] was opened for signature on 24 September 1996. As of June 2019, it has been signed by 184 states, and ratified by 167 states, including France, Russia and the United Kingdom ('UK'), but not China or the United States.

Despite the sheer number of ratifications, the *CTBT* is yet to enter into force. This is due to its extremely strict entry into force clause (art XIV), which stipulates that the *CTBT* will enter into force 180 days after the 44 states listed in annex 2 to the Treaty ('annex 2 states') ratify the Treaty. The 44 annex 2 states include not only the five *de jure* nuclear-weapon states but also such other states as India, Pakistan and Israel (the three de facto nuclear-weapon states), as well as the Democratic People's Republic of Korea ('DPRK') (the only state continuing nuclear testing in this century). With this select list of states, one can easily understand the difficulties the *CTBT* must overcome prior to its entry into force.

The fundamental argument for the requirement of such a strict entry into force clause[3] was that the *CTBT* could hardly serve any meaningful purpose

1 *Comprehensive Nuclear-Test-Ban Treaty*, opened for signature 24 September 1996, 35 ILM 1439 (not yet in force) ('*CTBT*').

2 UN GAOR, 51st sess, 6th plen mtg, UN Doc A/51/PV.6 (24 September 1996) 3.

3 It is argued elsewhere that the *CTBT*'s strict entry into force clause was adopted to 'ensure that participation in the treaty regime would not put one of these 44 states in an unfavourable position in respect to the other states', and therefore that 'it could not be maintained that, by signing a treaty, a state could assume the obligation not to carry out a nuclear weapons test explosion': Paolo Palchetti, 'Article 18 of the 1969 Vienna Convention: A Vague and Ineffective Obligation or a Useful Means for Strengthening Legal Cooperation?' in Enzo Cannizzaro (ed), *The Law of Treaties beyond the Vienna Convention* (Oxford University Press, 2011) 25, 29. However, this argument does not necessarily reflect the circumstances surrounding the drafting of the *CTBT*'s entry into force clause as described in the text; nor is it in line with the view of many states, as we will see below in this chapter.

without the participation of all nuclear test-capable states (that is, the five *de jure* nuclear-weapon states plus the three de facto nuclear-weapon states at that time).[4] This argument was put forward by the UK, Russia, China, Pakistan and Egypt during the *CTBT* negotiations.[5] Indeed, the *CTBT* is redundant for the non-nuclear-weapon states parties to the *Treaty on the Non-Proliferation of Nuclear Weapons* ('*NPT*'),[6] which have already been prohibited from possessing nuclear weapons in the first place, let alone testing them.[7] Thus, the drafters of the *CTBT* had to find an 'objective' criterion which could cover all of the above eight states, an endeavour which resulted in annex 2 to the Treaty.[8]

While the *CTBT* has not entered into force, it is interesting to consider whether there are any ways that the prohibition on nuclear testing in the *CTBT* could be deemed binding on states. Shortly after the signing of the *CTBT*, the author wrote an article on this subject which set out two possible ways that this question could be answered positively.[9] First, it was possible that a customary international law rule comprehensively prohibiting nuclear testing could emerge from the treaty, although the author argued that such a rule had not yet developed. Second, it was possible that the rules provided in art 18 of the *Vienna Convention on the Law of Treaties* ('*VCLT*')[10] could require states that had signed the *CTBT*, as well as those that had ratified it, to respect a comprehensive ban on nuclear testing. While the status (absence) of a comprehensive test ban under customary international law remains essentially the same today,[11] there have been some developments over the last 17 years in relation to the art 18 route. In particular, there are interesting issues that have arisen around when the requirement under art 18 will cease.

4 At that time, the DPRK was still to conduct its first nuclear test.

5 Rebecca Johnson, 'A Comprehensive Test Ban Treaty: Signed But Not Sealed' (Report No 10, Acronym Institute, May 1997) 62. The United States and France preferred a more flexible entry into force provision in order not to allow specific states to take the treaty hostage and delay its implementation indefinitely: at 63.

6 *Treaty on the Non-Proliferation of Nuclear Weapons*, opened for signature 1 July 1968, 729 UNTS 161 (entered into force 5 March 1970) ('*NPT*').

7 *NPT* (n 6) art II.

8 *CTBT* (n 1) annex 2 lists states members of the Conference on Disarmament which appear in Table 1 of the IAEA's April 1996 edition of 'Nuclear Power Reactors in the World' or Table 1 of the IAEA's December 1995 edition of 'Nuclear Research Reactors in the World'.

9 Masahiko Asada, '*CTBT*: Legal Questions Arising from Its Non-Entry-into-Force' (2002) 7(1) *Journal of Conflict and Security Law* 85.

10 *Vienna Convention on the Law of Treaties*, opened for signature 23 May 1969, 1155 UNTS 331 (entered into force 27 January 1980) ('*VCLT*').

11 This can be confirmed by referring to the text of the Final Declarations of the Article XIV Conferences, which continue to admit that the permanent and legally binding ban on nuclear weapon testing and all other nuclear explosions 'can only be achieved with the entry into force of the Treaty': Conference on Facilitating the Entry into Force of the Comprehensive Nuclear-Test-Ban Treaty, *Report of the Conference*, *CTBT*-Art.XIV/2017/6, 16 November 2017, annex ('*Final Declaration and Measures to Promote the Entry into Force of the Comprehensive Nuclear-Test-Ban Treaty*') [5]. For the Article XIV Conference, see below.

Article 18 of the *VCLT* provides:

> A State is obliged to refrain from acts which would defeat the object and purpose of a treaty when:
>
> a it has signed the treaty or has exchanged instruments constituting the treaty subject to ratification, acceptance or approval, until it shall have made its intention clear not to become a party to the treaty; or
> b it has expressed its consent to be bound by the treaty, pending the entry into force of the treaty and provided that such entry into force is not unduly delayed.

According to these provisions, both signatory and ratifier states are legally obliged not to carry out 'acts which would defeat the object and purpose of a treaty' (the 'art 18 obligation'). The obligation on the signatory states lasts until they make it clear that they do not intend to become parties to the treaty, while that on the ratifiers persists so long as the treaty's 'entry into force is not unduly delayed'.[12]

This chapter will focus on how the art 18 obligation applies to the *CTBT* and when it may cease to be applicable. In order to do this, Part II will explore what acts are prohibited by the art 18 obligation in the *CTBT* context and will argue that there is good evidence to suggest that the testing of nuclear weapons is. Part III will discuss whether art 18 of the *VCLT* amounts to customary international law. It will argue that there is strong support for the idea that it does. Part IV will then deal with the circumstances and conduct that may lead to the termination of the art 18 obligation in relation to the *CTBT.* It will argue that while there is no evidence to suggest that the art 18 obligation has been terminated by the entry into force of the *CTBT* being unduly delayed, there are a number of complexities that arise in relation to individual signatory states making it clear that they do not intend to become parties to the *CTBT.* Regard will be had to the practice of the US in relation to the *CTBT* over the last 20 years and the fact that it appears to have switched on and off the art 18 obligation under different Administrations. In so doing, the author tries to indicate how fragile the art 18 obligation is and therefore how imperative it is to make the *CTBT* enter into force.

II The art 18 obligation in the *Comprehensive Nuclear-Test-Ban Treaty* context

The first question to be asked when considering the art 18 obligation in relation to the *CTBT* is what constitutes 'acts which would defeat the object and purpose of [the] treaty' in the *CTBT* context. What this expression means in general terms was set out during the drafting of the *VCLT* by Professor Humphrey

12 Asada (n 9) 94.

Waldock, who participated in the United Nations ('UN') Conference on the Law of Treaties as an Expert Consultant. He said that '[i]t meant that the treaty was rendered meaningless by such acts and lost its object'.[13] With this, as well as with the object and purpose of the *CTBT* in mind, there is a strong case to say that in the context of the *CTBT* the above phrase includes conducting a nuclear test.

In support of this view, there have been a number of statements made by signatories to the *CTBT*, including Japan, the United States and Malta. On 5 June 1997, during the deliberations about the *CTBT* in the Diet (Parliament) before ratification, the Japanese government was asked whether a nuclear test is allowed before the entry into force of the *CTBT*. The Foreign Ministry's Director-General for Arms Control and Scientific Affairs, Takekazu Kawamura, answered by citing art 18 of the *VCLT* and stating that an '[a]ct which defeats the object and purpose of a treaty is, with regard to the *CTBT*, ***conducting a nuclear test***'. He also responded positively when asked whether he could confirm that 'those states which had joined the [*CTBT*] could no longer conduct a nuclear test by virtue of the Vienna Convention'.[14]

The United States was the first country to sign the *CTBT* (on 24 September 1996)[15] but it has not ratified the treaty yet due to the fact that when the *CTBT* was put to a vote in the US Senate on 13 October 1999, the senators voted by a wide margin[16] of 51-48 to repudiate the ratification of the *CTBT*.[17] Soon after this event, in order to reassure the world community about the US intention regarding the *CTBT*, Secretary of State Madeleine K Albright under the Clinton Administration sent a letter (the 'Albright letter') to several foreign ministers, including those of China and Russia, in which she said 'I want to assure you that the United States will continue to act in accordance with its obligations as a signatory under international law'.[18]

13 *Summary records of the plenary meetings and of the meetings of the Committee of the Whole*, United Nations Conference on the Law of Treaties Official Records, 1st sess, UN Doc A/CONF.39/11 (1969) 104 [26].

14 *Minutes of the Committee on Foreign Affairs* (State of Japan) House of Councillors, 140th Diet, No 15, 5 June 1997, 22 (emphasis added), discussed in Asada (n 9) 95.

15 Domestically, the Clinton Administration in August 1995 established six safeguards as conditions for US entry into the nuclear test ban: Craig Cerniello, 'Senate Rejects Comprehensive Test Ban Treaty; Clinton Vows to Continue Moratorium' (1999) 29(6) *Arms Control Today* 26, 27.

16 According to the US Constitution, a two-thirds majority is required for the 100-member Senate to give advice and consent to the ratification of a treaty: *United States Constitution* art II § 2 cl 2.

17 See, eg, Cerniello (n 15) 26. It is said that of the treaties submitted to the Senate over the course of US history, 1,523 have been ratified and, including the *CTBT*, only 21 rejected: Sean D Murphy, 'Contemporary Practice of the United States Relating to International Law' (2000) 94(1) *American Journal of International Law* 102, 139.

18 Letter from Secretary of State Madeleine Albright to key foreign governments, quoted in 'Prepared Statement of Stephen G Rademaker, Principal, The Podesta Group', in *The Administration's Proposal for a UN Resolution on the Comprehensive Nuclear Test-Ban Treaty* (hearing before the Committee on Foreign Relations, Senate Hearing 114–724, 114th Congress, 2nd Session, 7 September 2016) 13 ('Albright letter').

It was not necessarily clear what was meant by 'obligations as a signatory', but judging from subsequent statements of Clinton Administration officials it seems that the wording was intended as a reference to art 18. For example, John Holum, State Department Senior Adviser for Arms Control and International Security, said during a Foreign Press Center briefing that

> There is a general view, I think, under the Vienna [C]onvention that countries that have signed but not ratified are nonetheless obliged not to take any steps that would defeat the object and purpose of the treaty, which probably implies that even signature would create *legal obstacles to testing*.[19]

Malta, a state that has both signed and ratified the treaty, has the same view. At the second Article XIV Conference,[20] it stated that

> Under Article XVIII of the [*VCLT*], signatory states are bound not to take actions that violate the 'purpose or intent' [sic] of the Treaty to which they are signatories, which in effect, in the case of the *CTBT*, means they cannot conduct a nuclear test explosion.[21]

More recently, more important developments have taken place among the five nuclear-weapon states and in the UN Security Council. On 15 September 2016, the five nuclear-weapon states adopted a Joint Statement on the *CTBT* (the 'N5 Statement'), reaffirming their 'moratoria on nuclear weapons test explosions or any other nuclear explosions pending the CTBT's entry into force'.[22] The statement called on other states to do likewise, recognising that 'a nuclear-weapon test explosion or any other nuclear explosion would defeat the object and purpose of the CTBT'.[23]

19 Federal News Service, 'Transcript: Foreign Press Center Briefing by John Holum on the Comprehensive Test Ban Treaty' (Transcript, 9 November 1999) (emphasis added), discussed in Asada (n 9) 96.

20 Article XIV Conferences are convened by the United Nations Secretary-General and are designed to promote the treaty's entry into force. Specifically, Article XIV(2) of the *CTBT* (n 1) provides that if the treaty has not entered into force three years after its opening for signature, a Conference of ratifiers shall be convened to consider and decide by consensus what measures may be taken to facilitate the treaty's entry into force. In accordance with this provision, the 'Conference on Facilitating the Entry into Force of the *Comprehensive Nuclear-Test-Ban Treaty*' was first held in 1999 and has since been held every two years.

21 Joe Borg, 'Malta: Statement by The Hon Dr Joe Borg, Minister of Foreign Affairs' (Statement, Conference on Facilitating the Entry into Force of the Comprehensive Nuclear-Test-Ban Treaty, New York, 11 November 2001) 1.

22 Governments of China, France, the Russian Federation, the United Kingdom and the United States, 'Joint Statement on the Comprehensive Nuclear-Test-Ban Treaty by the Nuclear Nonproliferation Treaty Nuclear-Weapon States' (15 September 2016) (Web Page) <https://2009-2017.state.gov/r/pa/prs/ps/2016/09/261993.htm> ('N5 Statement').

23 Ibid.

This last phrase was subsequently quoted verbatim and '[n]ote[d]' in Security Council Resolution 2310,[24] which was adopted without any negative vote.[25] It is remarkable to see that not only was the Resolution co-sponsored by 45 UN member states,[26] but no divergent opinion was expressed on this point in the Council debate. This was a result of President Obama's international promotion of this position. Originally, the Obama Administration had wanted the Security Council to pass a Chapter VII resolution banning nuclear testing.[27] However, faced with opposition from a number of Senators domestically,[28] as well as by China and Russia in the Council,[29] Resolution 2310 was passed as a

24 SC Res 2310, UN SCOR, 7776th mtg, UN Doc S/RES/2310 (23 September 2016) para 4 ('Resolution 2310').

25 The Resolution was adopted by 14 votes in favour, none against and one abstention (Egypt). The reasons for abstention by Egypt were related to its following concerns: the Security Council is not the appropriate forum to address the *CTBT* in light of the existence of the CTBTO Preparatory Commission; the *NPT* is completely overlooked in the Resolution's operative paragraphs; the issue of nuclear disarmament is not adequately addressed; special responsibility ought to have been placed on the nuclear-weapon states and states not party to the *NPT*; the Resolution's intrusive nature in the work of the Preparatory Commission is counterproductive; and progress on the *CTBT* verification regime falls within the prerogative of the Preparatory Commission. UN SCOR, 7776th mtg, UN Doc S/PV.7776 (23 September 2016) 4–6.

26 Ibid., 2. The 45 co-sponsoring states included Israel but not China or Russia. However, the latter two states voted in favour of the Resolution. During the Council debate, China expressed its support for the object and purpose of the *CTBT*, and Russia also expressed its commitment to the implementation of the *CTBT* while, at the same time, cautioning about the possibility that the Security Council creates 'obligations under an international treaty for those States that have not joined that treaty': at 8–9.

27 The Japanese newspaper *Yomiuri Shimbun* reported that the White House originally tried to introduce a legally binding resolution to ban nuclear testing but, faced with Republican Senators' fierce opposition, abandoned such an idea: *Yomiuri Shimbun* (Japan) 24 September 2016. See also Josh Rogin, 'Obama Will Bypass Congress, Seek UN Resolution on Nuclear Testing', *Washington Post* (online, 4 August 2016) (Web Page) < https://www.washingtonpost.com/news/josh-rogin/wp/2016/08/04/obama-will-bypass-congress-seek-u-n-resolution-on-nuclear-testing/>. According to a senior official of the Obama Administration the author interviewed on this subject, the idea to adopt a Security Council resolution prohibiting nuclear weapon tests binding on all UN member states was in fact considered as one of the options.

28 For instance, as late as in September 2016, as many as 33 Senators signed and sent to President Obama a letter saying, 'It is [...] disturbing that [his] administration appears to be trying to circumvent the Senate's constitutional treaty role, this time by seeking to use the United Nations Security Council to endorse the Comprehensive Nuclear Test Ban Treaty (*CTBT*), which the Senate rejected in 1999': Letter from Senators to President Obama, 8 September 2016 (Web Page) <https://www.rubio.senate.gov/public/_cache/files/5144be8b-4cfc-422a-8017-cc19d362a778/6971525E619F533B35207A7868DEB787.*CTBT*-letter-final-2016.pdf>.

29 It was reported that the US draft Security Council resolution on the *CTBT* contained a Chapter VII decision to require UN member States to *report* on the progress in *CTBT* monitoring. However, due partly to the opposition by China and Russia, the reference to Chapter VII and the part dealing with the mandatory reporting system were deleted from the resolution: *Kyoto Shinbun* (Japan), 15 September 2016; Dan Joyner, 'UNSCR 2310 and the *CTBT*: Some Thoughts' *Arms Control Law* (Blog Post, 17 October 2016) (Web Page) < https://armscontrollaw.com/2016/10/17/unscr-2310-and-the-ctbt-some-thoughts/>. See also UN SCOR, 7776th mtg, UN Doc S/PV.7776 (23 September 2016) 8.

non-Chapter VII resolution and simply '[c]all[ed] upon all States to refrain from conducting any nuclear-weapon test explosion or any other nuclear explosion',[30] as well as noting the N5 Statement that recognised that a nuclear-weapon test explosion or any other nuclear explosion would defeat the object and purpose of the *CTBT*, as mentioned above.

Although neither the N5 Statement nor the Resolution was legally binding,[31] they are nonetheless noteworthy in light of the fact that they were agreed to by all of the nuclear-weapon states, which are all signatories to the *CTBT* and are all likely to have a far greater interest than many others in conducting a nuclear-weapon test explosion.[32]

III The customary nature of art 18 of the *Vienna Convention on the Law of Treaties*

One further point that requires consideration is whether the rules embodied in art 18 of the *VCLT* are binding on all of the states that have signed the *CTBT*. There are a number of signatories to the *CTBT* that are not states parties to the *VCLT*. Chief among them are states that are believed to have the capability to conduct nuclear testing: the United States, Israel and France.[33] However, the rules in art 18 may still be binding on these states if it has acquired customary international law status. On this point, there may be little need for a detailed discussion. Around the time of the conclusion of the *VCLT*, there were different views as to the customary status of art 18,[34] despite a view from the International Law Commission ('ILC') that it was in fact generally accepted

30 SC Res 2310, UN SCOR, UN Doc S/RES/2310 (23 September 2016) para 4.

31 Secretary of State John Kerry's letter to Senate Foreign Relations Committee Chairman Bob Corker before the adoption of Resolution 2310 said that '[t]he Resolution [...] would take note of [the] political statement by the *NPT's* nuclear-weapon states; it would not impose that view as a legal matter, or place any other legal prohibition on nuclear testing on UN member states': Letter from Secretary of State John Kerry to Senator Bob Corker, 7 September 2016, cited in *The Administration's Proposal for a UN Resolution on the Comprehensive Nuclear Test-Ban Treaty* (n 18) 44 ('Kerry Letter'). See also UN SCOR, 7776th mtg, UN Doc S/PV.7776 (23 September 2016) 2.

32 This is not to say that the views of nuclear-weapon states carry more weight than those of non-nuclear-weapon states. But it also seems true that it is unlikely that the non-nuclear-weapon *CTBT* signatories or ratifiers would oppose the idea that the art 18 obligation forbids nuclear testing.

33 Among the other states whose ratification is necessary for the *CTBT* to enter into force and which are not states parties to the *VCLT* are Bangladesh, Indonesia, Iran, Norway, Romania, South Africa and Turkey. All of these states have ratified the *CTBT*: United Nations, *Multilateral Treaties Deposited with the Secretary-General*, chap XXIII, no 1 (Web Page) <https://treaties.un.org/pages/ViewDetailsIII.aspx?src=TREATY&mtdsg_no=XXIII-1&chapter=23&Temp=mtdsg3&clang=_en>.

34 See, eg, Shabtai Rosenne, *Developments in the Law of Treaties 1945–1986* (Cambridge University Press, 1989) 148–9; Ian Sinclair, *The Vienna Convention on the Law of Treaties* (Manchester University Press, 2nd ed, 1984) 43; D P O'Connell, *International Law* (Stevens & Sons, 2nd ed, 1970) vol 1, 223; Hans Kelsen, *Principles of International Law* (Holt, Rinehart and Winston, 2nd ed, 1967) 466–8.

by states as custom.[35] However, with art 18 in force for nearly 40 years, with more than 110 states parties, and with the fact that many non-states parties to the *VCLT* seem to have accepted the rules provided in art 18, commentators are now almost unanimous in arguing that art 18 generally reflects customary international law.[36]

That this should be the correct understanding of the situation can also be confirmed in relation to the *CTBT*. The Article XIV Conferences have consistently reaffirmed the need not to defeat the object and purpose of the treaty. For example, at the first such conference in 1999, at which 92 ratifier and signatory states participated, the Final Declaration (adopted by consensus) stated that the ratifiers:

> *reaffirm[ed]* [their] commitment to the Treaty's basic obligations and [their] undertaking to refrain from acts which would defeat the object and purpose of the Treaty pending its entry into force.[37]

35 The ILC's Commentary to the final draft articles on the Law of Treaties stated, '[t]hat an obligation of good faith to refrain from acts calculated to frustrate the object of the treaty attaches to a State which has signed a treaty subject to ratification appears to be generally accepted': 'Draft Articles on the Law of Treaties with Commentaries' [1966] II *Yearbook of the International Law Commission* 187, 202.

36 Oliver Dörr, 'Article 18' in Oliver Dörr and Kirsten Schmalenbach (eds), *Vienna Convention on the Law of Treaties: A Commentary* (Springer, 2nd ed, 2018) 243, 245; Robert Kolb, *The Law of Treaties: An Introduction* (Edward Elgar, 2016) 45; Laurence Boisson de Chazournes, Anne-Marie La Rosa and Makane Moïse Mbengue, '1969 Vienna Convention Article 18: Obligation Not to Defeat the Object and Purpose of a Treaty Prior to Its Entry into Force' in Olivier Corten and Pierre Klein (eds), *The Vienna Convention on the Law of Treaties: A Commentary* (Oxford University Press, 2011) 369, 380–3; Mark E Villiger, *Commentary on the 1969 Vienna Convention on the Law of Treaties* (Martinus Nijhoff, 2009) 252–3; Edward T Swaine, 'Unsigning' (2003) 55(5) *Stanford Law Review* 2061, 2065 n 20; Jan Klabbers, 'Strange Bedfellows: The "Interim Obligation" and the 1993 Chemical Weapons Convention' in Eric P J Myjer (ed), *Issues of Arms Control Law and the Chemical Weapons Convention: Obligations Inter Se and Supervisory Mechanisms* (Martinus Nijhoff, 2001) 11, 12–3; Joni S Charme, 'The Interim Obligation of Article 18 of the Vienna Convention on the Law of Treaties: Making Sense of an Enigma' (1991) 25(1) *George Washington Journal of International Law and Economics* 71, 76–8, 85, 113; Mark E Villiger, *Customary International Law and Treaties* (Martinus Nijhoff, 1985) 318; Paul V McDade, 'The Interim Obligation between Signature and Ratification of a Treaty' (1985) 32(1) *Netherlands International Law Review* 5, 13, 25, 28; Michael J Glennon, 'The Senate Role in Treaty Ratification' (1983) 77(2) *American Journal of International Law* 257, 274–5; Martin A Rogoff, 'The International Legal Obligations of Signatories to an Unratified Treaty' (1980) 32(2) *Maine Law Review* 263, 271–2, 284, 287. See also Curtis A Bradley, 'Treaty Signature' in Duncan B Hollis (ed), *The Oxford Guide to Treaties* (Oxford University Press, 2012) 208, 212–3; Bin Cheng, *General Principles of Law* (Grotius Publications, 1987) 111–2 n 28; The American Law Institute, *Restatement of the Law (Third): The Foreign Relations Law of the United States* (American Law Institute Publishers, 1987) vol 1, 172; Lord McNair, *The Law of Treaties* (Oxford University Press, 1961) 199, 204; Dionisio Anzilotti, *Cours de droit international*, tr Gilbert Gidel (Recueil Sirey, 1929) 372–3.

37 Final Declaration, *CTBT*-Art.XIV/1999/5 (8 October 1999) annex para 8 (emphasis added). It is important to note that this Declaration used the words 'reaffirm' and 'undertaking'.

It is notable that the Final Declaration included a precise reproduction of art 18 of the *VCLT*. This is despite the fact that more than 30 of the 92 participating states were not party to the *VCLT* at that time, yet they did not object to the consensus Declaration reaffirming the art 18 obligation.

It should be noted that, strictly speaking, the Article XIV Conference mechanism concerns only ratifiers and not signatories. Under the treaty, signatories may attend the Conference as observers,[38] but according to the *Rules of Procedure of the Conference* they do not formally participate in the decision-making process that leads to the adoption of the Final Declaration.[39] As such, the reaffirmation of the art 18 obligation by the Article XIV Conference can only be formally attributed to the ratifiers and does not necessarily extend to the signatories. However, the practice of reaffirming the art 18 obligation in the context of the *CTBT* by adopting a Final Declaration in successive Article XIV Conferences has continued for 20 years now with increasing numbers of ratifiers participating in each Declaration and, as far as the author knows, with no divergent opinions being voiced. This has undoubtedly contributed to the confirmation of the customary law nature of the art 18 obligation.

IV How the art 18 obligation may cease in the *Comprehensive Nuclear-Test-Ban Treaty* context

As set out in the introductory section, the art 18 obligation is not a perpetual obligation but an interim one that may cease to exit. On its own terms, the art 18 obligation terminates for a signatory state when such a state makes its intention clear not to become a party to the treaty. The obligation ends for ratifier states when the entry into force of the treaty is unduly delayed. However, there is some uncertainty about how these aspects of art 18 should be understood. This part will explore these issues in the context of the *CTBT*. It will become apparent that while the Article XIV Conferences have been able to resolve the issues around the meaning of undue delay in the *CTBT* context, uncertainties remain as to how the signatories can declare that they are no longer going to become parties to the treaty.

A How the art 18 obligation may cease in circumstances of undue delay of entry into force

Article 18(b) provides that the art 18 obligation binds the ratifiers of a treaty pending its entry into force, 'provided that such entry into force is not unduly

38 *CTBT* (n 1) art 14(4).

39 Rule 30 of *The Rules of Procedure of the Conference* provides, '[d]ecisions on the measures referred to in paragraph 2 of Article XIV of the Treaty shall be taken by consensus of ratifiers, taking into account, to the maximum extent possible, views expressed at the Conference by signatories': *Rules of Procedure*, Conference on Facilitating the Entry into Force of the Comprehensive Nuclear-Test-Ban Treaty, *CTBT*-Art.XIV/2017/1 (30 June 2017) rule 30(1).

delayed'. Here, the central uncertainty lies in the question of how long is 'undue'. During the drafting of the *VCLT*, a proposal to set a limit of 12 months was suggested in order to provide clarity on this point but it was not adopted.[40] This result is understandable because the idea of what constitutes undue delay may well differ in each treaty. Indeed, in response to a clarification request about how long a time 'undue delay' would be, Expert Consultant Professor Waldock replied by saying that 'that was a question which could only be answered in the light of the circumstances of each case'.[41]

In the case of the *CTBT*, there is a unique mechanism which may contribute to alleviating or dispelling this uncertainty. According to art XIV(3), of the *CTBT*, it is envisaged that the Article XIV Conferences will be convened repeatedly, annually in principle,[42] until the entry into force of the treaty. In practice, the Conference has been convened every two years. Even with this frequency, the process has provided an extremely useful means to regularly confirm that the ratifier states are not permitted to conduct acts which would defeat the object and purpose of the treaty by adopting a Final Declaration containing the art 18 language. The successive convening of the Article XIV Conferences and the repeated reaffirmation of the art 18 undertaking by the *CTBT* ratifiers effectively negate the possible argument that the entry into force of the *CTBT* is now 'unduly delayed' and thus art 18 obligation has ceased to exist.

The relevant language in the Final Declarations of the Conferences has evolved.[43] From the first Conference in 1999 to the seventh in 2011, the Final

40 Proposal by Argentina, Ecuador and Uruguay: *United Nations Conference on the Law of Treaties: First and Second Sessions,* UN Doc A/CONF.39/11/Add.2 (1971) 131 [164(vi)].

41 *United Nations Conference on the Law of Treaties: Summary Records of the Plenary Meetings and of the Meetings of the Committee of the Whole*, 2nd sess, UN Doc A/CONF.39/11/Add.1 (1970) 29 [27]–[28].

42 *CTBT* (n 1) art 14(3) provides that '[u]nless otherwise decided by the [first Article XIV Conference] or other such conferences, this process shall be repeated at subsequent anniversaries of the opening for signature of this Treaty, until its entry into force'.

43 The second Article XIV Conference in 2001 adopted a Final Declaration containing exactly the same language as in the 1999 Final Declaration. From the 2003 to the 2009 Conferences, the relevant language read as follows: 'We [the ratifiers] reaffirm our commitment to the Treaty's basic obligations and call on all States to refrain from acts which would *defeat the object and purpose* of the Treaty pending its entry into force'. Conference on Facilitating the Entry into Force of the Comprehensive Nuclear-Test-Ban Treaty, *Report of the Conference, CTBT*-Art.XIV/2009/6, 8 October 2009, annex ('*Final Declaration and Measures to Promote the Entry into Force of the Comprehensive Nuclear-Test-Ban Treaty*')[8] (emphasis added). In 2011, the language further changed to read as follows:

> Pending the entry into force of the *CTBT*, we [the ratifying States] reaffirm our commitment, as expressed in the conclusions of the 2010 NPT Review Conference, and call on all States, to refrain from nuclear weapon test explosions or any other nuclear explosions, the use of new nuclear weapon technologies and any action that would *defeat the object and purpose* of the *CTBT*.

Conference on Facilitating the Entry into Force of the Comprehensive Nuclear-Test-Ban Treaty, *Report of the Conference*, *CTBT*-Art.XIV/2011/6, 13 December 2011, annex ('*Final Declaration*

Declaration used exactly the same language as art 18 of the *VCLT* (that is, 'defeat the object and purpose'). A change took place in the 2013 Final Declaration, which was repeated in the 2015 and 2017 Declarations. Those Declarations read:

> Pending the entry into force of the *CTBT*, we [the ratifying states] reaffirm our commitments, as expressed in the conclusions of the 2010 NPT Review Conference,[44] and call on all states to refrain from nuclear weapon test explosions or any other nuclear explosions, the development and use of new nuclear weapon technologies and any action that would ***undermine*** the object and purpose and the implementation of the provisions of the *CTBT*.[45]

The most salient difference of legal significance in this context is that while the language of 1999 to 2011 used the art 18 term 'defeat', it was replaced by the term 'undermine' in the 2013 to 2017 Declarations. It is not known how the language was changed, by whom, or for what purposes. However, the following interpretative and circumstantial evidence suggests that the change was intended for the ratifiers' commitment to cover not only nuclear explosions but also non-explosive nuclear testing.

First, the word 'undermine' seems to cover something more than the word 'defeat' as the former is clearly broader than the latter.[46] If acts which would 'defeat' the object and purpose of the *CTBT* cover nuclear test explosions, as Resolution 2310 enunciated, those which would 'undermine' its object and purpose could entail more than nuclear explosions (including non-explosive tests). Second, Indonesia, one of the co-chairs of the 2013 Article XIV Conference where that change took place,[47] strongly advocated for a ban on sub-critical

---

and Measures to Promote the Entry into Force of the Comprehensive Nuclear-Test-Ban Treaty') [8] (emphasis added). For the language in the 2013 to the 2017 Final Declarations, see the text.

44 The 2010 *NPT* Review Conference's Final Document in the 'conclusions and recommendations for follow-on actions' section includes the following language:

> Pending the entry into force of the Comprehensive Nuclear-Test-Ban Treaty, all States commit to refrain from nuclear-weapon test explosions or any other nuclear explosions, the use of new nuclear weapons technologies and from any action that would *defeat the object and purpose* of that Treaty, and all existing moratoriums on nuclear-weapon test explosions should be maintained.

Review Conference of the Parties to the Treaty on the Non-Proliferation of Nuclear Weapons, *Final Document*, NPT/CONF.2010/50 (vol I), 2010, 23 action 11 (emphasis added).

45 *Final Declaration and Measures to Promote the Entry into Force of the Comprehensive Nuclear-Test-Ban Treaty*, *CTBT*-Art.XIV/2017/6, annex [5] (emphasis added).

46 According to the *Oxford English Dictionary*, 'defeat' means to bring to nought or nullify while 'undermine' signifies to weaken or destroy by degrees: *Oxford English Dictionary* (2nd ed, 1989) 'defeat'; 'undermine'. *Webster's New World College Dictionary* indicates almost the same, by stating that 'defeat' means to bring to nothing while 'undermine' signifies to injure, weaken or impair by subtle, stealthy or insidious means: *Webster's New World College Dictionary* (5th ed, 2014) 'defeat'; 'undermine'.

47 Conference on Facilitating the Entry into Force of the Comprehensive Nuclear-Test-Ban Treaty, *Report of the Conference*, *CTBT*-Art.XIV/2013/6, 10 October 2013, [9].

(non-explosive) testing.[48] It is conceivable that Indonesia aimed to accomplish this ban at that Article XIV Conference, as it had not been able to realise it in the *CTBT* negotiations.[49]

In order to have the clearest possible legal prohibition on conducting nuclear tests, it would be advisable both to keep the expressions 'reaffirm' and 'undertaking' as found in the 1999 Declaration and to use the language of the *VCLT*. In this way a legal nexus could be maintained between the Final Declarations of the Article XIV Conferences and the art 18 obligation in the *CTBT* context.

B How the art 18 obligation may cease for signatory states

According to art 18 of the *VCLT*, the signatories can be released from the art 18 obligation not only when the entry into force of the treaty is 'unduly delayed' just as the ratifiers can be,[50] but also when they 'have made [their] intention clear not to become a party to the treaty'.[51] While the desire to prevent the art 18 obligation lapsing because of 'undue delay' has been tackled by the regular holding

48 In 1995, when Australia presented a simplified text on the scope of the prohibition for the *CTBT* (providing that 'Each State Party undertakes not to carry out any nuclear weapon test explosion or any other nuclear explosion'), Indonesia insisted that the word 'explosion' be bracketed because it wanted to ban all techniques of nuclear weapon tests, both explosive and non-explosive: Jaap Ramaker, *The Final Test: A History of the Comprehensive Nuclear-Test-Ban Treaty Negotiations* (Preparatory Commission for the Comprehensive Nuclear-Test-Ban Treaty Organization, 2003) 65.

49 Another piece of circumstantial evidence supporting the hypothesis put forward in the text is that the UN General Assembly resolution on the *CTBT* adopted in the same year (in 2013) continued to use the word 'defeat' as before: GA Res 68/68, UN GAOR, 68th sess, 60th plen mtg, Agenda Item 105, Supp No 49, Un Doc A/RES/68/68 (11 December 2013) para 4. The Resolution was sponsored by Australia: *Comprehensive Nuclear-Test-Ban Treaty: Report of the First Committee*, UN GAOR, 1st Comm, 68th sess, Agenda Item 105, UN Doc A/68/417 (22 November 2013) para 5.

50 Article 18 of the *VCLT* refers to the 'undue delay' of the entry into force of a treaty in relation to the obligation of ratifiers only: *VCLT* (n 10) art 18(b). However, it would be logical to say that the same rule also applies to the obligation of signatories. While it is true that signatories have another tool (making their intention clear not to become a party to the treaty) to release themselves from the obligation, it is difficult to justify a situation where ratifiers are freed from the art 18 obligation but signatories are not, in case of undue delay in the entry into force of the treaty, particularly because the ratifiers have expressed greater commitment to the treaty than the signatories.

51 This act is sometimes called 'unsign[ing] the treaty' or 'withdraw[ing] the signature': John R Worth, 'Globalization and the Myth of Absolute National Sovereignty: Reconsidering the "Un-signing" of the Rome Statute and the Legacy of Senator Bricker' (2004) 79(1) *Indiana Law Journal* 245. However, it does not mean physically unsigning the treaty; nor does it mean that the state will become a non-signatory to the treaty. The state will simply be freed from the art 18 obligation. In fact, the United States is still listed as a signatory to the *Rome Statute* in the UN Treaty Collection even after it sent the relevant letter to the UN Secretary-General: United Nations, *Multilateral Treaties Deposited with the Secretary-General*, chap XVIII, no 10 (Web Page) <https://treaties.un.org/Pages/ViewDetails.aspx?src=TREATY&mtdsg_no=XVIII-10&chapter=18&clang=_en>. See also Bradley (n 36) 217.

of Article XIV Conferences, the signatories' option of unilaterally terminating the art 18 obligation cannot be prevented by those Conferences.

Moreover, here again, there is some uncertainty. It is not set out in art 18 who has the authority to make an intention not to become a party clear, to whom they have to make that intention known and how. As these questions are precisely what the international community has been faced with, when and since the *CTBT* ratification was rejected by the US Senate, we will take up what has happened in the United States to provide an example of how they might be resolved.

1 The United States and art 18 of the Vienna Convention on the Law of Treaties

The United States Senate turned down the proposed ratification of the *CTBT* in 1999 because of concerns about the verifiability of the *CTBT* and the need to maintain a safe and reliable nuclear arsenal.[52] Our concern here is whether the United States as a signatory to the *CTBT* is (still) bound by the art 18 obligation in relation to the treaty. To answer this question affirmatively, it is necessary to address some preliminary points.

The first point is whether the rules embodied in art 18 of the *VCLT* are in fact applicable to the United States. This question arises not only because the United States has not ratified the *VCLT*, but also because there is a possibility that the US may not even be bound by the customary international law rule arising from art 18 as it may be a 'persistent objector'.[53]

The United States Senate has long opposed the idea that international treaties can be binding on the United States without the Senate's advice and consent. Specifically, it has raised objections to the idea that executive agreements can bind the United States.[54] Under this logic, it would appear that the art 18

52 See *Congressional Digest*, Vol. 78, No. 12 (December 1999) 301–13; Murphy (n 17) 137–9. See also Cerniello (n 15) 27.

53 Although the validity of this doctrine has been subject to controversy, the recently adopted ILC's *Draft Conclusions on Identification of Customary International Law with Commentaries* state, 'Where a State has objected to a rule of customary international law while that rule was in the process of formation, the rule is not opposable to the State concerned for so long as it maintains its objection': International Law Commission, *Draft Conclusions on Identification of Customary International Law*, UN GAOR, 73rd sess, Supp No 10, UN Doc A/73/10 (2018) [65] conclusion 15(1), [66] 152–3.

54 The precise language of the Senate's proposed interpretation and understanding was as follows:

> it is a rule of internal law of the United States of fundamental importance that no treaty (as defined by paragraph 1(a) of Article 2 of the [Vienna] Convention) is valid with respect to the United States, and the consent of the United States may not be given regarding any such treaty, unless the Senate of the United States has given its advice and consent to such treaty, or the terms of such treaty have been approved by law, as the case may be.

Arthur W Rovine, *Digest of the United States Practice in International Law* (Office of the Legal Advisor, Department of State, 1974) 195, 195.

obligations cannot bind the United States as the Senate would not have the occasion to give its advice and consent to such obligations.

However, members of the executive arm of the US government have repeatedly acted on the assumption that the rules in art 18 are expressive of customary international law binding on the United States. For instance, Ambassador Adam M Scheinman, Special Representative of the President for Nuclear Nonproliferation, US Department of State, stated, in relation to the then prospective Resolution 2310, that 'the United States does not consider the entire Vienna Convention to represent customary international law, only Article 18 which deals with signatory obligations'.[55] From this and other statements,[56] it is beyond doubt that the United States government has considered art 18 as representing customary international law.

Further, even some Senators have recognised that art 18 of the *VCLT* represents customary international law. For example, Chairman Bob Corker of the Senate Foreign Relations Committee, a Republican Senator who opposed the idea of passing a UN resolution that could impose international legal restrictions on the United States in nuclear testing without Senate approval, has admitted that art 18 obligations 'have been recognized by successive U.S. administrations as customary international law that present a binding restriction on the United States'.[57]

It thus appears that the Senate has not applied its reasoning about executive agreements to art 18 of the *VCLT*. Given this, there seems to be little difference of opinion between the Senate and the executive regarding the validity of art 18 rules vis-à-vis the United States.

These two branches of government do, however, have completely different ideas on the question of *who* has the power to make the US intention clear not to become a party to a treaty for the purpose of terminating its obligation as a signatory. The Senate rejection of *CTBT* ratification in 1999 generated a bitter controversy on this point. This issue will be addressed in the next section.

55 Adam M Scheinman (Discussion Panel, '20 Years Later: The United States and the Future of the *CTBT*', Stimson Center — Arms Control Association Event, 13 September 2016) (Web Page) <https://www.armscontrol.org/events/2016-09-13/RSVP-20-Years-Later-The-United-States-and-the-Future-of-the-CTBT>.

56 David S Jonas, General Counsel of the National Nuclear Security Administration, US Department of Energy, writes in relation to the *CTBT* that '[d]espite not being a party to the *VCLT*, the United States has long maintained the view that the *VCLT*'s interpretation of the obligation of signatories is expressive of customary international law': David S Jonas, 'The Comprehensive Nuclear Test Ban Treaty: Current Legal Status in the United States and the Implications of a Nuclear Test Explosion' (2007) 39(4) *New York University Journal of International Law and Politics* 1007, 1033. Similarly, Secretary of State John Kerry writes in his letter to Senator Bob Corker that '[a]s a matter of international law, treaty signatories are obliged to refrain from acts which would defeat the object and purpose of a treaty, unless they make their intention clear not to become a party to the treaty': Kerry Letter (n 31).

57 Letter from Chairman of the Committee on Foreign Relations Bob Corker to President Barack Obama, 12 August 2016 (Web Page) <https://www.foreign.senate.gov/press/chair/release/corker-strongly-opposes-obama-promoting-ratification-of-nuclear-test-ban-treaty-at-un>.

2 The authority to make a state's intention clear not to become a party to a treaty

One of the key issues in the 1999 controversy in the United States was who in a given State can make its intention clear not to become a party to a treaty and how. As mentioned earlier, Secretary of State Albright sent a letter to foreign ministers, just after the Senate's refusal to give consent to the US ratification of the *CTBT*, to the effect that despite that rejection the United States was still bound by its art 18 obligations as a signatory of the *CTBT*.[58]

Some Senators firmly rebuffed this position. For instance, Senator Trent Lott, Senate Majority Leader, argued that:

> If the Senate does not consent to ratification of a treaty — and in this case we didn't — it has no status for the United States in international law. … In fact, the Senate vote serves to release the United States from any possible obligations as a signatory of the negotiated text of the treaty.[59]

Senator Jesse Helms, Chairman of the Senate Foreign Relations Committee, expressed the same position in more legal terms. He said that:

> Article 18 of the Vienna Convention … makes clear that the obligation of a signatory State terminates when the State 'shall have made its intention clear not to become a party to the treaty.' … Since the Senate is a co-equal in treaty-making and the Senate has overwhelmingly vetoed the *CTBT*, the intention to never become a party has been made crystal clear.[60]

However, it is not clear that what these Senators said had any legal effect in this situation.[61] As art 18 of the *VCLT* does not specify which organ of a state must make 'its intention clear not to become a party', this question should be treated as a matter falling within the domestic jurisdiction of each state. The US Constitution does not contain any provision specifying which organ is empowered to address this issue. It is logical, however, to assume that the organ which would make such an intention clear should be the same as that which is authorised to express the state's consent to be *bound* by a treaty.[62]

58 Albright letter (n 18).
59 Bill Gertz, 'lott Hits Clinton's Stance on Nuke Pact; Says He's Risking Ties with Senate', *Washington Times* (Washington DC), 3 November 1999.
60 Ibid. Discussed in Asada (n 9) 101.
61 This could somewhat be confirmed by the action subsequently taken by Senator Helms. In March 2001, he wrote a letter to Secretary of State Colin Powell, saying that it is time 'for the Executive Branch … to withdraw the US signature from the *CTBT*': Oliver Meier, 'The *CTBT* Verification System: Entering Rough Waters?' (Briefing Paper No 01/04, VERTIC, September 2001) 7 n 25.
62 Asada (n 9) 101–2.

On this latter point, there is a provision in the US Constitution. Article II § 2 provides that '[The President] shall have Power, by and with the Advice and Consent of the Senate, to make Treaties'. This is to say that the President cannot make treaties without the Senate's advice and consent. But all the Senate is expected to do is to give advice and consent to the President about treaty-making and nothing more. Thus, in the United States, the power seems to be with the President to make his or her intention clear to be or not to be a party to a treaty.[63]

This conclusion can be confirmed by the practice of the United States. In US Constitutional history, there are quite a few instances where the President decided not to conclude a treaty where the Senate had already given advice and consent in favour of ratification.[64] This indicates that the President holds the requisite power. Indeed, all that the President cannot constitutionally do is to make a treaty without the advice and consent of the Senate.[65]

In the case of making clear the intention not to become a party to a treaty after signature, there is nothing in the US Constitution that suggests that the President must get the advice and consent of the Senate before making that intention known. Moreover, there are important precedents in the United States in which an announcement of such an intention was made by the President or his delegate without the advice or consent of the Senate. In relation to the 1998 *Rome Statute of the International Criminal Court* ('*Rome Statute*'),[66] the Under-Secretary of State for Arms Control and International Security, John R Bolton, in May 2002 sent UN Secretary-General Kofi Annan, the depositary of the Statute, a letter saying that 'the United States does not intend to become a party to the treaty. Accordingly, the United States has no legal obligations arising from its signature on December 31, 2000'.[67]

More recently in January 2017, the United States sent a similar letter to the depositary of the *Trans-Pacific Partnership Agreement* ('*TPP Agreement*'),[68] New Zealand, informing the latter that 'the United States does not intend to become a party to the TPP Agreement. Accordingly, the United States has no legal obligations arising from its signature on February 4, 2016'.[69] This letter was signed

63 Ibid.

64 Samuel B Crandall, *Treaties: Their Making and Enforcement* (John Byrne & Co, 2nd ed, 1916) 97–9; Congressional Research Service, *Treaties and Other International Agreements: The Role of the United States Senate* (U.S. Government Printing Office, 2001), 147, 152–3.

65 We are not talking about executive agreements here. See Asada (n 9) 102.

66 *Rome Statute of the International Criminal Court*, opened for signature 17 July 1998, 2187 UNTS 90 (entered into force 1 July 2002) ('*Rome Statute*').

67 *Multilateral Treaties Deposited with the Secretary-General* (n 51) n 12.

68 *Trans-Pacific Partnership Agreement*, opened for signature 4 February 2016, 2016 ATNIF 2 (not yet in force) ('*TPP Agreement*').

69 Letter from María L Pagán, Acting United States Trade Representative, to the Trans-Pacific Partnership Depositary, 30 January 2017 (Web Page) <https://ustr.gov/sites/default/files/files/Press/Releases/1-30-17%20USTR%20Letter%20to%20TPP%20Depositary.pdf>. See also Office of the United States Trade Representative, 'The United States Officially Withdraws from

by the Acting US Trade Representative of the Executive Office of the President. These instances clearly indicate that in the view of the United States, it is the President (or an executive official acting under his instruction), without the involvement of the Senate, who has the authority to make the state's intention clear not to become a party to a treaty after signing it.[70]

3 *Current US status under the* Comprehensive Nuclear-Test-Ban Treaty *and the revolving art 18 obligation*

Having determined that the President, or an executive official to whom the President has delegated his power, can make the state's intention not to become a party to a treaty known, it is now necessary to consider whether the United States has made its intention clear not to become a party to the *CTBT*. There have been some interesting developments in relation to this issue across successive US Administrations.

To start with, during the George W Bush Administration, Senators (led by Senator Jon Kyl) pressed the President to repudiate the Albright letter, which had asserted that the US continued to have obligations as a signatory to the *CTBT* despite the Senate's refusal to give consent to ratification of the treaty in 1999.[71] On 5 June 2008, Secretary of State Condoleezza Rice sent a letter (the 'Rice letter') back to Senator Kyl assuring him that

> the United States has no international legal obligations resulting from the 1996 signature of the *CTBT*, and we do not believe that such obligations would arise unless the treaty was to be ratified by the United States.[72]

She seems to have meant to convey the view that as the United States had already made its intention clear not to become a party to the *CTBT*, the art 18 obligation had ceased to exist vis-à-vis the United States in accordance with the rule stipulated in art 18(a) of the *VCLT*. However, should the US ratify the *CTBT* in the future, the obligation would be re-imposed upon it as a ratifier, pending the treaty's entry into force.

The question is whether the Rice letter is sufficient to conclude that the United States has in fact made it clear that it does not intend to become a party to the *CTBT* or whether, despite the Rice letter, the United States is still bound by the art 18 obligation as a signatory to the *CTBT*. The Rice letter repeatedly claimed that the 'Administration has made clear that the United States does not

---

the Trans-Pacific Partnership' (Press Release, January 2017) (Web Page) <https://ustr.gov/about-us/policy-offices/press-office/press-releases/2017/january/US-Withdraws-From-TPP>.

70 This seems a consensus view on this point. See Jonas (n 56) 1033.

71 Albright letter (n 18).

72 Letter from Secretary of State Condoleezza Rice to Senator Jon Kyl, 5 July 2008 in *The Administration's Proposal for a UN Resolution on the Comprehensive Nuclear Test-Ban Treaty*, above n 18, 45, 46 [question 9] ('Rice letter').

intend to become a party to the *CTBT*'.[73] However, there is no information in the Rice letter that indicates that the US government had sent a letter to the UN Secretary-General, as the depositary of the *CTBT*, to the effect that it had no intention to become a party to the treaty. This was in marked contrast to the practice followed with both the *Rome Statute* and the *TPP Agreement*.

A further complication is that the next Administration under President Obama took a fundamentally different approach to the *CTBT*. President Obama was enthusiastic about a comprehensive ban on nuclear testing, as exemplified by his Prague speech of 5 April 2009, in which he declared that '[t]o achieve a global ban on nuclear testing, my Administration will immediately and aggressively pursue U.S. ratification of the Comprehensive Test Ban Treaty'.[74] Despite this, he did not ask the Senate to reconsider the ratification of the Treaty. It was speculated that he feared that if he had asked the Senate to reconsider the Treaty, the result would have been the same as in 1999.[75]

Instead, he pursued, ***internationally***, the path of a Security Council resolution prohibiting nuclear testing as discussed above. ***Domestically***, Secretary of State John Kerry sent a letter (the 'Kerry letter') to the Senate Foreign Relations Committee Chairman Bob Corker on 7 September 2016, stating:

> As a matter of international law, treaty signatories are obliged to refrain from acts which would defeat the object and purpose of a treaty, unless they make their intention clear not to become a party to the treaty. A ***future*** Administration could make clear that the United States no longer intends to become a party to the treaty, ***in which case*** the United States would no longer have such obligations.[76]

These passages can not only be taken as reaffirming the customary law nature of the art 18 obligation binding on the United States, but also imply that the United States had not yet made its intention clear not to become a party to the *CTBT*.

Which of the Rice and Kerry letters is the correct understanding of the legal status of the United States vis-à-vis the *CTBT*? Or is there any way of understanding the US position consistently throughout the different Administrations? Evidence that the United States has made clear its intention not to become a

73 Ibid., 46 [question 1]–[question 2], 47 [question 7].

74 President Barak Obama, 'Remarks By President Barak Obama in Prague as Delivered' (Speech, Hradcany Square, Prague, 5 April 2009) (Web Page) <https://obamawhitehouse.archives.gov/the-press-office/remarks-president-barack-obama-prague-delivered>.

75 *The Administration's Proposal for a UN Resolution on the Comprehensive Nuclear Test-Ban Treaty* (n 18) 14.

76 Kerry letter (n 31) (emphasis added). See also Shervin Taheran, *UN Security Council Backs CTBT* (October 2016) Arms Control Association (Web Page) <https://www.armscontrol.org/ACT/2016_10/News/UN-Security-Council-Backs-*CTBT*>.

party to the Treaty includes a number of statements (enumerated in the Rice letter) made by the US delegations to the Comprehensive Nuclear-Test-Ban Treaty Organization's ('CTBTO') Preparatory Commission, the First Committee of the UN General Assembly and to the *NPT* Review Conference and its Preparatory Committee. Examples of what these statements have said include that '[the United States] has no plans to reconsider the *CTBT* for ratification',[77] and that 'the United States does not support the [*CTBT*], and will not become a party to it'.[78]

These may be seen as substantially different from what the United States did in relation to the *Rome Statute* in 2002 (before the Rice letter) and the *TPP Agreement* in 2017 (after the Rice letter) both in form and content. First, in the latter two cases, the US government sent a formal letter to the respective depositaries to make its intention clear not to become a party to the relevant treaty, while the Bush Administration did not do this in the *CTBT* case.[79] Second, in terms of content, it is crystal clear that the language used in the *Rome Statute* and the *TPP Agreement* cases was taken from art 18 of the *VCLT* with the intention to produce the prescribed legal effect provided therein,[80] while the statements made in the *CTBT* context were less clear in this respect.

However, since the *VCLT* does not specify the exact procedure to be followed in making one's intention clear not to become a party to a treaty, it is ultimately up to each signatory how to proceed. While it is true that the normal and perhaps desirable way would be to send a diplomatic note to the depositary as was the case with the United States sending a letter to the UN Secretary-General concerning the *Rome Statute*, as a matter of legal requirement that does not seem to be an absolutely indispensable step.[81] A common view seems to be that

77 Rice letter (n 72).

78 Ibid. See also UN GAOR, 1st Comm, 58th sess, 3rd mtg, Agenda Items 62–80, UN Doc A/C.1/58/PV.3 (7 October 2003) 4.

79 In replying to the question as to whether the President has provided written notice of this fact (that is, the fact that Secretary Albright's 1999 assurances regarding US obligations under the *CTBT* are not consistent with US policy) to the foreign governments that received the assurances, Secretary Rice stated that

> the United States circulated a written Information Paper on May 2, 2003 to the Second Session of the Preparatory Committee for the 2005 NPT Review Conference, and the text of the US statement at the UN General Assembly on October 7, 2003, is set forth in the Official Records of that meeting.

Rice letter (n 72) 46 [question 3]

80 See above IV(B)(2).

81 During the United Nations Conference on the Law of Treaties, a Malaysian amendment proposal to replace the words 'made its intention clear' by the words 'expressed its intention in the clearest terms' was not adopted: *United Nations Conference on the Law of Treaties: First and Second Sessions,* UN Doc A/CONF.39/11/Add.2 (1971) 131–2. Legal opinions on lines similar to that shown in the text tend to rely on the above fact. See, eg, Dörr (n 36) 252 n 53; Villiger, *Commentary on the 1969 Vienna Convention* (n 36) 250.

a simple but formal announcement by the government clarifying that it will not proceed with ratification may be enough to terminate the art 18 obligation.[82]

If this is the case, and since the United States made its intention clear several times in relation to the *CTBT* under the Bush Administration,[83] it could not be concluded other than that the United States was, in accordance with the rule set out in art 18(a) of the *VCLT*, released from its obligation not to defeat the object and purpose of the *CTBT*. Unlike the *Rome Statute* and the *TPP Agreement* cases, however it is difficult to specify the exact timing of that release.[84] What is more, whether the US approach is desirable is another story.

There are a couple of further questions that warrant attention here. First, from a political perspective, it is curious why the United States did not follow the procedure it had taken with regard to the *Rome Statute*. Although it is not possible to have access to firsthand background information about the decision, the Administration may have been concerned that if the United States had taken the conspicuous step of sending a formal letter to the UN Secretary-General, which would have then been circulated to all of the other signatories,[85] some of the signatory states (or even ratifiers)[86] may have followed suit. This could have led to a collapse of the whole *CTBT* regime, which would not have been in the interests of the United States.

Second, assuming that what was written in the Rice letter regarding the absence of the art 18 obligation for the United States corresponded to the legal reality at that time, and also assuming that the Kerry letter provided an equally correct description of the prevailing legal status of the United States in this respect, it would logically follow that one state can, with the change of Administration, switch on and off the obligation not to defeat the object and purpose of a treaty. One may question whether this is possible at all (as former Assistant Secretary of State Stephen G Rademaker did).[87] While this may appear irreconcilable with the spirit of art 18 or with good faith as a fundamental principle of international law, it is also true that there seems to be no rule of international law

82 Hans Blix, 'Developing International Law and Inducing Compliance' (2002) 41(1) *Columbia Journal of Transnational Law* 1, 5. A more liberal view that such an intention can also be made clear through implied conduct has been advocated in Villiger, *Commentary on the 1969 Vienna Convention* (n 36) 250. However, this view is not shared by many others. See, eg, Dörr, (n 36) 251–3; Swaine (n 36) 2082–3.

83 Rice letter (n 72). The Rice letter refers to five instances as such, including the two quoted in the text.

84 It is symbolic that in answering the question asking for a description of steps taken by President Bush to terminate the obligations that existed in 1999 when the assurances letter was sent by Secretary Albright, Secretary of State Rice referred to '[t]he various communications by the Bush Administration to representatives of foreign governments': ibid., 47 [question 5].

85 See *VCLT* (n 10) art 77(1)(e).

86 There are a number of instances where a state withdraws its prior instrument of ratification before the treaty's entry into force and resubmits one after adding a (new) reservation. See Dörr (n 36) 254–5.

87 *The Administration's Proposal for a UN Resolution on the Comprehensive Nuclear Test-Ban Treaty* (n 18) 10.

that prohibits it. Even in the case of a treaty *in force*, one state can withdraw from it and then rejoin it later.[88] *A fortiori*, there is no reason to believe that switching on and off the art 18 obligation is legally impossible. It may be seen as dishonest behaviour if one state switches off the art 18 obligation, conducts a nuclear test 'legally' and then switches on the obligation again. But, here again, the same logic applies in the case of a treaty *in force*. The Rice letter quoted above can also be read as indicating that the United States considers the art 18 system does indeed work in this way.[89]

The difficulty that remains in relation to the US position vis-à-vis the *CTBT* is that, to the best of the author's knowledge, there seems to have been no marked US action, after the Rice letter, to 'switch on' the art 18 obligation again during the Obama Administration. President Obama's Prague speech in which he declared his wish for the prompt ratification of the *CTBT* might be considered as such a switch, although he did not directly mention the art 18 obligation in this speech. One possible reason there was no clear action to switch on the obligation may have been that the Obama Administration thought that the United States had continuously been bound by the art 18 obligation in relation to the *CTBT* since 1996.

Whatever the reason is for the lack of a clear 'switching on' action by the Obama Administration, Secretary Kerry's 2016 letter clearly indicates that the United States is now under the art 18 obligation. The Kerry letter stated, after referring to Resolution 2310, that:

> [A] future Administration could make clear that the United States no longer intends to become a party to the treaty, in which case the United States would no longer have … obligations [to refrain from acts which would defeat the object and purpose of the *CTBT*].

The plain meaning of these words is that now, and until a future Administration takes steps to show it does not want to become a party to the *CTBT*, the United States is under the art 18 obligation.[90]Accordingly, it can be concluded that the United States is now legally prohibited from conducting a nuclear test.

88 For instance, on 26 May 1998, Trinidad and Tobago denounced the *First Optional Protocol to the International Covenant on Civil and Political Rights* and, on the same day, it re-acceded, including in its instrument of re-accession a reservation to Article 1 thereof. This process as such was not questioned by the Human Rights Committee. See Human Rights Committee, *Communication No 845/1999*, 67th sess, UN Doc CCPR/C/67/D/845/1999 (31 December 1999) [6.1]–[6.8] ('*Kennedy v Trinidad and Tobago*').

89 Rice letter (n 72). The letter stated that the art 18 obligation would not arise 'unless the treaty was to be ratified by the United States', meaning that if the United States ratifies the *CTBT*, the art 18 obligation would arise again.

90 It may be argued that the *Nuclear Posture Review ('NPR')* published early in 2018 under the Trump Administration can be seen as another instance where the United States made its intention clear not to become a party to the *CTBT*. The *NPR* states that 'the United States will not seek Senate ratification of the Comprehensive Nuclear Test Ban Treaty': Office of the Secretary

The United States' experience with the *CTBT* reveals the complexities and uncertainties surrounding the operation of art 18. Since the art 18 obligation is a legal obligation, there should be a clear way of all states knowing whether it is switched on or off for the sake of legal clarity and stability. To assist with this, it would be helpful for a coherent practice to emerge in which the state concerned sends a diplomatic note to the treaty's depositary if it wants to be released from the art 18 obligation. Similarly, if the state wants to re-engage the art 18 obligation after declaring its termination, it would send another diplomatic note to the depositary.

V Conclusions

Article 18 of the *VCLT* provides for an extraordinary rule. Contrary to the intuition that a treaty will not have any legal validity until it comes into force, the rule enables a treaty not yet in force to legally bind its signatories and ratifiers to 'refrain from acts which would defeat the object and purpose of [the] treaty'.

As has become apparent in this chapter, this rule has numerous weaknesses. Not only is its practical meaning sometimes ambiguous, but its legal force is fragile as well. First, it is not always clear what acts would 'defeat the object and purpose' of a treaty. While, in the abstract, it could be said that acts that would render the treaty meaningless would constitute such acts, in concrete cases it is not so easy to say exactly what kind of acts this would include. As far as the *CTBT* is concerned, there have been several relevant instances of practice, including a Security Council resolution and a joint statement by the five nuclear-weapon states as well as statements by individual signatory/ratifier states, which indicate that conducting a nuclear-weapon test explosion or any other nuclear explosion would constitute an act that defeats the object and purpose of the *CTBT*.

More issues arise in relation to the fact that the art 18 obligation is interim in nature and could terminate or be terminated in a couple of ways. It will cease to exist when the entry into force of the treaty is 'unduly delayed'. It is difficult

of Defense, *Nuclear Posture Review* (February 2018), XVII, 63, 72. This statement may also be understood as a mere announcement of the US Administration's domestic policy and not as an announcement required under art 18 (a) of the *VCLT*. In addition to the US practice concerning the *Rome Statute* and the *TPP Agreement*, Secretary Rice in her 2008 letter hinted that for an announcement to be as such, it is necessary to communicate a state's intention to the United Nations and/or foreign governments, by saying that 'this Administration has clearly expressed to the United Nations and foreign governments that the United States does not intend to become a party to the [CTBT]': Rice letter (n 72). During the general debate in the 2017 Session of the First Committee of the UN General Assembly, the US delegate did not even mention the *CTBT*. In 2018, the US delegate again did not mention the *CTBT* though she maintained that the United States continued to abide by its moratorium on nuclear explosive testing and support the International Monitoring System (one of the verification mechanisms of the *CTBT*). In March 2019, four US Senators sent a letter to President Trump asking him if he would consider 'unsigning' the *CTBT*. This fact may be taken as circumstantial evidence showing that the United States is still to make its intention clear not to become a party to the *CTBT*: Daryl Kimball, 'U.S. Questions Russian CTBT Compliance' (2019) 49(6) *Arms Control Today*, 22.

to indicate how long is long enough to be 'unduly delayed'. In the case of the *CTBT*, thanks to the Article XIV Conferences being held every two years to facilitate the treaty's entry into force, and to the language of their Final Declarations reflecting that of art 18 of the *VCLT*, it can persuasively be argued that the delay of entry into force of the *CTBT* is not yet 'undue'. As long as the Conference continues to adopt a Final Declaration that contains language supportive of the art 18 obligation, this will continue although the Conference would be well advised to stick more closely to the exact wording of art 18 than it has in recent years.

Another fragile aspect of the art 18 obligation is that a signatory may be able to terminate the obligation with immediate effect by making its intention clear not to become a party to the treaty.[91] Here again, there is uncertainty about what is expected to be done in order to make that intention clear. The US experience shows that one individual state may take different approaches at different times depending on the prevailing circumstances and which Administration is in power. Strictly speaking, the US approach cannot be considered unlawful. Nevertheless, since the art 18 obligation is a legal one, it is hoped, for the sake of legal clarity and stability, that there emerges a coherent practice in which the state concerned sends a diplomatic note to the treaty's depositary in order to be released from the obligation. Encouragingly such a trend seems to be emerging in some quarters.[92]

There is a further possibility that a state will switch on and off the art 18 obligation like a revolving door. In such a case, there may well be uncertainty surrounding both whether the obligation has been terminated and whether it has been re-engaged as was the case with the United States under the Obama Administration.

Thus, although one cannot deny its importance and undoubted legal nature, the art 18 obligation is both ambiguous and fragile. It would thus be best if states ratified treaties and brought them into force so that they did not need to rely on it. This, of course, applies to the *CTBT*.

91 Lisa Tabassi, 'The Nuclear Test Ban: *Lex Lata* or *de Lege Ferenda*?' (2009) 14(2) *Journal of Conflict & Security Law* 309, 320–1.

92 In relation to the *Rome Statute*, Israel (28 August 2002), Sudan (26 August 2008) and Russia (30 November 2016) each sent a letter to the UN Secretary-General, informing him of their intention not to become a party to the *Rome Statute*. See *Multilateral Treaties Deposited with the Secretary-General* (n 51).

8 Not a love affair

The relationship between the *Treaty on the Prohibition of Nuclear Weapons* and the *Nuclear Non-Proliferation Treaty*

Barry de Vries and Thilo Marauhn

I Introduction

Ever since the atomic bombings of Hiroshima and Nagasaki there have been consistent calls to ban the use of nuclear weapons and to negotiate complete nuclear disarmament.[1] Over the years, numerous efforts have been made to reduce the risk of nuclear war, the effectiveness of which has been debatable.[2] The most notable instrument addressing the dangers of nuclear weapons has been the *Treaty on the Non-Proliferation of Nuclear Weapons* ('*NPT*').[3] Arguably, this has at least led to fewer states developing nuclear weapons.[4] However, although the *NPT* includes a provision calling upon states to work towards nuclear disarmament, only limited steps have been taken to this end. Even worse, some pro-

1 See, eg, *Establishment of a Commission to Deal with the Problems Raised by the Discovery of Atomic Energy*, GA Res 1 (I), UN GAOR, 1st sess, 17th plen mtg, UN Doc A/RES/1 (I) (24 January 1946); *Declaration on the Prohibition of the Use of Nuclear and Thermo-Nuclear Weapons,* GA Res 1653 (XVI), UN GAOR, 16th sess, 1063rd plen mtg, UN Doc A/RES/1653 (XVI) (24 November 1961); GA Res 34/83G, UN GAOR, 34th sess, 97th plen mtg, UN Doc A/RES/34/83G (11 December 1979); *Non-Use of Nuclear Weapons and Prevention of Nuclear War,* GA Res 35/152D, UN GAOR, 35th sess, 94th plen mtg, UN/RES/35/152D (12 December 1980); *Non-Use of Nuclear Weapons and Prevention of Nuclear War*, GA Res 16/92I, UN GAOR, 36th sess, 91st plen mtg, UN Doc A/RES/36/92I (9 December 1981); *Convention on the Prohibition of the Use of Nuclear Weapons*, GA Res 37/100C, UN GAOR, 37th sess, 101st plen mtg, UN Doc A/RES/37/100C (13 December 1982); *Convention on the Prohibition of the Use of Nuclear Weapons*, GA Res 45/59B, UN GAOR, 45th sess, 54th plen mtg, UN Doc A/RES/45/59B (4 December 1990); *Convention on the Prohibition of the Use of Nuclear Weapons,* GA Res 46/37D, UN GAOR, 46th sess, 65th plen mtg, UN Doc A/RES/46/37D (6 December 1991).

2 Chris Peloso, 'Crafting an Updated Nuclear Non-Proliferation Treaty: Applying the Lessons Learned from the Success of Similar International Treaties to the Nuclear Arms Problem' (2011) 9(2) *Santa Clara Journal of International Law* 309, 315.

3 *Treaty on the Non-Proliferation of Nuclear Weapons*, opened for signature 1 July 1968, 729 UNTS 161 (entered into force 5 March 1970) ('*NPT*').

4 Gro Nystuen and Torbjørn Graff Hugo, 'The Nuclear Non-Proliferation Treaty' in Gro Nystuen, Stuart Casey-Maslen and Annie Golden Bersagel (eds), *Nuclear Weapons Under International Law* (Cambridge University Press, 2014) 374, 393.

liferation has occurred since the treaty was agreed, with India, Pakistan, Israel and the Democratic People's Republic of Korea ('DPRK') joining the ranks of nuclear-weapon possessor states.[5] In the current political climate, it seems unlikely that the nuclear-weapon states will effectively work towards nuclear disarmament. In fact, several have openly talked about updating their nuclear arsenal and developing new types of nuclear weapons.[6] It is against this background that many non-nuclear-weapon states came together to develop a treaty text banning nuclear weapons. The text of the *Treaty on the Prohibition of Nuclear Weapons* ('*TPNW*')[7] was adopted in July 2017 with the near unanimity of the participating states.[8]

The text, however, has received significant criticisms from the nuclear-weapon states and their allies and, as matters stand, it is unclear whether the *TPNW* will enter into force.[9] It is even less likely that the nuclear-weapon states and their close allies will become parties to this treaty.[10] This means that for now the *NPT* will continue to govern not only non-proliferation but also nuclear disarmament for most of the nuclear-weapon possessor states. Indeed, both nuclear-weapon states and the non-nuclear-weapon states, even after the adoption of the *TPNW* text, still see the *NPT* as the cornerstone for any discussion of nuclear

5 In this chapter, the following terminology is adopted: 'nuclear-weapon states' refers to the five states which are party to the *NPT*, and which had manufactured and exploded a nuclear weapon or other nuclear explosive device prior to 1 January 1967, as per art IX(3) of the *NPT*, namely China, France, Russia, the UK and the US; 'nuclear-weapon possessor states' refers to all states which currently possess nuclear weapons regardless of whether they are party to the *NPT* and regardless of when they developed their nuclear weapons programme, namely China, the Democratic People's Republic of Korea ('DPRK'), France, India, Israel, Pakistan, Russia, the UK and the US; 'non-nuclear-weapon states' refers to all states in the world that do not possess nuclear weapons today.

6 Office of the Secretary of Defense, *Nuclear Posture Review* (Special Report, February 2018) 48–55 (Web Page) <https://dod.defense.gov/News/SpecialReports/2018NuclearPostureReview.aspx>; Vladimir Putin, 'Presidential Address to the Federal Assembly' (Speech, Moscow, 1 March 2018) (Web Page) < http://en.kremlin.ru/events/president/news/56957>; Ministry of Defence, *The United Kingdom's Future Nuclear Deterrent: The 2018 Update to Parliament* (Corporate Report, 20 December 2018) (Web Page) < https://www.gov.uk/government/publications/the-united-kingdoms-future-nuclear-deterrent-the-2018-update-to-parliament>.

7 *Treaty on the Prohibition of Nuclear Weapons*, opened for signature 20 September 2017 (not yet in force) ('*TPNW*').

8 *Voting Results. Draft Treaty on the Prohibition of Nuclear Weapons*, UN GOAR, UN Doc *Item 9 A/CONF.229/2017/L.3/Rev.1* (7 July 2017).

9 Fifty states are required to ratify in order to trigger entry into force: *TPNW* (n 7) art 15(1).

10 Spokeswoman of the Ministry for Europe and Foreign Affairs, France, 'Adoption of a Treaty Banning Nuclear Weapons' (Official Statement, Permanent Mission of France to the United Nations and the International Organisations in Vienna, 7 July 2017) (Web Page) <https://onu-vienne.delegfrance.org/On-the-adoption-of-a-treaty-banning-nuclear-weapons-New-York-7-July-2017>; Foreign & Commonwealth Office, 'UK Statement on Treaty Prohibiting Nuclear Weapons' (Official Statement, 8 July 2017) (Web Page) <https://www.gov.uk/government/news/uk-statement-on-treaty-prohibiting-nuclear-weapons>.

disarmament and non-proliferation.[11] Because of this, it is important to consider one of the main criticisms voiced against the adoption of the *TPNW*, namely that it would weaken the *NPT*.[12] In order to assess this claim it is necessary to look at how provisions of the *NPT* and the *TPNW* are likely to affect one another and whether conflicts will arise.

This chapter, therefore, looks at the interaction between the *NPT* and the *TPNW*, developing three main arguments. First, even though the two treaties differ in numerous respects, there is no formal incompatibility between the two agreements. This follows from the *TPNW*'s conflict clause, which addresses the relationship between the *TPNW* and other pertinent instruments. Second, while there is no formal incompatibility, there is potential for conflict. However, any such conflicts can be managed by way of interpretation. In this regard our chapter will focus on specific issues where conflicts could occur and assess the possibility of such conflicts having a detrimental effect on either treaty regime. We will discuss the existing dichotomy between the nuclear-weapon states and the non-nuclear-weapon states arising from the *NPT*, and we will consider whether the *TPNW* may affect the safeguards system and its contribution to nuclear non-proliferation under the *NPT*. The *TPNW* will also be assessed in light of art VI of the *NPT*, and furthermore, assistance by the nuclear-weapon states with respect to peaceful nuclear use will be discussed, specifically whether such assistance is compatible with art 1(1)(e) of the *TPNW*. The third main argument of our chapter is that the two treaty regimes may develop in different directions given their respective institutional settings. We conclude that there

11 See, eg, Christopher A Ford, 'Statement by the United States in General Debate' (Statement, Third Session of the Preparatory Committee for the 2020 Review Conference of the Parties to the Treaty on the Non-Proliferation of Nuclear Weapons, 29 April 2019) (Web Page) <http://statements.unmeetings.org/media2/21491712/us.pdf>; Dell Higgie, 'New Zealand Statement' (Statement, Third Preparatory Committee of 2020 Review Conference of the Parties to the Treaty on the Non-Proliferation of Nuclear Weapons, General Debate, New York, 29 April 2019) (Web Page) <http://statements.unmeetings.org/media2/21491752/new-zealand.pdf>; 'Statement by France' (Statement, Third Preparatory Committee of 2020 Review Conference of the Parties to the Treaty on the Non-Proliferation of Nuclear Weapons, General Debate, New York, 29 April 2018) (Web Page) <http://statements.unmeetings.org/media2/21491754/france-e-.pdf>; Sovann Ke, 'Cambodian Statement' (2019 Preparatory Committee for the 2020 Nuclear Non-Proliferation Treaty Review Conference, New York, 30 April 2019) (Web Page) <http://statements.unmeetings.org/media2/21491818/cambodia-new.pdf>; Vitavas Srivihok, 'Thailand Statement' (General Debate of the Third Session of the Preparatory Committee for the 2020 Review Conference of the Parties to the Treaty on the Non-Proliferation of Nuclear Weapons, New York, 30 April 2019) (Web Page) <http://statements.unmeetings.org/media2/21491793/thailand.pdf>; Stockholm Ministerial Meeting on Nuclear Disarmament and the Non-Proliferation Treaty, *Ministerial Declaration*, 11 June 2019 (Web Page) < https://www.government.se/statements/2019/06/the-stockholm-ministerial-meeting-on-nuclear-disarmament-and-the-non-proliferation-treaty/>.

12 Spokeswoman of the Ministry for Europe and Foreign Affairs, France (n 10); Foreign & Commonwealth Office, (n 10); 'Explanation of vote of the Netherlands on the text of Nuclear Ban Treaty' *The Netherlands at International Organizations* (Web Page, 7 July 2017) <https://www.permanentrepresentations.nl/latest/news/2017/07/07/explanation-of-vote-of-ambassador-lise-gregoire-on-the-draft-text-of-the-nuclear-ban-treaty>.

are no indications of irreconcilable differences between the two treaties, and that it is unlikely that the *TPNW* will weaken the *NPT* in legal terms. Any impact of the *TPNW* on the *NPT* will rather be of a political nature, analyses of which are available elsewhere.[13]

II The *Treaty on the Non-Proliferation of Nuclear Weapons* and the *Treaty on the Prohibition of Nuclear Weapons* compared: (in)compatible approaches?

For decades now, the *NPT* has been the main instrument governing nuclear disarmament and non-proliferation. It came about after a very volatile period dominated by concerns about the Cuban missile crisis and nuclear tests conducted by China and France. The text was agreed upon in 1968, and the treaty entered into force in 1970. Originally, it was adopted for a limited period of 25 years.[14] In 1995, however, states parties agreed to extend its duration indefinitely.[15]

The main objectives of the *NPT* were to limit the further spread of nuclear weapons, while simultaneously protecting the peaceful uses of nuclear energy and moving towards nuclear disarmament. The *NPT* is therefore based upon three pillars: non-proliferation, peaceful use and disarmament.[16] In the eyes of the nuclear-weapon states, non-proliferation has always been considered a priority.[17] To prevent the proliferation of nuclear weapons, the *NPT* prohibits states that had not detonated a nuclear weapon or nuclear explosive device prior to 1 January 1967 from developing or acquiring nuclear weapons in the future.[18] It furthermore prohibits any form of assistance in the development or procurement of nuclear weapons.[19] In order to effectively ensure non-proliferation, the treaty provides for the International Atomic Energy Agency ('IAEA') to contribute to the verification of compliance with the non-proliferation obligations by non-nuclear-weapon states.[20] The *NPT* does not prohibit the use of nuclear

13 Paul Meyer and Tom Sauer, 'The Nuclear Ban Treaty: A Sign of Global Impatience' (2018) 60(2) *Survival Global Politics and Strategy* 61, 69–70; Kjølv Egeland et al., 'The Nuclear Weapons Ban Treaty and the Non-proliferation Regime' (2018) 34(2) *Medicine, Conflict and Survival* 74, 85–8; Rebecca Davis Gibbons, 'Addressing the Nuclear Ban Treaty' (2019) 42(1) *The Washington Quarterly* 27.

14 *NPT* (n 3) art 10(2).

15 *Final Document (Part I),* 1995 Review and Extension Conference of the Parties to the Treaty on the Non-Proliferation of Nuclear Weapons, UN Doc NPT/CONF.1995/32 (Part I) (1995) annex, Decision 3.

16 Jonathan L Black-Branch and Dieter Fleck, 'Nuclear Weapons, Non-Proliferation and Disarmament: A Comprehensive Audit of Relevant Legal Issues and International Concerns' in Jonathan L Black-Branch and Dieter Fleck (eds), *Nuclear Non-Proliferation in International Law* (T.M.C. Asser Press, 2014) vol. 1, 1, 3; Nystuen and Hugo (n 4) 386.

17 Andrew Grotto, 'Why Do States That Oppose Nuclear Proliferation Resist New Nonproliferation Obligations? Three Logics of Nonproliferation Decision-Making' (2010) 18(1) *Cardozo Journal of International and Comparative Law* 1, 11–2; Daniel H Joyner, *Interpreting the Nuclear Non-Proliferation Treaty* (Oxford University Press, 2011) 41–7.

18 *NPT* (n 3) art 2.

19 Ibid., arts 1–2.

20 Referenced in ibid., art 3. However, verification necessitated further arrangements and is centred on the *IAEA Statute* and Safeguards Agreements between the IAEA and the non-nuclear-weapon states.

weapons nor their possession in respect of states that had detonated a nuclear explosive device prior to 1 January 1967,[21] effectively meaning the UK, the US, the Soviet Union (now the Russian Federation),[22] China and France. Finally, the treaty includes a provision calling for the end of the nuclear arms race, nuclear disarmament and general and complete disarmament, which is interpreted as an obligation to negotiate in good faith to bring about this result.[23] It is noteworthy that, in art IV, the *NPT* recognises the inherent right of states to develop peaceful uses of nuclear energy, supplemented by an obligation specifically focusing on nuclear capable states to support such peaceful nuclear uses, 'with due consideration for the needs of the developing areas of the world'. This obligation was considered a trade-off for developing states not to develop nuclear weapons.[24]

The *TPNW* was negotiated against a somewhat similar background, in that there were heightened concerns about nuclear weapons. There were growing tensions between different nuclear powers, modernisation of nuclear weapons by the nuclear-weapon states and fears of further proliferation.[25] While these fears were perhaps more imminent during the creation of the *NPT*, the fears at the time of the adoption of the text of the *TPNW* were quite real, with the DPRK having developed nuclear weapons and indications that Iran was developing nuclear capabilities. In contrast to the *NPT*, the object of the *TPNW* is to comprehensively prohibit the use and possession of nuclear weapons.[26] The *TPNW* thus goes beyond the *NPT*. It clearly abandons the discriminatory regime of the *NPT*, prohibiting the possession of nuclear weapons for *all* states parties. Art 1 of the *TPNW* furthermore includes a prohibition on the use or the threat of use of nuclear weapons. It includes a list of further prohibitions, similar to the *NPT*, such as the production, development, transfer or receipt of nuclear explosive devices.[27] But, unlike the *NPT*, these prohibitions apply to all states parties. Nevertheless, the *TPNW* acknowledges the existence of the nuclear-weapon states and thus includes, in art 4, a mechanism for such states to work with a competent international authority towards dismantling their nuclear arsenal, supplemented by an obligation to enter into a Safeguards Agreement with the IAEA.[28] Thus, the treaty

21 Ibid., art 9(3).

22 After the dissolution of the Soviet Union there were three more states that had access to nuclear weapons as inheritor states, Belarus, Kazakhstan and Ukraine, but all these have given up being nuclear powers and joined the *NPT* as non-nuclear-weapon states according to the Lisbon Protocol to the 1991 Strategic Arms Reduction Treaty: *Protocol to the Treaty between the United States of America and the Union of Soviet Socialist Republics on the Reduction and Limitation of Strategic Offensive Arms*, signed 23 May 1992 (entered into force 5 December 1994).

23 *NPT* (n 3) art 6; *Legality of the Threat or Use of Nuclear Weapons (Advisory Opinion)* [1996] ICJ Rep 226, 263–4 [99].

24 Joyner, *Interpreting the Nuclear Non-Proliferation Treaty* (n 17) 17–8.

25 Nystuen and Hugo (n 4) 372–7.

26 *TPNW* (n 7) preamble.

27 Ibid., arts 1(1)(a)–1(1)(c).

28 Ibid., art 4.

does not only prohibit the use of nuclear weapons, but it provides a roadmap for complete nuclear disarmament.[29]

III The conflict clause of *Treaty on the Prohibition of Nuclear Weapons*

The *TPNW* and the *NPT* deal with similar subject matter and it is therefore possible for conflicts to arise between the two treaties. During the *TPNW* negotiations there was a dispute about how any such conflict — as well as possible conflicts between the *TPNW* and other relevant treaties — should be resolved. Ultimately, the negotiating states decided to insert a conflict clause in the treaty because there was broad agreement among the negotiators that the relationship between the two treaties should be addressed by the new treaty text.[30]

Thus, art 18 provides: 'The implementation of this Treaty shall not prejudice obligations undertaken by States Parties with regard to existing international agreements, to which they are party, where those obligations are consistent with the Treaty'.

Any discussion of the relationship between the *NPT* and the *TPNW* must take this provision as a starting point. Art 18 of the *TPNW* is fairly broad, not limited to specific treaties, but instead referring to any obligations undertaken by states parties in existing international agreements. This covers obligations arising from a broad variety of treaties, such as those establishing the nuclear-weapon-free zones,[31] the *NPT*, the *Partial Nuclear Test Ban Treaty* ('*PNTBT*'),[32] the *Comprehensive Nuclear-Test-Ban Treaty* ('*CTBT*')[33] and any other

29 The *TPNW* also goes beyond the *NPT* in other respects, such as with regard to victim assistance and international cooperation: ibid., arts 6–7.

30 This can be seen in the original General Assembly Resolution deciding to convene the conference: *Taking Forward Multilateral Nuclear Disarmament Negotiations*, GA Res 71/258, UN GAOR, 71st sess, 68th plen mtg, UN Doc A/RES/71/258 (23 December 2016) and in statements made by multiple states during the conference, records of which can be found at 'United Nations Conference to Negotiate a Legally Binding Instrument to Prohibit Nuclear Weapons, Leading Towards their Total Elimination', *United Nations* (Web Page) https://www.un.org/disarmament/tpnw/ ('*Conference Statements*'). See, eg, Statement by Argentina (1st plen mtg, 27 March 2017); Guatemala (3rd plen mtg, 28 March 2017); Brazil and Colombia (9th plen mtg, 31 March 2017), all available on the above website.

31 See, eg, *Treaty for the Prohibition of Nuclear Weapons in Latin America and the Caribbean*, opened for signature 14 February 1967 (entered into force 22 April 1968); *South Pacific Nuclear Free Zone Treaty*, signed 6 August 1985, 1445 UNTS 177 (entered into force 11 December 1986); *Treaty on the Southeast Asia Nuclear Weapon-Free Zone*, opened for signature 15 December 1995, 1981 UNTS 129 (entered into force 27 March 1997); *African Nuclear-Weapon-Free Zone Treaty*, signed 11 April 1996 (entered into force 15 July 2009); *Treaty on a Nuclear-Weapon-Free Zone in Central Asia*, opened for signature 8 September 2006, 2970 UNTS (entered into force 21 March 2009).

32 *Treaty Banning Nuclear Weapon Tests in the Atmosphere, in Outer Space and Under Water*, signed 9 August 1963, 480 UNTS 43 (entered into force 10 October 1963) ('*Partial Nuclear Test Ban Treaty*').

33 *Comprehensive Nuclear-Test-Ban Treaty*, opened for signature 24 September 1996, 35 ILM 1439 (not yet in force) ('*CTBT*').

relevant treaty. Art 18 of the *TPNW* does not prioritise the *TPNW* vis-à-vis all existing international agreements but includes a qualifier ensuring the continued applicability of obligations consistent with the *TPNW*. Even as states agreed to adopt this provision, there remained disagreements as to its precise meaning. In this part we set out the drafting history of the article, the nature of the disagreements that exist around its interpretation and our views on how the provision may be applied in practice to the *TPNW* and the *NPT*.

A Drafting art 18

A provision that outlined the relationship between the *TPNW* and other treaties, especially the *NPT*, was seen by many as a crucial inclusion from the start of the negotiations. During the first round of deliberations, many delegations expressed the view that any possible text should state how it would interact with the *NPT*, and all were agreed that the *TPNW* should reinforce and complement existing agreements.[34] The President of the Conference interpreted the different statements as indicating a need for a specific provision,[35] and this was phrased in the first draft as follows: 'This Convention does not affect the rights and obligations of the States Parties under the Treaty on the Non-Proliferation of Nuclear Weapons'.[36]

Many states were unhappy with the wording, as it was thought that it could possibly create a loophole allowing nuclear-weapon states to retain their nuclear arsenals.[37] Subsequently, two different options were discussed: either deleting the provision as a whole[38] or re-drafting it on the basis of language drawn from art 26 (1) of the *Arms Trade Treaty* ('*ATT*').[39] The significantly re-phrased provision in the second draft followed the wording of art 26 (1) of the *ATT*:

34 For states specifically referring to the need to include a provision stipulating the exact relationship between the *TPNW* and other instruments, see above n 30. For further statements of a more general nature, see, eg, Libya, Fiji, Iran, Switzerland (9th plen mtg, 31 March 2017), *Conference Statements* (n 30).

35 Elayne Whyte Gomez, 'Briefing by the President of the Conference' (President's Briefing, United Nations Conference to Negotiate a Legally Binding Instrument to Prohibit Nuclear Weapons, Leading Towards Their Total Elimination, 12 June 2017).

36 *Draft Convention on the Prohibition of Nuclear Weapons*, UN Doc A/CONF.229/2017/CRP.1 (22 May 2017) art 19.

37 That is, if the *NPT* was to be read as conferring a right to possess nuclear weapons, then this wording would have confirmed that purported right, an argument which will be discussed in Part IV(A). See also statements by Ecuador and Brazil (19th plen mtg, 21 June 2017): *Conference Statements* (n 30).

38 Suggested by Egypt with support from states such as Mexico and Indonesia (19th plen mtg, 21 June 2017), *Conference Statements* (n 30).

39 Suggested by Malaysia with support from states such as Brazil, Mexico, New Zealand, Ireland, Sweden and Switzerland (19th plen mtg, 21 June 2017): *Conference Statements* (n 30). The text of art 26(1) is: 'The implementation of this Treaty shall not prejudice obligations undertaken by States Parties with regard to existing or future international agreements, to which they are parties, where those obligations are consistent with this Treaty': *Arms Trade Treaty*, opened for signature 3 June 2013, 3013 UNTS (entered into force 24 December 2014).

> 'The implementation of this Treaty shall not prejudice obligations undertaken by States Parties with regard to existing or future international agreements, to which they are parties, where those obligations are consistent with this Treaty'.[40]

This change was well received by several states. This is interesting in light of the fact that it no longer included a reference to the rights of states, but only referred to obligations. Earlier in the discussion, several states insisted on a reference to the rights of states within the conflict clause to ensure the protection of the right to develop peaceful nuclear activities.[41] The importance of the right to peaceful nuclear activities was underlined by the draft text's preamble referring to the 'inalienable right of its States Parties to develop research, production and use of nuclear energy for peaceful purposes without discrimination', which is similar to the phrasing used in art IV of the *NPT*.[42] This was an important inclusion within the preamble for many states, regardless of the exact wording of the conflict clause.[43] During the negotiations it was recognised that this right was not a right granted by the *NPT*, but an inherent, sovereign right of states.[44] As the right does not flow from the *NPT*, the focus on obligations within the conflict clause does not have any effect on how the *TPNW* interacts with the right to peaceful uses of nuclear energy. Therefore, because the right was referred to in the preamble, the importance of referring to rights in the conflict clause diminished.

While the change was positively received by most states, the Netherlands vehemently opposed the new text as 'undermining the authority of the *NPT*, by subordinating it to the prohibition'.[45] This opposition was not shared by most other states, evidenced by the fact that the only subsequent alteration was the elimination of the words 'or future' from the provision as ultimately adopted.[46] That being said, some states remained unsatisfied with the provision as included in the final draft. They wanted to delete the final phrase 'where those obligations are consistent with this treaty',[47] arguing that the effect of this phrase was to place the *TPNW* in a superior position to the *NPT*, rather than being complementary to it.[48] Other states responded by stating that the deletion of this phrase

40 *Draft Treaty on the Prohibition of Nuclear Weapons*, UN Doc A/CONF.229/2017/CRP.1/Rev.1 (27 June 2017) art 19.

41 See, eg, Brazil (9th plen mtg, 31 March 2017); Austria, Iran, Indonesia and Singapore (19th plen mtg, 21 June 2017): *Conference Statements* (n 30).

42 *TPNW* (n 7) preamble para 21.

43 See, eg, Philippines on behalf of the Association of Southeast Asian Nations (11th plen mtg, 15 June 2017); Algeria, Brazil, Cuba, South Africa, Mexico, Iran and Venezuela (14th plen mtg, 16 June 2017): *Conference Statements* (n 30).

44 See, eg, Algeria, Brazil and Cuba (14th plen mtg, 16 June 2017), *Conference Statements* (n 30).

45 Netherlands (21st plen mtg, 27 June 2017), *Conference Statements* (n 30).

46 *Draft Treaty on the Prohibition of Nuclear Weapons*, Agenda Item 9, UN Doc A/CONF.229/2017/L.3 (3 July 2017).

47 See, eg, Switzerland, Netherlands, Sweden and Singapore (26th plen mtg, 5 July 2017), *Conference Statements* (n 30).

48 Ibid.

would lessen the importance of the *TPNW*.[49] In any event, the provision was adopted as part of the final text.

B Interpreting art 18

All treaty interpretation builds on the general rules laid down in art 31 of the *Vienna Convention on The Law of Treaties* ('*VCLT*'), which reflects customary international law.[50] Apart from considering the plain meaning of a provision, its context and the object and purpose of a treaty have to be taken into account. Art 32 of the *VCLT* provides for the preparatory works and the circumstances of a treaty's conclusion to be used as supplementary means of interpretation.

Interpreting art 18 of the *TPNW* could be fairly straightforward, as the wording of the provision clearly mirrors its underlying intention, namely that any obligations that states have undertaken in already existing treaties remain intact, as long as their fulfilment is not inconsistent with the *TPNW*. The focus on obligations arising from 'existing international agreements' ensures that the treaty can and should be seen as complementing previous efforts to govern nuclear weapons. The context, namely the reference to the *NPT* in the preamble of the *TPNW*, also illustrates that art 18 of the *TPNW* aims to reduce the risk of conflicts between the *NPT* and the *TPNW*. Additional support for this understanding follows from the negotiations of the treaty text, where the complementarity of the *TPNW* to the *NPT* was stressed continuously.[51] Indeed, the fact that a conflict clause was included at all is evidence that this was the desired outcome.

During the negotiations there were some criticisms of the inclusion of the qualifying phrase, 'where those obligations are consistent with the treaty', because of the way in which it purports to give the *TPNW* primacy. Given the broad scope of art 18 of the *TPNW*, covering all existing international agreements, this would have wide ramifications. As an example, it was pointed out that this formulation would mean that the agreement among some member states of the North Atlantic Treaty Organization ('NATO') to store and/or deploy nuclear weapons on their territory (which according to some states is allowed under the *NPT*, but which would conflict directly with art 1(1)(c) of the *TPNW*) would be superceded by the *TPNW*.[52] Most importantly, it is clear that, in principle at least, the *NPT* may need to give way to the *TPNW*.

49 See, eg, Austria, Argentina, Chile, South Africa and Brazil (26th plen mtg, 5 July 2017), *Conference Statements* (n 30).

50 *Territorial Dispute (Libyan Arab Jamahiriya v Chad) (Judgment)* [1994] ICJ Rep 6, 21 [41]; *Oil Platforms (Islamic Republic of Iran v United States of America) (Preliminary Objection)* [1996] ICJ Rep 803, 812 [23].

51 See, eg, Brazil, Nepal, Trindad and Tobago and Fiji (9th plen mtg, 31 March 2017), *Conference Statements* (n 30); President's Briefing (n 35).

52 Nystuen and Hugo (n 4) 387–8. This argument was implicitly acknowledged in the explanation of the vote by the Netherlands: Explanation of vote of the Netherlands on the text of Nuclear Ban Treaty (n 12).

The following part considers some specific aspects of the two instruments in order to determine whether, and if so how, conflicts might arise in practice between the two regimes.

IV Interaction or conflict?

The criticisms voiced against the *TPNW* and its conflict clause require us to take a more detailed look at how specific provisions of the *NPT* and the *TPNW* are likely to interact. Therefore, this part considers possible conflicts which might arise in practice between the *TPNW* and the *NPT* and assesses those in the light of art 18 of the *TPNW*.[53] We argue that while there may be political difficulties in reconcilings the two texts, no legal issues will arise that cannot be resolved by interpretation.

A The status of nuclear-weapon states

One of the issues in considering the relationship between the *TPNW* and the *NPT* is whether, or the extent to which, the *TPNW* affects any purported right of nuclear-weapon states to possess nuclear weapons. If it can be said that those states do have such a right under the *NPT*, then a conflict arises between the two treaties because the *TPNW* clearly prohibits all states parties, whatever their status under the *NPT*, from possessing nuclear weapons.

States that believe such a right exists rely on two provisions of the *NPT*. First, they point to art IX(3) of the *NPT*, which provides: 'For the purposes of this Treaty, a nuclear-weapon State is one which has manufactured and exploded a nuclear weapon or other nuclear explosive device prior to 1 January 1967'.

Second, they point to art II of the *NPT*, which explicitly prohibits non-nuclear-weapon states from developing or possessing nuclear weapons.[54] They argue that because the treaty acknowledges as a matter of fact that nuclear-weapon states possess nuclear weapons, and that non-nuclear-weapon states are prohibited from doing so, as a matter of logic, nuclear-weapon states have a legal right to possession.

In our view, there is no such right and therefore no conflict arises on this point. First, art IX(3) is a definitional provision, establishing what is meant by the term 'nuclear-weapon state'. That acknowledgement of fact cannot and does not create a legal right. Second, while it is correct that the *NPT* prohibits all

53 In light of art 18 of the *TPNW*, there is no need to refer back to the general rules included in art 30 of the *Vienna Convention on the Law of Treaties*, opened for signature 23 May 1969, 1155 UNTS 331 (entered into force 27 January 1980) ('*VCLT*'). For discussion, see Mark Villiger, *Commentary on the 1969 Vienna Convention on the Law of Treaties* (Martinus Nijhoff Publishers, 2009) 404–5 and Kerstin Von der Decken, 'Article 30' in Oliver Dörr and Kristen Schmalenbach (eds) *Vienna Convention on the Law of Treaties: A Commentary* (Springer, 2nd ed, 2018) 539, 546–7.

54 *NPT* (n 3) art 2.

non-nuclear-weapon states from possessing nuclear weapons, that cannot be read as therefore implicitly conferring a right of possession on other states. Third, this reasoning is strongly supported by the negotiating history of art 18 of the *TPNW* as noted above.[55] Although the first iteration of what became art 18 included a reference to 'rights and obligations' of states parties under the *NPT*, the reference to rights was removed in order to avoid any suggestion that the *NPT* gives rise to such a right.

Consequently, as there is no right in the *NPT*, there cannot be any conflict with the *TPNW*.

B The safeguards system

A second specific concern regarding possible conflict between the *TPNW* and the *NPT* concerns the way in which verification of non-proliferation of nuclear weapons will be managed. There are material differences between the two treaties but our argument is that these do not constitute a conflict.

The *NPT* requires verification of compliance by the non-nuclear-weapon states of their non-proliferation obligations. That verification is achieved through the mechanism of Comprehensive Safeguards Agreements ('CSA'), which are individually agreed upon between states parties and the IAEA.[56] The CSAs allow the IAEA to verify that nuclear material is used only for peaceful uses and is not diverted to nuclear weapons programmes. The system also allows for checks on the existence of any undeclared nuclear material.[57] Following the discovery of Iraq's nuclear weapons programme, despite a CSA operating between Iraq and the IAEA, improved and strengthened safeguards were developed in the form of the Model Additional Protocol.[58] Again this only applied to the non-nuclear-weapon states. At the time of writing, 134 states parties to the *NPT* had entered into an Additional Protocol agreement with the IAEA, thus subjecting themselves to these strengthened verification procedures.[59] The *NPT* contains

55 Above Part III.(A).

56 *NPT* (n 3) art 3(1).

57 International Atomic Energy Agency, *The Structure and Content of Agreements between the Agency and States Required in Connection with the Treaty on the Non-Proliferation of Nuclear Weapons* (Information Circular, IAEA Doc INFCIRC/153/Corr., 1 June 1972); Tariq Rauf, 'The General Framework of IAEA Safeguards' in Jonathan L Black-Branch and Dieter Fleck (eds), *Nuclear Non-Proliferation in International Law* (T.M.C. Asser Press, 2016) vol 2, 11, 15–8.

58 International Atomic Energy Agency, *Model Protocol Additional to the Agreement(s) Between State(s) and the International Atomic Energy Agency for the Application of Safeguards* (Information Circular, IAEA Doc INFCIRC/540/Corr., 1 September 1997).

59 'Additional Protocol' *International Atomic Energy Agency* (Web Page) <https://www.iaea.org/topics/additional-protocol. Of the states that participated in the negotiations 83 had already entered into an Additional Protocol, while only seven states participating had not entered into a Comprehensive Safeguards Agreement yet. See: Zia Mian, Tamara Patton and Alexander Glaser, 'Addressing Verification in the Nuclear Ban Treaty' (2017) 47(5) *Arms Control Today* 14, 16.

no verification obligations for the nuclear-weapon states which is logical because the treaty itself does not require non-proliferation on the part of those states.

The *TPNW* approaches verification differently in that it requires *all* states parties to be subjected to verification. For non-nuclear-weapon states, it essentially preserves the status quo: it does not specifically differentiate between the original Safeguards Agreements and the Additional Protocol regime, but it requires states to maintain, as a minimum, the safeguards already in place at the time of the entry into force of the *TPNW*.[60] The nuclear-weapon states are also required to submit to verification and this is a significant departure from the *NPT*. Arts 4(1) and (3) of the *TPNW* require states that have nuclear weapons at the time of accession to the *TPNW*, or states which possessed nuclear weapons on 7 July 2017, to enter into a Safeguards Agreement with the IAEA in order to verify the non-diversion of declared nuclear material from peaceful nuclear activities and of the absence of undeclared nuclear material or activities.[61]

An argument has been made that, due to the differences between the two regimes in terms of the verification provisions, a conflict can arise. That argument rests on the content of Action 30 of the Action Plan agreed by the states parties to the *NPT* at the 2000 Review Conference of the Parties to the *NPT*.[62] Action 30 stipulates:

> The Conference stresses that comprehensive safeguards and additional protocols should be universally applied once the complete elimination of nuclear weapons has been achieved. In the meantime, the Conference calls for the wider application of safeguards to peaceful nuclear facilities in the nuclear weapon States under the relevant voluntary-offer safeguards agreements in the most economic and practical way possible, taking into account the availability of IAEA resources.[63]

That is, Action 30 provides that once nuclear disarmament has been achieved, the highest standards of safeguards should be applied to all states — the highest

60 *TPNW* (n 7) art 3(1). See Eirini Giorgou, 'Safeguards Provisions in the Treaty on the Prohibition of Nuclear Weapons' *Arms Control Law* (Blog Post, 11 April 2018) (Web Page) <https://armscontrollaw.com/2018/04/11/safeguards-provisions-in-the-treaty-on-the-prohibition-of-nuclear-weapons>. Currently, 134 states parties to the *NPT* have entered into an Additional Protocol. Of the states that participated in the *TPNW* negotiations, 83 are subject to Additional Protocol level safeguards. Only seven states had not completed a Comprehensive Safeguards Agreement and of course they would be required to do so now as well by the *TPNW*: *TPNW* (n 7) art 3(2).

61 Many negotiating states felt that there was a missed opportunity in not further strengthening this provision and requiring such states to enter into an Additional Protocol Arrangement. See, eg, Statements of Switzerland and Sweden (28th plen mtg, 7 July 2017), *Conference Statements (n 30).*

62 Giorgou (n 60).

63 *Final Document Parts I and II*, 2000 Review Conference of the Parties to the Treaty on the Non-Proliferation of Nuclear Weapons, UN Doc NPT/CONF.2000/28 (Parts I and II) (2000) 4 [12]; restated in *Final Document Volume I,* 2010 Review Conference of the Parties to the Treaty on the Non-Proliferation of Nuclear Weapons, UN Doc NPT/CONF.2010/50 (Vol. I) 25.

standard being the Additional Protocol. As explained above, the *TPNW* does not require its states parties to enter into an Additional Protocol — it merely requires that non-nuclear-weapon states which were party to an Additional Protocol prior to its entry into force maintain that level of verification and it is silent entirely as regards the nuclear-weapon states. This 'lower standard' in the *NPT* is argued to be a conflict.

In our view, while there are clearly differences between the *NPT* and the *TPNW* in terms of verification obligations, these differences do not constitute a conflict. First, while the *TPNW* does not require its states parties to submit to the Additional Protocol standard (even when all disarmament is complete), it certainly does not preclude states from doing so. That the *TPNW* does not go as far as the Action Plan is not a conflict. Second, in any event, arts 3 and 4 of the *TPNW* specifically anticipate possible additional relevant verification instruments that may be adopted in the future. This demonstrates that the development of stronger safeguards (within the treaty regime or externally in the *NPT*) would not conflict with the treaty; rather, it would simply strengthen the verification aspect. A third reason why the differences in verification requirements do not constitute a conflict is found within the terms of art 18. That states that pre-existing obligations of states parties remain in force and this reinforces art 3(1) of the *TPNW*, which requires non-nuclear-weapon states to maintain existing safeguards. Finally, the frequent mentions throughout the *TPNW* to the effect that the *NPT* was to be complemented and strengthened negate any conflict thesis. For example, the 18th preambular paragraph provides that the states parties to the treaty reaffirm:

> that the full and effective implementation of the Treaty on the Non-Proliferation of Nuclear Weapons, which serves as the cornerstone of the nuclear disarmament and non-proliferation regime, has a vital role to play in promoting international peace and security.

C *The* Treaty on the Prohibition of Nuclear Weapons *in light of art VI of the* Treaty on the Non-Proliferation of Nuclear Weapons

The third area where concern has arisen about a conflict between the *TPNW* and the *NPT* is around nuclear disarmament. Both treaties make provisions for nuclear disarmament. Article 1 of the *TPNW* requires complete nuclear disarmament of its states parties. Article VI of the *NPT* provides:

> Each of the Parties to the Treaty undertakes to pursue negotiations in good faith on effective measures relating to cessation of the nuclear arms race at an early date and to nuclear disarmament, and on a treaty on general and complete disarmament under strict and effective international control.

The primary argument advanced as to why these provisions conflict with each other is that art VI of the *NPT* requires nuclear disarmament to be achieved through a particular sequence.[64] First, the nuclear arms race must cease; this is to be followed by nuclear disarmament; and then a treaty on general and complete disarmament will be developed. The *TPNW*'s requirement for complete nuclear disarmament, the argument goes, disrupts this sequence.[65] According to this argument, a treaty requiring complete nuclear disarmament cannot precede the cessation of the nuclear arms race nor the existence of total nuclear disarmament. Such a treaty could only accord with art VI of the *NPT* if it led to worldwide nuclear disarmament or came after the achievement of worldwide nuclear disarmament.

There are several flaws with this reasoning. First, there is nothing in the plain text of art VI of the *NPT*, nor in its context, indicating such a chronological sequencing.[66] Second, even if it were accepted that art VI of the *NPT* requires a sequential approach, the *TPNW* would still not be in violation of art VI of the *NPT*. This is because the *TPNW* can be understood as fitting within the sequencing of art VI of the *NPT* as its requirement for complete nuclear disarmament can be interpreted either as a means towards a cessation of the nuclear arms race, or as a step towards nuclear disarmament.[67] The position that the *TPNW* is properly considered as a step towards fulfilling the requirements of art VI of the *NPT* was adopted by different states during *TPNW* negotiations.[68] These states considered the negotiations as part of the good faith efforts being addressed by art VI of the *NPT*. Indeed, some states explained that their participation in the negotiations was to fulfil their obligations under art VI of the *NPT*.[69]

In conclusion then, it is clear that there is no conflict between the *TPNW* and art VI of the *NPT*. Indeed far from contravening the *NPT*, the *TPNW* can be understood as a vehicle for adhering to the nuclear disarmament obligations laid out in art VI of the *NPT*.

64 Joyner, *Interpreting the Nuclear Non-Proliferation Treaty* (n 17) 99–101; see, eg, Netherlands (4th plen mtg, 28 March 2017), *Conference Statements* (n 30).

65 It is noteworthy that the above criticism of the *TPNW* largely came from nuclear-weapon states and some of their close allies, who arguably had earlier hampered discussions on nuclear disarmament and now feared that the new treaty might deprive them of controlling the debate about disarmament and the development of international law in this respect: see Foreign & Commonwealth Office (n 10).

66 Daniel H Joyner, 'The Legal Meaning and Implications of Article VI of the Non-Proliferation Treaty', in Gro Nystuen, Stuart Casey-Maslen and Annie Golden Bersagel (eds), *Nuclear Weapons Under International Law* (Cambridge University Press, 2014) 397, 406.

67 Ibid., 412.

68 Many states made remarks on how this treaty was a step towards nuclear disarmament, even if not all directly referenced art VI of the *NPT*. See, eg, Statements of Lebanon representing the Arab Group, South Africa, Trinidad and Tobago on behalf of CARICOM, Cuba, Chile, Venezuela, Iran, Brazil, Malaysia and Peru (28th plen mtg, 7 July 2017), *Conference Statements* (n 30).

69 Note that art VI of the *NPT* applies equally to nuclear-weapon states and non-nuclear-weapon states. See, eg, Statements of Chile and the Philippines on behalf of the Association of Southeast Asian Nations (1st plen mtg, 27 March 2017); Ecuador and Ireland (2nd plen mtg, 27 March 2017), *Conference Statements* (n 30).

D Nuclear-weapon states assistance for peaceful use

Another conflict that has been argued to exist between the treaties relates to the relationship between art IV(2) of the *NPT* and art 1(1)(e) of the *TPNW*. Art IV(2) of the *NPT* provides:

> All the Parties to the Treaty undertake to facilitate, and have the right to participate in the fullest possible exchange of equipment, materials and scientific and technological information for the peaceful uses of nuclear energy. Parties to the Treaty in a position to do so shall also co-operate in contributing alone or together with other States or international organizations to the further development of the applications of nuclear energy for peaceful purposes, especially in the territories of non-nuclear-weapon States Party to the Treaty, with due consideration for the needs of the developing areas of the world.

Art 1(1)(e) of the *TPNW* states that it is prohibited to: 'Assist, encourage or induce, in any way, anyone to engage in any activity prohibited to a State Party under this Treaty'.

Those who suggest that these provisions are in conflict with each other point to the fact that the term 'assist' in art 1(1)(e) of the *TPNW*, read with the words 'in any way', means that the prohibition on assistance refers not only to direct assistance but also to assistance that is rendered indirectly. Therefore, the argument goes, the *TPNW* provision must be read as prohibiting the transfer of nuclear material to a state that might re-direct such nuclear material towards military nuclear facilities. Meanwhile, art IV(2) of the *NPT* puts in place an obligation on states parties to the *NPT* to facilitate prohibiting assistance for peaceful uses of nuclear energy and to co-operate for the further development of applications of nuclear energy for peaceful purposes.[70] As such, it is argued that there is a conflict between the prohibition on indirect assistance arising from art 1 of the *TPNW* and the obligation to provide assistance in art IV(2) of the *NPT*. This claim requires us to interpret both provisions carefully and it is our view that the two provisions can be read to be consistent with each other, and therefore avoid any conflict.

The plain wording of art 1(1), and the object and purpose of the *TPNW* as a whole, make it clear that the underlying purpose of art 1(1) is to prevent assistance in developing nuclear weapons or other nuclear explosive devices. However, the text itself does not specify how broadly assistance should be understood and, in particular, whether it would include supplying nuclear materials for peaceful uses to states that have nuclear weapons programmes. Neither

70 And indeed, this was explicitly noted as one of the necessary components of the *TPNW* during negotiations: see, eg, Statements of Vietnam (3rd plen mtg, 28 March 2017) and Nepal (9th plen mtg, 31 March 2017), *Conference Statements* (n 30).

the preparatory works nor the circumstances of the *TPNW*'s conclusion[71] assist us because among the publicly available documents there is little reference to this issue in the publicly available documents on, or records of, the negotiations. Most states discussed the interaction between the *TPNW* and the *NPT* in general terms, rather than in light of particular problems. This means that there is little clarity from within the *TPNW* as to how it was intended that this issue should be approached.[72]

Similarly, there has been little research into the meaning of 'assistance' in the context of the *NPT*, and this could well reflect the fact that assistance for peaceful uses to a state that is known to have nuclear weapons is, understandably, a relatively unusual situation. However, a particular instance is the Agreement between India and the United States pertaining to peaceful uses of nuclear energy.[73] The *Agreement* allows for nuclear cooperation and transfer of nuclear materials,[74] but restricts such cooperation to only peaceful nuclear use,[75] and obliges India to put its civilian nuclear facilities under *IAEA* safeguards.[76]

While that *Agreement* has been controversial especially because it created a form of nuclear cooperation outside of the *NPT* regime,[77] it does show an instance by which it is possible to retain nuclear cooperation between states parties to the *TPNW* and the nuclear-weapon states of the *NPT*. It is notable that the Agreement has enjoyed the support of the IAEA,[78] as well as the Nuclear Suppliers Group.[79] Furthermore, the obligation to provide assistance set out in art IV of the *NPT* does not restrict itself to cooperation only with states parties to

71 *VCLT* (n 53) art 32.

72 Some remarks did focus on certain specific aspects; however, none did so with regard to this specific issue.

73 *Agreement for Cooperation between the Government of the United States of America and the Government of India Concerning Peaceful Uses of Nuclear Energy*, United States-India, signed 10 October 2008 ('*United States-India Agreement*' or '*the Agreement*').

74 Ibid., art 2.

75 Ibid., art 9.

76 Ibid., art 5(6)(c). India subsequently entered into an Additional Protocol: International Atomic Energy Agency, *Protocol Additional to the Agreement between the Government of India and the International Atomic Energy Agency for the Application of Safeguards to Civilian Nuclear Facilities*, IAEA Doc INFCIRC/754/Add.6 (1 August 2014).

77 The *123 Agreement* has often been criticised for significantly harming the *NPT*: Surabhi Ranganathan, *Strategically Created Treaty Conflicts and the Politics of International Law* (Cambridge University Press, 2014) 308; Faustin Z Ntoubandi, 'Reflections on the USA-India Atomic Energy Cooperation' (2008) 13(2) *Journal of Conflict & Security Law* 273, 277–8.

78 'IAEA Board Approves India-Safeguards Agreement' *International Atomic Energy Agency* (Web Page, 1 August 2008) <https://www.iaea.org/newscenter/news/iaea-board-approves-india-safeguards-agreement>.

79 Nuclear Suppliers Group, 'Statement on Civil Nuclear Cooperation with India' (Statement, 7 September 2008) <https://www.armscontrol.org/system/files/20080906_Final_NSG_Statement.pdf>; Jack I Garvey, *Nuclear Weapons Counterproliferation: A New Grand Bargain* (Oxford University Press, 2013) 46; Kate Deere, 'The Obligations of Nuclear-Weapon States Not to Transfer Nuclear Weapons and Devices (Article I NPT)' in Jonathan L Black-Branch and

the *NPT.* [80] This has led some commentators to point out that the *Agreement* has set a precedent for other states to provide nuclear assistance outside of the *NPT* framework. [81]

Considering all of this in the light of the argument that there is a conflict between art 1(1)(e) of the *TPNW* and art IV(2) of the *NPT*, it seems that any conflict can be avoided if the *India-United States Agreement* approach is followed. That is, if the recipient state is required to enter into a Safeguards Agreement to ensure that the assistance is only directed towards peaceful use. Since this approach would be replicating the practice (limited though it is) in the *NPT* regime, it could not be said to be creating a conflict between the two treaties.

E Potentially competing institutional settings

A final potential conflict identified between the *TPNW* and the *NPT* is concerned with the way each treaty establishes a different institutional framework, both of which have a mandate to discuss nuclear disarmament. It is argued that divergences could arise between the two institutions and that this could lead to political and legal difficulties.[82]

In our view, there is merit to this argument, but the extent to which any actual conflicts will occur cannot be ascertained until implementation of the *TPNW* actually begins as the matter cannot be considered in the abstract. In this section, we explain the institutional structures of both systems to show how a conflict might emerge.

Art 8 of the *TPNW* establishes a Meeting of States Parties, which can discuss 'any matter with regard to the application or implementation of this Treaty' and can discuss and take decisions on 'further measures for nuclear disarmament'. Reading this latter provision broadly, it is clear that such matters could extend beyond the scope of the *TPNW.* Art VIII(3) of the *NPT* provides for five-yearly Review Conferences to be convened by the states parties to the *NPT* for the purposes of reviewing the operation of that treaty and being assured that its provisions are being realised. Thus, the *NPT* Review Conferences also have a mandate to discuss matters pertaining to nuclear disarmament. This means that, with the entry into force of the *TPNW*, there will be two separate treaty bodies with a mandate to discuss nuclear disarmament. Taking into consideration that

---

Dieter Fleck (eds), *Nuclear Non-Proliferation in International Law* (T.M.C. Asser Press, 2014) vol 1, 23, 33.

80 Ranganathan, above (n 83), 303–5; Daniel Rietiker, 'Between Prosperity and Destruction: A Modern Interpretation of the Right to Peaceful Use of Nuclear Energy in Light of the Protection of Human Rights and Future Generations' in Jonathan L Black-Branch and Dieter Fleck (eds), *Nuclear Non-Proliferation in International Law* (TMC Asser Press, 2016) vol 3, 21, 25 n 17. Although this has been contested: Ntoubandi (n 77) 280.

81 Peloso (n 2) 319–20; Deere (n 79) 33.

82 See, eg, Statements of Netherlands (26th plen mtg, 5 July 2017) and Switzerland (28th plen mtg, 7 July 2017), *Conference Statements* (n 30).

the nuclear-weapon states are unlikely to become parties to the *TPNW*, a divergence could arise between the two.

This situation could exacerbate a number of existing political tensions between the non-nuclear-weapon states and the nuclear-weapon states.[83] First, for many years, a large number of non-nuclear-weapon states have been dissatisfied with the lack of progress that the nuclear-weapon states have made towards nuclear disarmament,[84] and have also been concerned about the lack of assistance by nuclear-weapon states for developing states towards their peaceful use of nuclear energy.[85] In fact, this dissatisfaction was a driving force for many of the non-nuclear-weapon states to negotiate the *TPNW*. It is possible (perhaps even likely) that the Meeting of States Parties to the *TPNW* will be used as a forum in which to bring political pressure and draw attention to the perceived failures of the nuclear-weapon states.[86] When taking into consideration that it is unlikely that the nuclear-weapon states will become party to the *TPNW*, this could well generate new conflicts or exacerbate existing ones. Such a development could subsequently harm, rather than promote, the pursuit of nuclear disarmament.

Second, tensions could increase further in light of art 12 of the *TPNW* which requires states parties to work towards the treaty's universality.[87] If, during *NPT* Review Conferences, states parties to the *TPNW* insist that all other states parties to the *NPT* join the *TPNW*, this could generate even more friction. There is a significant probability that if this happens it will gridlock the *NPT* Review Conference and frustrate any further practical discussion in that forum about nuclear disarmament in general, and gradual or partial nuclear disarmament in particular. Looking at previous *NPT* Review Conferences, it has always been difficult to achieve consensus on a final document and the dichotomy between states strongly opposed to nuclear weapons and nuclear-weapon states has already caused significant conflict.[88] While the *TPNW* may not aggravate such

83 See, eg, Heather Nauert, US Department of State Spokesperson 'Conclusion of UN Negotiations on a Treaty to Ban Nuclear Weapons' (Press Statement, 7 July 2017).

84 Alexander Kmentt, 'The Development of the International Initiative on the Humanitarian Impact of Nuclear Weapons and Its Effect on the Nuclear Weapons Debate' (2015) 97 *International Review of the Red Cross* 681, 706; Joyner, 'The Legal Meaning and Implications of Article VI of the Non-Proliferations Treaty' (n 66), 402–4; Nystuen and Hugo (n 4) 392.

85 Peloso (n 2) 316–7.

86 See, eg, Philippines on behalf of the Association of Southeast Asian Nations, Algeria (1st plen mtg, 27 March 2017), Egypt (13th plen mtg, 16 June 2017), South Africa (2nd plen mtg, 27 March 2017), *Conference Statements* (n 30).

87 'Each State Party shall encourage States not party to this Treaty to sign, ratify, accept, approve or accede to the Treaty, with the goal of universal adherence of all States to the Treaty': *TPNW* (n 7) art 12.

88 Sarah J Swart, 'An African Contribution to the Nuclear Weapons Debate' (2015) 97 *International Review of the Red Cross* 753, 757; Arms Control Association 'Nuclear Nonproliferation Treaty Review Conference Outcome a Warning Sign, Say Arms Control Experts' (Press Release, 22 May 2015); Michal Smetana, 'Stuck on Disarmament: The European Union and the 2015 NPT Review Conference' (2016) 92(1) *International Affairs* 137, 140–2, 145–50.

tensions, this may be different if it is excessively instrumentalised. It seems unlikely that it will alleviate any of the existing issues under the *NPT*.

It has also been argued that the creation of competing institutional settings will not only be a political problem, but the duality may have legal effects.[89] This point was raised in the negotiations.[90] The question is whether art 18 of the *TPNW* (which, as discussed above, provides for primacy of the *TPNW*) should be read as only addressing actual treaty obligations vis-à-vis other treaty obligations, or whether it also captures decisions of the respective treaty bodies. It seems clear that decisions of a treaty body (such as the Meeting of States Parties) could not supersede provisions of the *NPT*; however, it was suggested that decisions of the Meeting of States Parties could supersede measures taken in the context of the *NPT*.[91] This would be the case if art 18 did apply beyond treaty provisions. There is merit in such an argument because decisions of the Meeting of States Parties are binding and thus constitute 'obligations' of the states parties.

As indicated above, in our view, it is not possible to assess whether such a legal conflict will arise in the absence of actual implementation practice. However, at this point, it must be conceded that this type of legal conflict is a possibility.

V Conclusions and perspectives

History does not provide evidence that disarmament agreements following earlier arms control agreements have undermined the latter's normativity. Rather the opposite is true: the new agreements have strengthened the earlier ones, often by following stricter standards. Even in cases of partial overlap only, there is no evidence that the earlier agreement was delegitimised or weakened. Thus, the *Anti-Personnel Landmines Convention*[92] did not weaken the *Amended Protocol II* to the 1980 CCW ('*Amended Protocol II*')[93] for those becoming parties to the *Anti-Personnel Landmines Convention* nor for those who only ratified *Amended Protocol II*. *Amended Protocol II* has not experienced reduced compliance; rather states supplemented their obligation to merely control anti-personnel landmines with an obligation to disarm themselves of the weapons.

While it is hard to predict the long-term impact of the *TPNW* on the *NPT*, our analysis of the various potential conflicts has demonstrated that, apart from

89 See, eg, Statements of Netherlands (26th plen mtg, 5 July 2017) and Switzerland (28th plen mtg, 7 July 2017), *Conference Statements* (n 30).

90 Ibid.

91 Ibid.

92 *Convention on the Prohibition of the Use, Stockpiling, Production and Transfer of Anti-Personnel Mines and on Their Destruction*, opened for signature 3 December 1997, 2056 UNTS 211 (entered into force 1 March 1999) ('*Anti-Personnel Landmines Convention*').

93 *Amended Protocol on Prohibitions or Restrictions on the Use of Mines, Booby-Traps and Other Devices*, opened for signature 31 May 1995, 35 ILM 1206 (entered into force 3 December 1998). ('*Amended Protocol II*')

the general and overarching dichotomy between nuclear-weapon states and non-nuclear-weapon states, there are no indications of irreconcilable differences between the two. It may thus be argued that it is unlikely that the *TPNW* will weaken the *NPT* regime in legal terms.

Concerns that the *TPNW* might weaken the *NPT* rather emerge from political considerations. Indeed, the *TPNW* will most likely affect the relationship between the nuclear-weapon states and the non-nuclear-weapon states most ardently opposed to nuclear weapons. It is likely that the already entrenched positions in this debate will not be alleviated and that further discussions of nuclear disarmament within the framework of the *NPT* will prove less viable. This is likely to impact the 2020 *NPT* Review Conference. Japan highlighted this when arguing that a treaty like the *TPNW* without nuclear-weapon states

> will only deepen the schism and division not only between nuclear-weapon states and non-nuclear-weapon states, but also among non-nuclear-weapon states, which will further divide the international community. Therefore, our common goal will be pushed away, a goal of reaching a world free of nuclear weapons.[94]

Even though nuclear-weapon states have occasionally taken up this conflict, this has not been the focus of their criticism. They have rather framed it in more general and sometimes even legal terms.[95] Notwithstanding the arguments of the nuclear-weapon states, it is debatable whether the *TPNW* itself will really heighten tensions beyond what has already emerged. Furthermore, such criticism raises questions in light of the unwillingness of nuclear-weapon states to work towards nuclear disarmament and some of the more recent statements suggesting a restart of a nuclear arms race.[96]

It is obvious that the *TPNW* will not achieve nuclear disarmament without participation of nuclear-weapon states, which remains unlikely. The *TPNW* therefore appears to be part of the politics of leverage by creating public pressure on the nuclear-weapon states and their closest allies rather than an in-depth legal instrument dealing with all the relevant aspects of nuclear disarmament.[97] Seen as a political instrument, it is unlikely to generate more disagreement within the *NPT* beyond what is already there. The *TPNW* thus emerges as a more formal

94 See, eg, Statement by Japan (1st plen mtg, 27 March 2017), *Conference Statements* (n 30).

95 Spokeswoman of the Ministry for Europe and Foreign Affairs, France (n 10); Foreign & Commonwealth Office (n 10).

96 Sophie Tatum, Ryan Browne and Kevin Bohn, 'Trump Says US Is Ending Decades-Old Nuclear Arms Treaty with Russia', *CNN* (online, 21 October 2018) (Web Page) <https://edition.cnn.com/2018/10/20/politics/donald-trump-us-arms-agreement-russia/index.html>.

97 Which has even been acknowledged or at least implied during the drafting of the text of the *TPNW*: see, eg, Philippines (1st plen mtg, 27 March 2017) and Brazil (9th mtg, 31 March 2017), *Conference Statements* (n 30).

and juridified restatement of positions that have already been on the negotiating table for many years.[98] From this perspective, it is unlikely that it will weaken the *NPT* more than the opposing positions of nuclear-weapon states and some non-nuclear-weapon states have already done and are likely to do during the 2020 NPT Review Conference.[99]

98 Ramesh Thakur, 'Japan and the Nuclear Weapons Prohibition Treaty: The Wrong Side of History, Geography, Legality, Morality, and Humanity' (2018) 1(1) *Journal for Peace and Nuclear Disarmament* 11, 12.

99 This can be seen by the multiple invocations of the lack of serious action under the *NPT* towards nuclear disarmament under the *NPT*. See, eg, Austria, the Philippines, Algeria (1st plen mtg, 27 March 2017), Egypt and Timor-Leste (2nd plen mtg, 27 March 2017), *Conference Statements* (n 30).

9 The OSCE

A study of the role of 'soft law' in disarmament

*Lisa Tabassi and Treasa Dunworth**

I Introduction

In 1975, 35 states adopted the *Helsinki Final Act*[1] with the objective of 'promoting better relations among themselves and ensuring conditions in which their people can live in true and lasting peace free from any threat to or attempt against their security'.[2] It put in place a mechanism to convene a series of summits between participating states to discuss the matters under its remit — the Conference on Security and Cooperation in Europe ('CSCE').[3] That system of conferences evolved over time to become the Organization for Security and Co-operation in Europe ('OSCE') — the subject matter of this chapter.

There were three so-called 'dimensions' of security in the CSCE/OSCE: a politico-security dimension; an economic and environmental dimension; and a human dimension. Disarmament fell within the politico-security dimension, and participating states agreed to 'take effective measures which by their scope and by their nature constitute steps towards the ultimate achievement of general and complete disarmament under strict and effective international control'.[4]

* We are grateful to Lucy England for her excellent research assistance on aspects of soft law as we prepared this chapter.

1 Conference on Security and Co-operation in Europe ('CSCE'), *Helsinki Final Act*, 1 August 1975 (Web Page) <https://www.osce.org/helsinki-final-act?download=true> ('the *Act*'). The original participating states were Austria, Belgium, Bulgaria, Canada, Cyprus, Czechoslovakia, Denmark, Finland, France, the German Democratic Republic, the Federal Republic of Germany, Greece, the Holy See, Hungary, Iceland, Ireland, Italy, Liechtenstein, Luxembourg, Malta, Monaco, the Netherlands, Norway, Poland, Portugal, Romania, San Marino, Spain, Sweden, Switzerland, Turkey, the Union of Soviet Socialist Republics, the United Kingdom, the United States and Yugoslavia. Today, as the world's largest regional security organization, wthere are 57 participating states with a further 11 states engaged as 'Partners for Co-operation'. See *Organization for Security and Cooperation in Europe* (Web Page) <www.osce.org>.

2 *Helsinki Final Act*, 3. On the history of the negotiations and the perceptions at the time, see Christian Nünlist, 'Helsinki+40 in the Historical Context' (2014) 25(2) *Security and Human Rights* 198, 201–3; David J Galbreath, *The Organization for Security and Co-operation in Europe* (Routledge, 2007), ch 2.

3 *Helsinki Final Act*, 57–8.

4 *Helsinki Final Act*, 9.

Thus, disarmament was an important component of the CSCE/OSCE mandate from the start and there have been significant disarmament achievements in the ensuing decades.[5] Those achievements — and the challenges being faced — have been written about elsewhere.[6] Our focus in this chapter is to explore some questions that arise from the fact that this work has taken place in a soft law paradigm. A soft law setting is unusual in disarmament which generally leans towards strong binding treaty commitments, with strict (obligatory) monitoring of those obligations and the ability of the participating states to impose effective sanctions in response to non-compliance.[7] In our view then, the disarmament work of the OSCE is worthy of study to see how a soft law paradigm might affect its work.

An explanation about our terminology is in order. In this chapter, we draw on and explore a number of closely inter-related concepts. The main term we use, and the one signalled in the title of the chapter, is 'soft law'. For the purposes of this chapter, we use this term to mean moral or political commitments that, notwithstanding their lack of a legally binding character, nevertheless influence the behaviour of actors in their international relations.[8] We use the closely related term 'informal law' to mean cross-border cooperation between public authorities, beyond a traditional international organisation or between non-traditional diplomatic actors (so that might include inter-agency cooperation).[9] Such interactions may or may not result in formal 'binding' law such as a treaty, but often result in what might be considered soft or 'non legally binding' law. In this way,

5 In particular, the 1996 OSCE Framework for Arms Control. See below Part II.

6 See, eg, Lucien Klenjan, 'Conventional Arms Control in Europe: Decline, Disarray, and the Need for Reinvention' (2016) 46(5) *Arms Control Today* 22; Victor-Yves Ghebali, 'Where Is the OSCE Going? Present Role and Challenges of a Stealth Security Organisation' in Thierry Tardy (ed), *European Security in a Global Context: Internal and External Dynamics* (Routledge, 2008) 75; Łukasz Kulesa, 'The Role of Arms Control in Future European Security' (2014) 25(2) *Security and Human Rights* 221; Peter van Ham, *Modernising Conventional Arms Control in the Euro-Atlantic Region* (Clingendael Report, 18 September 2018) (Web Page) <https://www.clingendael.org/sites/default/files/2018-10/Modernizing_CAC.pdf>.

7 See Christopher Daase, 'Coercion and the Informalization of Arms Control' in Oliver Meier and Christopher Daase (eds), *Arms Control in the 21st Century: Between Coercion and Cooperation* (Routledge, 2012) 67. See also Dinah Shelton et al., 'Multilateral Arms Control' in Dinah Shelton (ed), *Commitment and Compliance: The Role of Non-Binding Norms in the International Legal System* (Oxford University Press, 2003) 466, suggesting that we would expect soft law norms to have little role to play but providing case studies of several regimes in which this does in fact happen. See also the discussion by Lipson as to why formal treaties are a preferred route in the arms control context: Charles Lipson, 'Why Are Some International Agreements Informal?' (1991) 45(4) *International Organization* 495, 520.

8 For a detailed overview of soft law, see Christine Chinkin, 'Normative Development in the International Legal System' in Dinah Shelton (ed), *Commitment and Compliance: The Role of Non-Binding Norms in the International Legal System* (Oxford University Press, 2003) 21.

9 Joost Pauwelyn, 'Informal International Lawmaking: Framing the Concept and Research Questions' in Joost Pauwelyn, Ramses Wessel and Jan Wouters (eds), *Informal International Lawmaking* (Oxford University Press, 2012) 13, 22.

informal law is closely related to the idea of soft law, although they are conceptually distinct.[10]

We also refer to 'soft organisations' or 'informal organisations' in the course of the chapter. By this we mean regimes or systems of interstate cooperation that do not take place in a formally constituted organisation (by treaty or otherwise), and which generally (but not necessarily exclusively) create soft law. Both expressions are used in the academic commentary. Daase, for example, uses the term 'informal organisation', meaning 'cooperative arrangements between political actors, state and non-state, which are only weakly institutionalized and therefore less binding than traditional international organizations'.[11] Klabbers, however, refers to these arrangements as 'soft organizations', using the OSCE as an example[12] and explaining his understanding of the concept as being international cooperation which is organised through mechanisms that are 'deliberately kept at the fringes of international law, or even outside it altogether'.[13] For the purposes of this chapter, we use the terms 'soft organisation' and 'informal organisation' interchangeably.[14]

Soft law is the subject of a vast literature among international legal academics. There is a vibrant debate[15] canvassing such issues as whether it exists at all, the extent to which we can speak of soft law's normativity,[16] whether there is, in fact,

10 The differences between the two concepts are discussed in Olivia Herman and Jan Wouters, 'The OSCE as a Case of Informal International Law Making?' in Mateja Steinbrück Platise, Carolyn Moser and Anne Peters (eds), *The Legal Framework of the OSCE* (Cambridge University Press, 2019) 241. Referring to the dynamic between the two concepts as 'deformalisation', van Mulligen explains that deformalisation can often redefine the normative materials that make up international law, making a direct connection to soft law: Anne van Mulligen, 'Framing Deformalisation in Public International Law' (2015) 6(3–4) *Transnational Legal Theory* 635, 636.

11 Daase (n 7) 76. Herman and Wouters also use the term 'informal organizations' while noting that these arrangements are also called 'soft organizations': Herman and Wouters (n 10) 246.

12 There is very much a live debate about the legal status of the OSCE. See Lisa Tabassi, 'The Role of the Organisation in Asserting Legal Personality: The Position of the OSCE's Secretariat on the OSCE's Legal Status' in Mateja Steinbrück Platise, Carolyn Moser and Anne Peters (eds), *The Legal Framework of the OSCE* (Cambridge University Press, 2019) 48; and Carolyn Moser and Anne Peters, 'Legal Uncertainty and Indeterminacy: Immutable Characteristics of the OSCE?' in Mateja Steinbrück Platise, Carolyn Moser and Anne Peters (eds), *The Legal Framework of the OSCE* (Cambridge University Press, 2019) 3.

13 Jan Klabbers, 'Institutional Ambivalence by Design: Soft Organisations in International Law' (2001) 70(3) *Nordic Journal of International Law* 403, 405.

14 See, eg, Angela Di Stasi, 'About Soft International Organizations: An Open Question' in Roberto Virzo and Ivan Ingravello (eds), *Evolutions in the Law of International Organizations* (Brill Nijhoff, 2015) 44, 45.

15 For an outline of the views 'for and against' soft law, see Alexander Demin, 'Soft Law Concept in a Globalized World: Issues and Prospects' (2018) 4 *Journal of the Higher School of Economics* 49.

16 Christine Chinkin, 'The Challenge of Soft Law: Development and Change in International Law' (1989) 38(4) *International and Comparative Law Quarterly* 850.

a binary distinction between 'hard' and 'soft' law,[17] and what are the causes and consequences of the increasing incidence of soft law.[18] Our focus in this chapter is to critically engage with just two aspects of these debates in the specific context of the disarmament work of the OSCE. First, we explore concerns about the transparency and accountability of soft law and informal regimes. Second, we explore concerns about the way in which soft law and informal regimes might exacerbate existing inequalities among ostensibly equal sovereign states. We come to the conclusion that while these concerns are significant in the formation and application of soft law generally, we suggest that they might not have such traction in the OSCE context, although we take the view that there is a great deal more work to be done in the OSCE to guard against these concerns.

We start, in Part II, with a brief overview of the OSCE as a soft law system. As we will show, the OSCE regime can be characterised as 'soft' in two respects: first, in the way in which the OSCE is an informal, or soft, organisation;[19] and second, in the way in which decisions and resolutions emanating from the various bodies within the OSCE are avowedly 'non-binding', constituting only political commitments.

We then turn to consider two aspects of the soft law debates. The first, which we consider in Part III, addresses the concern that it is easier for actors involved in the generation of soft law to be less transparent about their activities and so it is easier to evade (political or legal) accountability. We test this critique in the context of the disarmament work of the OSCE. Our analysis leads us to conclude that while soft law presents additional barriers or complexities in achieving transparency and accountability, the example of the OSCE suggests that there are no *practical* obstacles to providing for greater transparency (because there are, in fact, examples of transparency practice). We argue, however, that there is a *conceptual* barrier to transparency and accountability. This is based on the perception that the OSCE does not generate 'binding law' with real-world impact, and thus, there is less need for transparency or accountability. We argue that this perception is wrong-footed because the OSCE is in fact exercising public functions (and thus does have real-world impact even if its actions are not formally binding) and therefore should be accountable for its work. We explain, and use, the concept of 'international public law' to support this analysis.

The second specific aspect of the soft law debates which we address in this chapter is the concern that soft law regimes might perpetuate and aggravate

17 László Blutman, 'In the Trap of a Legal Metaphor: International Soft Law' (2010) 59 *International and Comparative Law Quarterly* 605; Cynthia Lichtenstein, 'Hard v. Soft Law: Unnecessary Dichotomy?' (2001) 35(4) *International Lawyer* 1433.

18 Jean d'Aspremont, 'Softness in International Law: A Self-Serving Quest for New Legal Materials' (2008) 19(5) *European Journal of International Law* 1075; Eyal Benvenisti, '"Coalitions of the Willing" and the Evolution of Informal International Law' in Christian Calliess, Georg Nolte and Peter-Tobias Stoll (eds), *Coalitions of the Willing: Avantgarde or Threat?* (Carl Heymanns Verlag, 2007) 1. For a discussion on causes in the specific context of arms control, see Daase, (n 7) 68–71.

19 See Klabbers (n 13); Moser and Peters, 'Legal Uncertainty and Indeterminacy' (n 12) 4.

existing power inequalities between states. We explore this concern in Part IV. Drawing on the work of a number of academics challenging the phenomenon of 'coalitions of the willing' because of the way in which they privilege powerful states and marginalise weaker states, we examine how soft law systems can replicate this dynamic and therefore how existing inequalities between states can be exacerbated. In other words, we suggest that soft law regimes are susceptible to the same criticisms that have been levelled against 'coalitions of the willing'. However, when we assess those concerns in light of the disarmament work of the OSCE, we conclude that the concerns, while still relevant, do not have quite the same traction in this context. We suggest two reasons that explain this conclusion: first, the motives lying behind the creation of the OSCE are different to those underpinning many other 'coalitions of the willing'; and second, the *Helsinki Final Act* did not attempt to impinge on the existing rights of states outside the regime it was establishing. While we do not suggest that the OSCE is therefore free from inequality concerns, we do not think that its informal nature is exacerbating inherent inequalities in the system. We conclude in Part V.

II The OSCE as a soft organisation

From the beginning, the OSCE has been avowedly informal in its structure and soft in terms of its outputs. Reflecting this, the *Helsinki Final Act* was never registered as a formal treaty,[20] and no formal organisation was created. Further, the language employed by the drafters clearly signalled their understandings that they were engaged in recording political commitments, rather than binding legal obligations. For example, the language of voluntariness, rather than obligation, was pervasive in the section providing for participating states to allow the exchange of observers — one of the regime's important early confidence building measures. The relevant section provided:

> The participating States will invite other participating States, voluntarily and on a bilateral basis, in a spirit of reciprocity and goodwill towards all participating States, to send observers to attend military manoeuvres.
>
> The inviting State will determine in each case the number of observers, the procedures and conditions of their participation, and give other information which it may consider useful. It will provide appropriate facilities and hospitality.

20 *Helsinki Final Act*, (n1) 59 'The Government of the Republic of Finland is requested to transmit to the Secretary-General of the United Nations the text of this Final Act, which is not eligible for registration under Article 102 of the Charter of the United Nations, with a view to its circulation to all the members of the Organization as an official document of the United Nations'. For a brief account of the discussions at the time, see Galbreath (n 2) 28. For how this non-binding approach repeats through time in various outcome documents, see Moser and Peters, 'Legal Uncertainty and Indeterminacy' (n 12) 7–8.

> The invitation will be given as far ahead as is conveniently possible through usual diplomatic channels.[21]

Similarly, in the provisions relating specifically to disarmament,[22] the participating states recognised that 'this measure deriving from political decision rests upon a voluntary basis'.[23] The *Act* went on:

> The participating States recognize the interest of all of them in efforts aimed at lessening military confrontation and promoting disarmament which are designed to complement political détente in Europe and to strengthen their security. They are convinced of the necessity to take effective measures in these fields which by their scope and by their nature constitute steps towards the ultimate achievement of general and complete disarmament under strict and effective international control, and which should result in strengthening peace and security throughout the world.[24]

The soft nature of the regime prevailed in the post-Cold War world, even as more formal institutional structures were adopted through the *Charter of Paris for a New Europe* signed in 1990[25] and the name changed from the Conference on Security and Cooperation in Europe to the Organization for Security and Cooperation in Europe.[26] In the years since then, there has been gradual institutionalisation and growing formality of the system. For example, there is a permanent Secretariat located in Vienna and various decision-making bodies, including the Summit,[27] the Ministerial Council,[28] the Permanent Council[29] and the Forum for Security Cooperation ('FSC').[30] Despite this drift to

21 *Helsinki Final Act* (n 1), 12.
22 The *Helsinki Final Act* covered much more than disarmament, but the disarmament-related work of the CSCE/OSCE is the sole focus of this chapter. For a discussion of the entire scope of OSCE activities, see Galbreath (n 2).
23 *Helsinki Final Act* (n 1) 11.
24 *Helsinki Final Act* (n 1) 13.
25 Conference on Security and Co-operation in Europe ('CSCE'), *Charter of Paris for a New Europe*, 21 November 1990 (Web Page) <https://www.osce.org/mc/39516?download=true>.
26 CSCE, *Budapest Document 1994: Towards a Genuine Partnership in a New Era*, 6 December 1994, para 3. Note para 22 which provides: 'The Government of Hungary is requested to transmit to the Secretary-General of the United Nations the text of the Budapest Document, which is not eligible for registration under Article 102 of the Charter of the United Nations, with a view to its circulation to all the members of the Organization as an official document of the United Nations'. See also Klabbers (n 13) 413.
27 Summits are gatherings at the highest political level and generally result in a 'Summit Document' or similar, adopted by consensus: Galbreath (n 2) 58.
28 Which is the central decision-making and governing body, composed of the foreign ministers of participating states, which meets between Summits, generally annually.
29 The Permanent Council, is the principal decision-making body for regular political consultations and for governing the day-to-day operational work of the OSCE. Galbreath (n 2) 59–60.
30 The Forum for Security Cooperation is an autonomous decision-making body with a politico-military security mandate set by Summit or Ministerial Council decisions. Galbreath (n 2) 60–1.

formalisation over time, overall the regime has remained faithful to the soft approach signalled in the original *Helsinki Final Act*.[31]

The OSCE not only remains an informal regime, but it generates 'soft law'. All of its bodies adopt decisions by consensus and all such decisions have only a 'politically binding' character.[32] This is also the case with the disarmament work of the OSCE. For example, the FSC was established to specifically address security issues. It develops and helps to implement the various confidence and security building measures which have progressively developed and expanded since their original creation at the first Helsinki Summit. Devised as a platform for the exchange of views (yet another indication of the soft law paradigm), its decisions (taken by consensus) are only 'politically binding'.[33] For example, in the field of regulating small arms and light weapons ('SALW'), the OSCE adopted a *Document on Small Arms and Light Weapons*,[34] which went on to influence United Nations work on SALW, and ultimately the conclusion of the *Arms Trade Treaty*, opened for signature 3 June 2013, 3013 UNTS (entered into force 24 December 2014) opened for signature 3 June 2013, 3013 UNTS (entered into force 24 December 2014).[35] And yet, it was a soft law mechanism. Similarly, disarmament work within various OSCE assistance missions in the destruction of surplus stockpiles of SALW and conventional ammunition have emanated from soft law 'directives'.[36] Other important, and effective, soft law initiatives have taken place in eliminating, neutralising or converting stores of highly toxic, volatile and obsolete rocket fuel stored in deteriorated sites in corroded, partly leaking containers.[37]

31 Some writers refer to the 'shaky legal foundations' and this does raise a number of practical issues including working out the privileges and immunities available (or otherwise) to officials of the OSCE and identifying whether international responsibility can attach to the OSCE. Although undoubtedly important, these debates are not our focus here. See generally Moser and Peters, 'Legal Uncertainty and Indeterminacy' (n 12) 5.

32 OSCE, Ministerial Council, *Rules of Procedure of the Organization for Security and Co-Operation in Europe*, Doc No MC.DOC/1/06, 1 November 2006, II(A), para 2 on consensus, and paras 1 and 3 on the politically binding nature of decisions < https://www.osce.org/mc/22775?download=true> ('*Rules of Procedure*'). See also Moser and Peters, 'Legal Uncertainty and Indeterminacy' (n 16) 8.

33 CSCE, *Helsinki Document 1992: The Challenges of Change*, 9–10 July 1992, Part V, para 9. See also comments by Zdenek Matejka, 'OSCE and its Impact on State Policies' (1996) 6/7 *Perspectives* 101, 105.

34 *OSCE Document on Small Arms and Light Weapons*, Doc No FSC.DOC/1/00, 24 November 2000.

35 See the detailed discussion by Paul Holtom, 'The OSCE and the Arms Trade Treaty: Complementarity and Lessons Learned' in Institute for Peace Research and Security Policy at the University of Hamburg (ed), *OSCE Yearbook 2015* (Nomos-Verlag, 2016) 327.

36 See, eg, OSCE, *Destruction of Conventional Ammunition*, Doc No FSC.DEC/3/11, 23 March 2011. See also OSCE, *Stabillizing Measures for Localized Crisis Situations*, Doc No DOC.FSC/2/96, 25 November 1993; OSCE, *Code of Conduct on Politico-Military Aspects of Security*, Doc No DOC.FSC/1/95, 3 December 1994; OSCE, Update of the OSCE *Principles Governing Non-Proliferation*, Doc No FSC.DEC/7/13, 4 December 2013; OSCE, *Best Practice Guides on Small Arms and Light Weapons*, Doc No FSC.DEC/5/03, 18 June 2003.

37 OSCE, *Liquid Rocket Fuel in the OSCE Area: Overview of Disposal Aspects*, Doc No FSC.DEL/443/07/Rev.2, 23 October 2008.

Although fundamentally a soft law regime, there are two important arms control treaties which emerged under the umbrella of the OSCE: the *Treaty on Conventional Armed Forces in Europe* ('*CFE Treaty*')[38] which was concluded in 1990 and the *Treaty on Open Skies*[39] concluded in 1992. The *CFE Treaty* imposed numerical limits on its states parties in respect of five categories of heavy weapons and related technologies.[40] The *Treaty on Open Skies* provided for a system whereby states parties can conduct short-notice, unarmed observation flights over the territories of other states parties to collect data on military forces and activities.[41] These treaties, while not creatures of the OSCE, are intimately connected with that system in a number of ways. First, the negotiations for both were supported by the OSCE. Second, the implementing and oversight body created by the *Treaty on Open Skies*, the Open Skies Consultative Commission ('OSCC'), convenes its monthly meetings at the OSCE Headquarters. Similarly, the Joint Consultative Group ('JCG') created to oversee the implementation of the CFE also meets at OSCE Headquarters and comprises the heads of the OSCE delegations. In this way, the OSCE can be seen as a kind of guardian of both treaties, although of course it is not the direct implementing or enforcement body for either of them (and not all 57 OSCE states are party to them).

In more recent years, the OSCE has come under increasing pressure as the overall strategic environment, specifically NATO-Russian relations, has once again deteriorated.[42] Consideration of precisely why and how that has happened is beyond the scope of this chapter.[43] However, it is interesting to note that one

38 *Treaty on Conventional Armed Forces in Europe*, signed 19 November 1990, 30 ILM 1 (entered into force 17 July 1992) ('*CFE Treaty*'). Note that the dissolution of the Soviet Union and the *Warsaw Pact* resulted in making the system created by the *CFE Treaty* redundant, which in turn resulted in an *Adaptation Agreement* being agreed in 1999. However, this has not entered into force due to the deterioration of the strategic environment. The Russian Federation suspended its engagement with the *CFE Treaty* in 2007, and in 2015, it ended its participation in the Joint Consultative Group ('JCG'). For discussion, see Zdzislaw Lachowski, 'Conventional Arms Control' (2008) *SIPRI Yearbook* 471; Max Schterngel, 'Bucking Conventional Wisdom: Russia's Unilateral "Suspension" of the CFE Treaty' (2008) 33(3) *Brooklyn Journal of International Law* 1037; John Kierulf, *Disarmament under International Law* (Djøf Publishing, 2017) 176–9.

39 *Treaty on Open Skies*, signed 24 March 1992, [2002] UKTS 27 (entered into force 1 January 2002).

40 Being battle tanks, armoured combat vehicles, artillery, combat aircraft and combat helicopters: *CFE Treaty* (n 38) art I, para 1 and arts III–XII.

41 See discussion by Hartwig Spitzer, *News from Open Skies: A Co-operative Treaty Maintaining Military Transparency* (VERTIC Brief No 8, February 2009) 2.

42 See Wolfgang Richter, *Return to Security Cooperation in Europe: The Stabilizing Role of Conventional Arms Control* (Deep Cuts Working Paper No 11, September 2017).

43 For a variety of positions, see Wolfgang Richter, *The Implications of the State of Conventional Arms Control for European Security* (Deep Cuts Working Paper No 12, August 2018); Johan Engvall, Gudrun Persson (eds), Robert Dalsjö, Carolina Vendil Pallin and Mike Winnerstig, *Conventional Arms Control: A Way Forward or Wishful Thinking?* (Swedish Defence Research Agency Report No FOI-R--4586--SE, April 2018); Patricia Flor, Alexander Brushko and Alexander Vershbow, 'Revitalizing Arms Control' (2016) 3 *Security Community* 6. See also the collection of essays in the Special Issue of *Security and Human Rights*: 'Special

of the OSCE key responses to this deterioration – the Structured Dialogue – is a soft law mechanism. The Structured Dialogue was an initiative which started in 2016, led by the then German Foreign Minister and then Chair of the OSCE, Frank-Walter Steinmeier, and was supported by a number of other states (the 'Group of Like-Minded States'). Steinmeier called for a renewed dialogue on conventional arms control in Europe in response to the deteriorating strategic situation. It was thus an attempt to overcome the impasse at the time, to reverse the deterioration in the Russian-NATO relationship and specifically to create a platform to exchange ideas on threat perceptions and so diffuse tensions and re-build some trust and confidence.[44] On this last aim, it was a clear echo of the original Helsinki Process itself: an ideal of dialogue as a means of building a more trusting relationship. As to whether it will succeed on any level remains to be seen,[45] but for our purposes in this chapter, it shows an attempt to revert to dialogue and to do that in an informal, fluid and soft way.

Thus, we can see that the OSCE system generally, and its disarmament work specifically, has evolved and adapted over time to respond to fundamental changes in the strategic environment. The regime was soft and informal from the start, and has remained so over time. Even when the Cold War ended, and the new system was instituted, it did not turn to a 'harder' system in the sense of a shift to binding treaties and the creation of a formal organisation. Similarly, as the Russian-NATO relationship has deteriorated in more recent times, along with the essential collapse of the *CFE Treaty*, the soft law approach has persisted.

In the following parts of the chapter, drawing on existing critiques of soft law, we examine two possible implications about the prevalence of soft law in the OSCE regime. The first enquiry is whether the soft law nature of the system compromises or limits opportunities for accountability and transparency — we discuss this in Part III. The second concern about soft law which we discuss is whether it might exacerbate inequalities between states. We examine this concern in Part IV.

III Concerns about transparency and accountability

A Introduction

Concerns that are frequently expressed about soft law are, first, that it can be difficult to achieve transparency[46] in how soft law is formulated and applied, and

Issue: Helsinki+40: The Organization for Security and Co-operation in Europe Under a Stress Test' (2014) 25(4) *Security and Human Rights*.

44 Five key areas were defined for discussion: (1) to define regional ceilings, minimum distances and transparency measures; (2) to take into account new military capabilities and strategies; (3) to integrate new weapons systems; (4) to permit effective verification; and (5) to agree measures to be applied in areas whose territorial status is disputed.

45 See also the reservations expressed by van Ham (n 6).

46 As to the assumptions about transparency as a constituting a 'good', see Andrea Bianchi, 'On Power and Illusion: The Concept of Transparency in International Law' in Andrea Bianchi and Anne Peters (eds), *Transparency in International Law* (Cambridge University Press, 2013) 1.

second, that devising a means of accountability[47] for soft law's operation and impact can be challenging.[48] This part explores these concerns and considers the extent to which they have traction in the context of the OSCE generally and its disarmament work specifically. We take the view that there are indeed additional barriers to achieving transparency and accountability in soft law regimes (and thus in the OSCE). However, we conclude that the example of the OSCE shows that these barriers are not *practical* but rather are *conceptual* in that they stem from a mind-set that sees soft law as ineffectual and therefore not requiring the same (or any) level of transparency and/or accountability. We suggest that the frame of 'international public authority' might allow us to see that even in informal organisations, public authority is in fact being exercised (whether it results in 'binding' or 'soft' law), and that therefore there ought to be some mechanisms for greater transparency and accountability in such organisations.[49] While this framing does not itself suggest or present processes or mechanisms to achieve those outcomes, it does at least defend against the argument that such processes or mechanisms have no place in soft law regimes.

B *Transparency and accountability in soft law regimes*

A key criticism of soft law regimes is that they lack transparency, making it more difficult to render decision-makers accountable (or even identifiable).[50] Klabbers, for example, notes that while the shift to a soft approach can often be motivated by a perceived need for efficiency, the resulting organisations or regimes then tend to harbour executive power, which is exercised unchecked.[51] Moser (writing in the specific context of the OSCE) expresses concerns about the lack of accountability in informal organisations, pointing out that the legal status of an organisation is not the key factor in determining whether accountability is required, but rather the core question is whether the organisation in question

47 In this context we use the term 'accountability' to mean that those who exercise power should be required to report to the citizens who are affected by their actions: Beat Habegger, 'Democratic Accountability of International Organizations: Parliamentary Control within the Council of Europe and the OSCE and the Prospects for the United Nations' (2010) 45(2) *Cooperation and Conflict* 186, 188.

48 Klabbers (n 13); Carolyn Moser, 'Conceptualising Accountability in the Legal and Institutional Framework of the OSCE' in Mateja Steinbrück Platise, Carolyn Moser and Anne Peters (eds), *The Legal Framework of the OSCE* (Cambridge University Press, 2019) 273; Benvenisti (n 18).

49 For an introduction to the ideas of international public authority, see Armin von Bogdandy, Matthias Goldmann and Ingo Venzke, 'From Public International to International Public Law: Translating World Public Opinion into International Public Authority' (2017) 28(1) *European Journal of International Law* 115.

50 Klabbers (n 13) 420. Moser, 'Conceptualising Accountability' (n 48) 289 says that transparency is key to accountability because information-sharing and understanding is the first step in accountability.

51 Klabbers (n 13) 407.

actually exercises public power in the international realm.[52] If so, then there ought to be a corresponding accountability of that organisation.[53] Benvenisti also raises concerns about the way in which informal regimes raise issues of lack of accountability and transparency.[54] Van Mulligen discusses how deformalised systems undermine opportunities for political contestation which is usual, and beneficial, in the processes of norm-setting and decision-making.[55]

All of these general critiques have traction in the context of disarmament,[56] although of course it must be noted that questions of transparency and accountability are far from resolved even in the case of formal disarmament regimes and binding treaty law dealing with security issues.[57] In contrast to other areas of international law (for example, human rights, the environment, international criminal law to mention a few), disarmament organisations and regimes have been less open to civil society, and generally are less transparent about their work.[58] While there are important signs of change,[59] it remains the case that disarmament regimes remain generally less transparent and less amenable to accountability mechanisms.

However, in informal disarmament regimes which generate soft law, the traditional resistance to transparency and accountability is compounded. In addition to the existing wariness, there is also a sense that because the informal regimes are 'not binding', their decisions and resolutions are somehow inconsequential. That in turn can lead to the sense that those regimes and their resulting decisions do not give rise to the same need for transparency or accountability. In the next section, we explain how this dynamic plays out in the context of the OSCE, including in its disarmament work.

52 Moser, 'Conceptualising Accountability' (n 48) 282.

53 Ibid.

54 Benvenisti (n 18).

55 van Mulligen (n 10) 642.

56 And indeed, Moser's work is written in the specific context of the OSCE. She points out that accountability is rarely discussed in the OSCE context and when it has been discussed, it often relates to issues of responsibility and liability rather than being concerned with internal institutional accountability: Moser, 'Conceptualising Accountability' (n 48) 274. She further points out that, as with the Security Council, many of the inter-governmental bodies within the OSCE pass resolutions about accountability — but accountability of other entities, not its own work: Moser, 'Conceptualising Accountability' (n 48) 286. See as well Daase (n 7) 73.

57 See, eg, Treasa Dunworth, 'Towards a Culture of Legality in International Organizations: The Case of the OPCW' (2008) 5 *International Organizations Law Review* 119; Tobias Weise, 'Participation and Transparency in Intergovernmental Security Organizations: Resource and Norm Driven Opening in the IAEA and OPCW' (PhD Thesis, University of Bremen, 2016).

58 See the discussion by Treasa Dunworth, 'Accountability of International Organisations: The Potential Role of NGOs in the Work of Disarmament Bodies' 14 (2016) *New Zealand Journal of Public and International Law* 47, 55–7.

59 See the discussion by Weise (n 57) who traces the ways in which the Organisation for the Prohibition of Chemical Weapons and the International Atomic Energy Agency ('IAEA') have been, in his words, 'opening up'.

C *Transparency and accountability in the OSCE in practice*

The OSCE illustrates how concerns about transparency and accountability have traction in soft law settings although, as we will show, there have been some successful efforts to alleviate these concerns. Despite these efforts, there is clearly scope for further improvements.

Participation and even attendance in the inter-governmental bodies of the OSCE are relatively closed. For example, the rules of procedure make no provision for 'observers', and all meetings are closed unless decided otherwise by the participating states.[60] There is only brief admission for media in some circumstances.[61] There are some avenues for broader engagement. For example, the rules of procedure for the Ministerial Council meetings provide for participating states to invite states from the Mediterranean and Asian Partners for Cooperation[62] to attend, as well as some other international organisations and even non-governmental organisations.[63] However, overall, the OSCE tends towards being less open and transparent in the work of its decision-making bodies.[64]

This lack of transparency is even more pronounced in the specific context of the disarmament work of the OSCE. Meetings of the FSC are closed.[65] Even the meetings of the more recently established Structured Dialogue,[66] which is an informal working group of the OSCE, are open only to OSCE participating states with the press and public excluded.[67] There are no official records kept of the meetings.[68] Without the transparency that broader participation (or even record-keeping) would facilitate, accountability becomes much more difficult as the decision-makers, and the process through which decisions are arrived at, become much more difficult to identify and understand.

That being said, there have been attempts to, and calls for, greater transparency and accountability in the OSCE. A significant initiative in this respect was the creation, in 1991, of the OSCE Parliamentary Assembly ('Assembly') as part

60 OSCE, *Rules of Procedure* (n 32) IV.1(D), paras 2–6.

61 Ibid., para 6.

62 The Asian Partners for Cooperation (Afghanistan, Australia, Japan, Republic of Korea and Thailand) and the Mediterranean Partners for Cooperation (Algeria, Egypt, Israel, Jordan, Morocco and Tunisia) are groupings of states with which the OSCE has a 'privileged relationship' with in order to 'better address shared security challenges'. See 'Partners for Co-operation', *OSCE* (Web Page) <www.osce.org/partners-for-cooperation>.

63 OSCE, *Rules of Procedure* (n 32) IV. 2(B), paras 6–10.

64 See the detailed discussion by Moser, 'Conceptualising Accountability' (n 48) 286–9, making the point that there is some accountability within the bureaucracy in relation to operational actors in terms of reporting upwards (what she terms 'hierarchical accountability'). In contrast, the strategic decision-making organs appear to have no accountability other than to (perhaps) their domestic constituencies.

65 OSCE, *Rules of Procedure* (n 32) IV.2(C), para 5.

66 'The OSCE Structured Dialogue', *OSCE* (Web Page) <www.osce.org/structured-dialogue>.

67 OSCE, *Rules of Procedure* (n 32) V(B), para 5. Interestingly, one of the guiding principles of the Structured Dialogue is transparency.

68 OSCE, *Rules of Procedure* (n 32) V(B), para 2.

of the drive towards democratisation, which was a feature of the immediate post-Cold War period.[69] While the initial focus (and intention) was on parliamentary diplomacy, not oversight of the inter-governmental bodies, that has changed over time as the Assembly has become more assertive. For example, in 1999, the Assembly, noting the importance of democratic oversight and accountability within the OSCE, recommended that prior to making major decisions (a term that remained undefined), the OSCE Ministerial Council should be obliged to ask the opinion of the Assembly,[70] and proposed that members of the Assembly should have the right to submit written questions to the Chairman-in-Office of the Ministerial Council.[71] Two years later, the Assembly returned to the question of accountability and set out more detailed proposals to that end, including the creation of an ad hoc Committee to promote transparency and accountability in the OSCE.[72] Despite repeated calls over the years for the Assembly to have a stronger oversight role, this has yet to eventuate.[73]

There have also been attempts to engage more directly with the public. For example, the OSCE hosts 'Security Days' which gather civil society together with representatives of OSCE participating states and OSCE officials.[74] Further, the OSCE Network of Think Tanks and Academic Institutions publishes periodic research.[75]

While it remains the case that the OSCE continues to be less than transparent and accountable,[76] the developments above illustrate that there are steps available to the various OSCE bodies and organs to enhance transparency and

69 See Andreas Nothelle, 'The OSCE Parliamentary Assembly — Driving Reform' in Institute for Peace Research and Security Policy at the University of Hamburg (ed), *OSCE Yearbook 2006* (Nomos-Verlag, 2007), 347. On the role of parliamentary assemblies in addressing problems of democratic deficit generally, see Habegger (n 47).

70 OSCE Parliamentary Assembly, *Resolution on Correcting the Democratic Deficit of the OSCE* (St Petersburg, 1999), para 7. See Nothelle (n 69) 357.

71 OSCE Parliamentary Assembly, *Resolution on Correcting the Democratic Deficit of the OSCE* (n 70) para 10.

72 OSCE Parliamentary Assembly, *Resolution on Strengthening Transparency and Accountability in the OSCE* (Paris, 2001), paras 7–12. See Moser, 'Conceptualising Accountability' (n 48) 289 n 67 for a list of the resolutions passed by the Assembly on the question of transparency and accountability.

73 See, eg, OSCE Parliamentary Assembly, *Resolution on Strengthening Relations between the OSCE Parliamentary Assembly and the OSCE* (Tbilisi, 2016).

74 See Kurt Tudyka, 'Non-Governmental Organizations and the OSCE' in Institute for Peace Research and Security Policy at the University of Hamburg (ed), *OSCE Yearbook 2001* (Nomos-Verlag, 2002) 465, 468–74.

75 See generally, Wolfgang Zellner, 'The OSCE Network of Think Tanks and Academic Institutions: Baby Steps' in Institute for Peace Research and Security Policy at the University of Hamburg (ed), *OSCE Yearbook 2013* (Nomos-Verlag, 2014) 269.

76 The Parliamentary Assembly continues to express concern about the 'continuing democratic deficit'. See, eg, the Final Declarations from 2013 to 2016: discussed by Herman and Wouters (n 10) 253. This is also the assessment in the academic commentary: see Moser, 'Conceptualising Accountability' (n 48) 290; Habegger (n 47).

accountability.[77] Indeed, the informal nature of the OSCE may well have made it easier in some ways to promote accountability because its very informality makes it easier to change internal structures and would not necessitate, for example, treaty amendments nor would it have to overcome the political inertia which can stagnate more formalised systems.[78] Indeed, adaptability is a point of pride for the OSCE: it was designed as an informal structure precisely to allow for dialogue, change and adaptability. It has the capacity to adapt to become more transparent and accountable.

D *Transparency and accountability of the OSCE: the conceptual challenge*

Clearly then, as a matter of practice, some moves towards accountability have been achievable within the OSCE – however imperfect and incomplete. The fact that overall accountability is still woefully inadequate, particularly as regards the disarmament work of the OSCE, is probably in large part simply a reflection of the fact that decision-makers are inevitably reluctant to open up their work to scrutiny.[79] However, in our view, there is a further obstacle at play in this context, and that is a conceptual barrier. By this we mean that the idea that because the soft law which emerges from the regime is non-binding, and therefore purely political, it might be of less consequence and therefore there is less — or no — need for systems of accountability.[80] We reject this line of thinking and we argue that the need for transparency and accountability is apparent even in informal regimes generating 'only' soft law.

We find support for our position in the idea of an 'international public law', which has emerged from the work of the Heidelberg Project.[81] According to those authors, the exercise of international public authority by an international institution occurs where that institution claiming to pursue a common interest unilaterally acts in a way that determines the legal or factual situation of another

77 It is not possible (in this project at least) to judge whether or not these steps towards transparency and accountability have resulted in better decision-making, improved legitimacy, opportunities for redress or any other asserted tangible benefits of increased transparency and accountability. See, eg, Ngaire Woods, 'Good Governance in International Organizations' (1999) 5(1) *Global Governance* 39.

78 Moser, 'Conceptualising Accountability' (n 48) 292; Herman and Wouters (n 10) 250 discussing the failed attempt to formalise the relationship between the Parliamentary Assembly and the executive OSCE bodies. Klabbers questions the benefits of flexibility: Klabbers (n 13) 421.

79 Daase (n 7) 70.

80 This idea is a specific instance of the broader understanding that informal regimes exist extra-legally and therefore are not easily amenable to legal constraints. See, eg, Klabbers (n 13) 411 and Lipson (n 13) 500–1. See also the discussion, and sources mentioned, by von Bogdandy, Dann and Goldmann, 'From Public International to International Public Law' (n 49) 123.

81 Armin von Bogdandy, Philipp Dann and Matthias Goldmann, 'Developing the Publicness of Public International Law: Towards a Legal Framework for Global Governance Activities' (2008) 9(11) *German Law Journal* 1375.

legal subject.[82] Their key point is that international public authority can be exercised in informal (ostensibly non-binding) ways and contexts and still affect the rights and interests of members of the public.[83] On that basis, they argue that any act that significantly impacts upon individual freedom or political self-determination ought to be subject to scrutiny and accountability.[84] Moser has also explored this idea in her work and specifically in relation to the OSCE's work.[85] She argues that neither the legal status of an organisation, nor the categorisation of its resulting decisions or resolutions as extra-legal or non-binding is relevant in working out whether there should be accountability for those acts. She says that the question is only whether the decisions and resolutions are, in fact, exercises of public authority in the international realm.[86]

In our view, this way of thinking can be usefully applied to the OSCE's work on disarmament. In pursuing its disarmament activities (whether at the decision-making level, or operationally), the OSCE is claiming to pursue a common interest and it does affect members of the public. Think, for example, of its work in field operations on the collection of SALW, the rehabilitation of areas contaminated with explosives or overseeing the destruction of SALW and conventional ammunition.[87] In all of these situations, accountability is necessary regardless of whether those actions are taking place in a legally binding framework or not.[88]

However, even if this conceptual reframing is accepted that would not, by itself, provide the tools, processes or procedures to achieve greater accountability in practice. We take the view that there is no shortage of ideas about *how* transparency and accountability could be enhanced. A good start would be to implement the proposals by the Assembly in 2013 set out in its *Resolution on Enhancing Trust, Transparency and Accountability within the OSCE Institutions.*[89] These included suggestions that there be greater oversight of the OSCE budget and the appointment of the Secretary General of the OSCE including by means

82 Ibid., 1382. As the authors go onto explain this might happen through regulations or decisions, but also through the dissemination of information.

83 Ibid.

84 Ibid., 1383.

85 Moser, 'Conceptualising Accountability' (n 48) 274.

86 Ibid.

87 The activities of the OSCE in its various field operations are detailed at: 'Arms Control', *OSCE* (Web Page) <www.osce.org/arms-control>. Some of the problems that arise in the various missions are discussed by Pál Dunay, 'Improve What You Can – Ignore What You Can't: Reform and the Prospects of the OSCE' in Institute for Peace Research and Security Policy at the University of Hamburg (ed), *OSCE Yearbook 2004* (Nomos-Verlag, 2005) 41.

88 As to why accountability is desirable in this context see Moser, who argues that accountability promotes legitimacy and ultimately the effectiveness of the operation: Moser, 'Conceptualising Accountability' (n 48) 290–2.

89 OSCE Parliamentary Assembly, *Istanbul Declaration*, Doc No AS (13) D E, 29 June–3 July 2013, 18.

of the appointment of an external auditor,[90] and that the Assembly have the authority to organise its own fact-finding missions.[91]

IV Concerns about inequality

A Introduction

A second concern which arises in the context of soft law is that it can perpetuate and aggravate inequality among ostensibly equal sovereign states. Our view on this is that while there is clearly an increased risk that soft law systems might obscure power and power differentials, we also hold the view that soft law systems can operate not so much to perpetuate inequality but to provide a more open space for interaction and dialogue. We suggest that there is nothing inherently more unequal about informality, although we do acknowledge that informality carries with it a higher risk of perpetuating inequality (in part due to the transparency issues which we discussed in the preceding part).

In this part, we first explain in general terms the concern that informality can obscure power and we then turn to analyse the OSCE in particular to show why, in our view, this critique may not have complete traction in this particular context. While much of our analysis relates to the OSCE generally, we think that the same dynamics play out in the OSCE's disarmament work, although we concede that a closer study of the disarmament work of the OSCE would need to be done in order to make a more fully informed determination. For now, we suggest two reasons why the critique might not have so much traction in the context of the OSCE. These relate to the motives for establishing the soft regime and the fact that the OSCE (generally and in the context of disarmament) echoed and endorsed the prevailing rules of the contemporary multilateral system and did not attempt to impinge on the existing rights of states outside the regime. In our analysis, while we take the position that the OSCE can be favourably compared to other informal regimes (such as the Proliferation Security Initiative 'PSI') in terms of not exacerbating inequality among participating states, we should not be understood to be making an argument that there are no equality problems in the OSCE.[92]

Before we explore concerns about inequality in soft regimes, it is important to acknowledge that inequality is endemic even (or perhaps, especially) in formal organisations. Many commentators, particularly those from the critical schools of thought, have shown how despite the ostensible 'level playing fields' in international organisations, the fact is that not all states are in a position to participate equally. Chimni, for example, argues that international institutions are

90 Ibid. Paras 7–9.

91 Ibid. Para 10.

92 And indeed, in the light of the growing chasm between Russia and the NATO states within the OSCE, it is clear that there are difficulties: see van Ham (n 6).

an 'imperial global state in the making'[93] because of the way in which organisations perpetuate inequalities between states in the guise of multilateralism. Other commentators have shown how there is widespread concern that many formal organisations are failing to respect sovereign equality in practice, whether that is through some form of weighted voting, or more subtle forms of privileging the interests and values of some (more powerful) states than others.[94] Much inequality also lies in the very disparate levels of material resources available to states; in the ability of states to attend meetings and follow debates, report back to and receive instructions from capitals; and in the access that states have to documentation and even interpretation facilities.[95] All of the above factors lead Alvarez to conclude that state power, and therefore differentials in state power, continues to play out in formally equal international organisations.[96]

B *Informal regimes and inequality between states*

A number of academic commentators have explored the concern that informal regimes generating soft law obscure, and therefore exacerbate, power within soft regimes. For example, the scholars working within the Heidelberg Project point out that informality is frequently presented as a means of being efficient and 'getting things done', but argue that a consequence of such regimes (often 'mini-lateral' in nature) is that less powerful states can find themselves marginalised and unable to meaningfully participate in the work and decision-making of the organisation in question.[97] Daase, writing in the specific context of nuclear weapons possession, points out that informal inequality is endemic among states even in formal settings but argues that informalisation perpetuates that inequality, rather than being a leveller which can sometimes happen in domestic politics.[98] Benvenisti makes this point in the context of diverse settings including in the area of combating the proliferation of weapons of mass destruction ('WMD'), financial regulations and health regulations.[99] He argues that such systems can disguise and perpetuate inequalities between states.

Rodiles explores the point in detail in his study of the PSI, and shows how its mode of informal cooperation privileges the more powerful states.[100] The PSI

93 BS Chimni, 'International Institutions Today: An Imperial Global State in the Making' (2004) 15(1) *European Journal of International Law* 1.

94 José E Alvarez, 'International Organizations: Then and Now' (2006) 100(2) *American Journal of International Law* 324, 341–2.

95 This observation arises from the authors' own experiences in a range of different international settings and negotiations.

96 Alvarez (n 94) 346.

97 Bogdandy, Dann and Goldmann, 'Developing the Publicness of Public International Law' (n 81).

98 Daase (n 7) 71–2.

99 Benvenisti (n 18) 24–6.

100 Alejandro Rodiles, *Coalitions of the Willing and International Law: The Interplay between Formality and Informality* (Cambridge University Press, 2018) 98.

was launched by then United States President George W Bush in 2003 as an informal group of states, with a common goal of combating the proliferation of WMD. Specifically, the PSI provides for national authorities of participating states to co-ordinate efforts to combat the transfer of WMD to and from states and non-state actors that are considered by many in the international community to be proliferation risks. In operational terms, most of this co-ordination involves the interdiction of vessels at sea.[101] Importantly for our purposes here, the PSI gives rise to no formal law — the actions of participating states are guided (in fact, determined) by a Statement of Interdiction Principles ('Principles').[102] Rodiles traces how the initial core group of states, led by the United States, developed these Principles, what we might call the PSI 'rules of the road'. Even as the PSI evolved to include 'extended core members' and today has more than 100 'endorsing' states (allowing it to be presented as being genuinely multilateral),[103] the core operational rules and founding values remain as they were created and locked in by an exclusive and powerful group of states — the original 'coalition of the willing'.[104] Of particular concern in the PSI context is that the soft law which emerged from the original coalition ultimately was transformed into hard law in the form of binding Security Council resolutions.[105]

C Does soft law exacerbate inequality in the OSCE?

In our view, while these critiques of 'coalitions of the willing' are persuasive and concerning, we are not convinced that a soft law dynamic, or an informal regime, inevitably creates or perpetuates existing inequality among states. In this section, using the OSCE as our specific example, we set out two factors to consider as to why a soft law dynamic does not necessarily exacerbate inequalities between states.

1 Intention matters

First, intention matters. While we accept that the intention of the founders of a regime might not be determinative in whether or not inequalities arise, we suggest that the underlying motives or reasons for establishing an informal or

101 Ibid., 96.

102 Ibid., 98–104. The Principles are available at 'Statement of Interdiction Principles', *Proliferation Security Initiative* (Web Page, 14 May 2018) <https://www.psi-online.info/psi-info-en/botschaft/-/2077920>.

103 At the time of writing, there were 107 states listed on the PSI's webpage as being 'endorsing states': 'Endorsing States List', *Proliferation Security Initiative* (Web Page, 2 April 2019) <https://www.psi-online.info/psi-info-en/botschaft/-/2205942>.

104 Rodiles (n 100) 98–104.

105 Discussed by Benvenisti (n 18). The possibility of soft law becoming or evolving into a form of hard law (either in treaties, by Security Council resolutions or as customary international law) is often touted as one of its advantages, but the example here points to more worrying aspects of this dynamic: see generally, Demin (n 15) 67.

soft regime do influence the extent to which inequality among states is likely to result. For example, and as Rodiles explains, the motivation behind the PSI was a desire to *avoid* multilateralism with all its perceived inefficiencies and the need for consensus and compromise.[106] Almost inevitably then, the resulting informal exercise of 'mini-lateralism' operates as an exclusionary practice and therefore privileges the core states involved from the outset at the expense of the marginalised states, even those that subsequently joined the PSI on a 'take it or leave it' basis.

In contrast, the 'softness' of the OSCE was not devised as a means of aggregating power to a small cohort of states; rather, it was devised as a means of creating a space for East-West dialogue. It was aimed at dialogue, not division. As signalled earlier, the seeds of the OSCE lie in a time of tension between the NATO and *Warsaw Pact* states and arose out of the Helsinki Process — very much a fluid, soft and informal series of inter-governmental conferences convened from 1973 onwards. The *Helsinki Final Act* which emerged from this process was envisaged primarily as a mechanism of cooperation and dialogue between the two blocs. Indeed, far from being born of a 'dogma of efficiency', the *Helsinki Final Act* recognised the critical role that dialogue had to play in building trust and relationships, and thereby promoted better relationships between them. It was aimed at creating better conditions for multilateral relationships. In the *Act*, the states declared:

> Considering that solidarity among peoples, as well as the common purpose of the participating States in achieving the aims as set forth by the Conference on Security and Cooperation in Europe, should lead to the development of better and closer relations among them in all fields and thus to overcoming the confrontation stemming from the character of their past relations, and to better mutual understanding.[107]

We accept that the question of motive does not, by itself, preclude inequalities from emerging or even from being perpetuated. However, we do take the view that if the motive or intention at the outset is to preclude broader engagement so as to set the 'rules of the game' with little or no need to compromise with different state interests, then the resulting regime is likely to exacerbate inequalities between states. If this has not been the underlying motive, then we suggest that an informal system is not inevitably more prone to inequalities than any formal system.

2 Strengthening existing rules

A second factor to consider in assessing whether a soft regime is exacerbating inequality between states relates to the content of the rules in the new regime. This

106 Rodiles (n 100) 98.
107 *Helsinki Final Act*, 3.

matters because the informal regimes which do attempt to carve out their own special regime often do so at the expense of the legal rights of other states and in this way a dynamic of inequality is created. The PSI, again, is a good example of this. The system of interdiction established by the initiative arguably violates long-standing rules of the law of the sea including freedom of the high seas and the rights of states regarding their territorial seas.[108] This is despite the fact that the Principles refer to the need for participating states to act consistently with their international obligations.[109] In this way, the PSI represents a challenge to the rights of other states conferred by the law of the sea (by treaty or otherwise).

In contrast, the OSCE regime was an attempt to complement the international legal order, rather than carve out a special regime for its participating states. For example, the *Helsinki Final Act* echoed key provisions from the Charter of the United Nations ('*UN Charter*') with its references to developing 'friendly relations and co-operation' and specifically refers to the intention of the participating states to adhere to the principles of the *UN Charter*:

> Expressing their common adherence to the principles which are set forth below and are in conformity with the Charter of the United Nations, as well as their common will to act, in the application of these principles, in conformity with the purposes and principles of the Charter of the United Nations.[110]

Looking specifically at the disarmament provisions of the *Helsinki Final Act*, these also complemented existing disarmament law provisions (as they were at the time) and did not attempt to infringe on the existing rights of other states or curtail the responsibilities of its own participating states. Recall that the *Helsinki Final Act* provided:

> The participating States recognize the interest of all of them in efforts aimed at lessening military confrontation and promoting disarmament which are designed to complement political détente in Europe and to strengthen their security. They are convinced of the necessity to take effective measures in these fields which by their scope and by their nature constitute steps towards the ultimate achievement of general and complete disarmament under strict and effective international control, and which should result in strengthening peace and security throughout the world.[111]

108 See generally, Douglas Guilfoyle, 'The Proliferation Security Initiative: Interdicting Vessels in International Waters to Prevent the Spread of Weapons of Mass Destruction' (2005) 29 *Melbourne University Law Review* 733 and Douglas Guilfoyle, 'Maritime Interdiction of Weapons of Mass Destruction' (2007) 12 (1) *Journal of Conflict and Security Law* 1.

109 'Statement of Interdiction Principles' (n 102), Part IV.

110 *Helsinki Final Act*, 4.

111 *Helsinki Final Act*, 13.

This complemented the (admittedly scant) provisions in the *UN Charter* relating to disarmament[112] and in no way compromised the rights of any states not participating in the Helsinki Process.

For these reasons, our argument is that the OSCE shows that soft/informal regimes do not inevitably create or exacerbate inequality among states. In this section, we have suggested two factors which influence whether, or to what extent, a soft law approach necessarily exacerbates inequalities and have used the OSCE as an example. None of this is to suggest that existing inequalities among states are not continued within the OSCE. Rather, our point here is simply that an informal regime does not inherently or inevitably perpetuate inequality.

V Conclusion

In the last decade, the OSCE has faced a number of challenges and indeed, there are those who suggest that it may now be impotent or even defunct in light of the continuing deterioration in the relationships between Russia and NATO. In disarmament terms, progress has stalled in the FSC and in other OSCE decision-making bodies.[113] Even with the Structured Dialogue initiative from 2016, matters remain difficult and perhaps irremediably so.

The difficulties have been attributed to increasing military activities, growing military capabilities, lack of trust and ongoing debates about compliance. Most of the conditions necessary for progress on nuclear disarmament, articulated in 2018 in another forum by the United States, also apply to prospects for concrete achievements in the Structured Dialogue process. Thus, the impasse in OSCE efforts towards disarmament is largely attributable to global politics, rather than to regional elements or organizational format.

The focus of this chapter, however, has been to examine the OSCE as a soft/informal law regime and to see if some of the stated concerns about soft law are borne out. We have explored two fundamental concerns in detail — that of transparency and accountability, and that of perpetuating inequality between states. Our conclusions are that while those concerns are valid and important, it is not clear that they are inevitable in soft law systems, including in the OSCE. It is therefore our view that soft law and/or informal regimes may well offer a potential route in attempting to advance disarmament in other spheres and other regions.

112 The *UN Charter* itself set out no obligations regarding disarmament and in fact only mentions disarmament in passing as falling within the mandate of the General Assembly (art 11), the never-to-be-created Military Staffing Committee (art 47), and a passing reference in art 26.

113 Fred Tanner, 'Arms Control in Times of Crisis' in Dan Plesch, Kevin Miletic and Tariq Rauf (eds) *Reintroducing Disarmament and Cooperative Security to the Toolbox of 21st Century Leaders* (Stockholm International Peace Research Institute, 2017) 37, 41.

Index

For Product Safety Concerns and Information please contact our EU representative GPSR@taylorandfrancis.com
Taylor & Francis Verlag GmbH, Kaufingerstraße 24, 80331 München, Germany

www.ingramcontent.com/pod-product-compliance
Ingram Content Group UK Ltd.
Pitfield, Milton Keynes, MK11 3LW, UK
UKHW022128190926
475702UK00013B/1696
9780367610050